Interactive Music Systems

Interactive Music Systems

Machine Listening and Composing

Robert Rowe

The MIT Press
Cambridge, Massachusetts
London, England

A CD-ROM supplement to *Interactive Music Systems* is available. It contains audio and program examples that document a variety of systems and the music they produce. An extensive library of Macintosh software allows the user to experiment with or adapt existing interactive systems. Some parts of the library require the presence of underlying software environments such as SmallTalk, LISP, and Opcode's Max Language. The program discussed most extensively, Robert Rowe's Cypher, needs no additional software. Requires an Apple Macintosh computer with a MIDI interface. For more information, please contact Sales Department, The MIT Press, 55 Hayward Street, Cambridge, MA 02142 USA.

This book was formatted by The MIT Press from disks prepared by the author and was printed and bound in the United States of America.

Library of Congress Cataloging-in-Publication Data

Rowe, Robert.
Interactive music systems : machine listening and composing / Robert Rowe.
p. cm.
Includes bibliographical references (p.) and index.
ISBN 0-262-18149-5
1. Computer sound processing. I. Title.
MT723.R7 1993
780'.285--dc20 92-16388
CIP
MN

Contents

Preface

This book describes a range of interactive computer music systems, developing a framework for their discussion and evaluation in the process. Interactive systems exhibit changing behavior in response to human input. I consider the impact of three related fields (music theory, music cognition, and artificial intelligence) on the design of such systems, particularly as this impact affects their ability to function in ensembles including human performers. A companion CD-ROM of audio and program examples documents a variety of extant systems and the music they were used to produce. A series of examples illustrating the fundamentals and some advanced issues in interactive systems are written in Max, a graphic MIDI programming environment.

The most thoroughly reviewed program is my own Cypher. Cypher is an interactive music system with two major components: a listener and a player. The listener analyzes streams of MIDI data. The player uses various algorithmic techniques to produce new musical output. Both components are made up of many small, interconnected agents operating on several hierarchical levels. The listener classifies features in the input and their behavior over time, sending messages that communicate this analysis to the player. A user of Cypher can configure the player component to react to such messages, where a reaction is the execution of compositional methods producing new music in response. Features characterized include speed, density, dynamic, harmony, and rhythm. Collections of relations can be saved and recalled during performance by a score-orientation section, which tracks human performance and executes state changes at predetermined points in the score.

Interactive Music Systems is not an exhaustive account of the relationship between computer music and artificial intelligence, computer music and cognitive science, or computer music and music theory. Rather, it proposes a consideration of building artificial performers and improvisers that quickly recognizes the relevance and potential contribution of those other fields. Other texts will detail those relationships; this one points out why interactive music systems are unworkable without them.

Acknowledgments

Interactive Music Systems was written on the completion of my Ph.D. thesis at the MIT Media Laboratory, in April of 1991. Since then, many people have helped make this text a more general overview of the fundamental issues and the state of affairs surrounding interactive systems. I wish to thank those particularly responsible for helping to bring the work on Cypher to a good end, beginning with my thesis supervisor, Tod Machover, for his unwavering support of my research and composition. Marvin Minsky and John Harbison, the other members of my committee, were careful and insightful in their consideration and improvement of my efforts. The MIT Media Laboratory played an important part in shaping Cypher: the combination of people, facilities, and atmosphere provided a constant stimulus and challenge. I was blessed with a great musician and provocative debater as an officemate—Michael Hawley. My other (upstairs) officemate, Joseph Chung, was always a helpful source of code, ideas, discussion, and experience.

Terry Ehling of the MIT Press has been tremendously supportive and helpful during the transformation from thesis to book/CD-ROM. My students and colleagues at New York University listened to and corrected me as I tried out various ideas from these pages; particular thanks go to Lawrence Ferrara for his perceptive reading. The many people who supplied material, ideas, and music for this project made it possible—the index is perhaps a fair listing of the debt I owe. I only hope I have done justice to their efforts. Many more people again should have been discussed; though I have tried to identify the major dimensions of the field, I have learned that the scope and variety of work being done is far too immense to be covered completely in a volume like this one. Thanks to my wife Tamara for letting me use the computer once in a while, and for generally making my life a living heaven. *Interactive Music Systems* is dedicated with love to my parents, for showing me how to live.

This book describes research done at the Media Laboratory of the Massachusetts Institute of Technology. Support was granted by the Yamaha Corporation.

Interactive Music Systems

1 Interactive Music Systems

Interactive computer music systems are those whose behavior changes in response to musical input. Such responsiveness allows these systems to participate in live performances, of both notated and improvised music. This text reviews a wide range of interactive systems, from the perspectives of several different fields. Each field, particularly music theory, artificial intelligence, and cognitive science, has developed techniques appropriate to various facets of interactive music systems. In relating a large number of existing programs to established bodies of work, as well as to each other, a framework for discussing both individual contributions and the field as a whole will be developed.

This book grew out of a doctoral thesis describing my own interactive system, called Cypher. For that reason, extensive consideration is given to the theoretical foundations and practical use of that program. Though the attention devoted to Cypher is out of proportion to that given the other programs reviewed here, the lattice of perspectives through which interactive systems will be viewed is more easily constructed with one example serving to focus the effort. Nonetheless, the book covers many other current applications in considerable detail, particularly when used in conjunction with the companion CD-ROM of audio and program examples. Further, basic concepts and characteristic issues will be illustrated using the Max programming environment, a graphic language for building interactive music systems (Puckette 1991).

1.1 Introduction

The use of computers has expanded musical thought in two far-reaching directions, the first of which concerns the composition of timbre. Digital computers afford the composer or sound designer unprecedented levels of control over the evolution and combination of sonic events. The second expansion stems from the computer's ability to implement algorithmic methods for generating musical material. As in the case of timbral synthesis, the use of computers for algorithmic composition began with the earliest essays in the field (Koenig 1971). Recently, however, an important extension to this line of development has arisen from the realization of such processes in the context of live performance. By attaining the computation speeds needed to execute compositional algorithms in real time, current computer music systems are able to modify their behavior as a function of input from other performing musicians. Such changes of behavior in response to live input are the hallmark of interactive music systems. Interactivity qualitatively changes the nature of experimentation with compositional algorithms: the effect of different control variable values on the sounding output of the method can be perceived immediately, even as the variables are being manipulated (Chadabe 1989).

In this book, the musical motivations and possibilities accompanying interactive systems will occupy the forefront of the discussion. Second, I examine practical considerations of how to build, analyze, and extend these systems. Finally, I explore perspectives afforded by the viewpoints of artificial intelligence, cognitive science, and music theory in detail, both in terms of their actual contributions to the growth of the field to date, and of their potential impact on the continuing evolution of interactive music systems.

1.2 Machine Musicianship

In using a computer for composition or performance, the most fundamental question to be asked about any particular system is, What musical purpose does it serve? This book will cover several technical areas, some in considerable detail; however, the primary focus will be on the musical opportunities afforded by interaction and the ways in which these opportunities have been explored and elaborated by compositions and improvisations using them.

The responsiveness of interactive systems requires them to make some interpretation of their input. Therefore, the question of what the machine can hear is a central one. Most of the programs reviewed in this book make use of the abstraction provided by the MIDI standard (Loy 1985). An additional level of information can be gleaned from an analysis of the audio signal emitted by acoustic musical instruments. MIDI input and audio signals are low-level, weakly structured representations, which must be processed further by the program to advance any particular musical goals. How these low-level signals are interpreted and structured into higher-level representations is a research topic common to all interactive systems. The representations and processes available for constructing responses form the other broad area of inquiry.

Several of the systems we will review here interpret the input by emulating human musical understanding. Programming a computer to exhibit humanlike musical aptitude, however, is a goal with implications for a much broader range of applications. For almost any computer music program, in fact, some degree of musical understanding could improve the application's performance and utility. For example, in the automated editing of digital audio recordings, "simultaneous access to the low-level representations of the music in the signal and the higher-level constructs familiar to musicians would allow [automated editors] to perform operations and transformations whose realization by signal processing techniques alone would range from cumbersome to unimaginable" (Chafe, Mont-Reynaud, and Rush 1982, 537). With interactive systems, interpretation of the input is unavoidable. In non-real-time applications, such as sequencers or notation programs, an understanding by the program of concepts such as phrase, meter, direction, and so on could extend their function in the direction of a computer assistant, or interlocutor, able to suggest variations in tempo for the realization of a sequence or to locate points of significant change in a notated composition.

Capturing Musical Concepts

Communication between musicians, verbal as well as musical, assumes certain shared concepts and experiences. Observing, for example, a rehearsal of chamber music, or a piano lesson, one might hear a comment such as, "Broaden the end of the phrase." Interpreting that instruction engages a complex collection of listening and performing skills, which must be related to each other in a reasonably precise way. The necessary relations are rarely described verbally beyond the use of just such admonitions; if a student were to shape the phrase poorly, a typical next response for the teacher would be simply to play or sing it.

Pursuing such common musical effects in computer music systems often leads to alien and unwieldy constructions, precisely because the software does not share the concepts and experiences that underlie musical discourse. Many of the most persistent problems in computer music ("mechanical" sounding performances, lack of high-level editing tools) come from an algorithmic inability to locate salient structural chunks or describe their function. Although research has begun to show us systematic ways in which human performers add expression to their rendering of a score (Palmer 1988), a general application of the fruits of this research will be impossible until programs can find the appropriate structural units across which to apply expressive deformations. In other words, it does computer music systems little good to know how human players broaden phrase boundaries if those systems cannot find the phrases in the first place. Among the concepts the machine would have to employ to "broaden the end of the phrase" are beat, harmonic progression, meter, and decelerando (Figure 1.1). These concepts rely in turn, I maintain, on even more primitive perceptual features such as loudness, register, density, and articulation, and the way these change in time.

In their interpretation of musical input, interactive systems implement some collection of concepts, often related to the structures musicians commonly assume. Each interactive system also includes methods for constructing responses, to be generated when particular input constructs are found. As methods of interpretation approach the successful representation of human musical concepts, and as response algorithms move toward an emulation of human performance practices, programs come increasingly close to making sense of and accomplishing an instruction such as "broaden the end of the phrase."

Before embarking on the formidable task of trying to achieve such behavior, one could ask why it is important for a computer program to approach human performance practices. In fact, throughout the early stages of electronic and computer music development, an expressed goal was often the elimination of human performers, with all their limitations and variability. "About 1920, when the slogan 'objective music' was in vogue, some famous composers (Stravinsky, for instance) wrote compositions specifically for pianola, and they took advantage of all the possibilities offered by the absence of restraints that are an outcome of the structure of the human hand. The intent, however, was not to achieve superior performance but to restrict to an absolute minimum the intervention of the performer's personality" (Bartok 1937, 291).

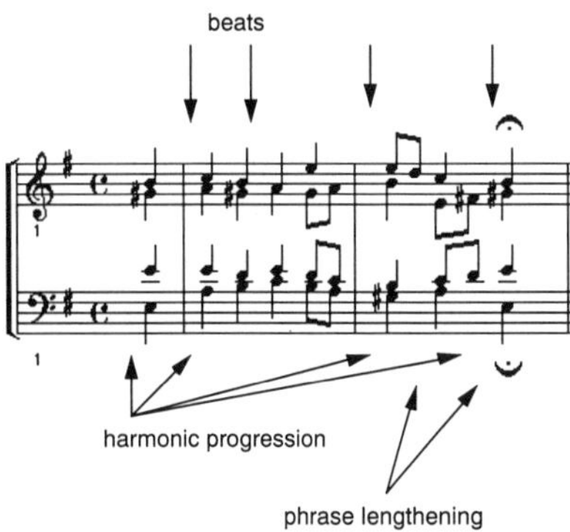

Figure 1.1

Computer music has, in fact, provided a perfect vehicle for eliminating the performer's personality. Compositions realized on tape can be painstakingly constructed by the composer, who in effect "performs" the work while entrusting it to a fixed realization, which is then played back without any further human intervention. Many of the most compelling and durable compositions in the field have been made in exactly this way. Eliminating performers entirely is hardly a desirable outcome, however, and one that few if any composers in the field would advocate. Their elimination is undesirable, beyond the purely social considerations, because human players understand what music is and how it works and can communicate that understanding to an audience, whereas computer performers as yet do not.

Works for performers and tape have been an expression of the desire to include human musicianship in computer music compositions. Coordination between the fixed realization of the tape and the variable, expressive performance of the human players, however, can become problematic. Such difficulties are more pronounced when improvisation becomes part of the discourse. And, as taped and performed realizations are juxtaposed, the disparity between levels of musicality evinced by the two often becomes untenable.

Composition by Refinement

Interactive music systems contribute to a process of composition by refinement. Because the program reacts immediately to changes in configuration and input, a user can develop compositional applications by continually refining initial ideas and sketches, up to the development of complete scripts for a performance situation in which the computer can follow the evolution and articulation of musical ideas and contribute to these as they unfold.

Further, many interactive systems can be considered *applied music theories*. Music theory, in its best form, is the scholarly attempt to describe the process of composing, or listening to music. Computer systems able to implement this work in real time allow the musician to assess the validity of the intellectual enterprise by hearing it function in live musical contexts. The construction of formal processes is judged by the ear and sound, not through more words and paper. Moreover, implementation in a computer program demands the formalization of a theory to the point where a series of machine instructions can realize it. For suitable theories, the added rigor of realization by computer can clarify their formulation and make them available in a form from which they can be extended or used in other computational tasks. When a theory has been brought to the point of interactivity, it can be applied to the production and analysis of music in its native environment—that is, performed and experienced as live music has always been.

1.3 Classification of Interactive Systems

A primary objective of this book is to provide a framework within which interactive systems may be discussed and evaluated. Many of the programs developed to date have been realized in relative isolation from one another, with little scope for building on the work of earlier efforts. Now, several fundamental tools of the trade have become standardized and are no longer so subject to ad hoc solutions. Here I will propose a rough classification system for interactive music systems. The motivation for building such a set of classifications is not simply to attach labels to programs but to recognize similarities between them and to be able to identify the relations between new systems and their predecessors.

This classification system will be built on a combination of three dimensions, whose attributes help identify the musical motivations behind types of input interpretation, and methods of response. The dimensions will be described using some points along the continuum of possibilities for that dimension, points generally close to the extremes. The points used should not be considered distinct classes, however. Any particular system may show some combination of the attributes outlined here; however, these metrics do seem to be useful in identifying characteristics that can often distinguish and draw relations between interactive programs.

The first dimension distinguishes *score-driven* systems from those that are *performance-driven.*

• Score-driven programs use predetermined event collections, or stored music fragments, to match against music arriving at the input. They are likely to organize events using the traditional categories of beat, meter, and tempo. Such categories allow the composer to preserve and employ familiar ways of thinking about temporal flow, such as specifying some events to occur on the downbeat of the next measure or at the end of every fourth bar.

• Performance-driven programs do not anticipate the realization of any particular score. In other words, they do not have a stored representation of the music they expect to find at the input. Further, performance-driven programs tend not to employ traditional metric categories but often use more general parameters, involving perceptual measures such as density and regularity, to describe the temporal behavior of music coming in.

Another distinction groups response methods as being *transformative, generative,* or *sequenced.*

• Transformative methods take some existing musical material and apply transformations to it to produce variants. According to the technique, these variants may or may not be recognizably related to the original. For transformative algorithms, the source material is complete musical input. This material need not be stored, however—often such transformations are applied to live input as it arrives.

• For generative algorithms, on the other hand, what source material there is will be elementary or fragmentary—for example, stored scales or duration sets. Generative methods use sets of rules to produce complete musical output from the stored fundamental material, taking pitch structures from basic scalar patterns according to random distributions, for instance, or applying serial procedures to sets of allowed duration values.

• Sequenced techniques use prerecorded music fragments in response to some real-time input. Some aspects of these fragments may be varied in performance, such as the tempo of playback, dynamic shape, slight rhythmic variations, etc.

Finally, we can distinguish between the *instrument* and *player* paradigms.

• Instrument paradigm systems are concerned with constructing an extended musical instrument: performance gestures from a human player are analyzed by the computer and guide an elaborated output exceeding normal instrumental response. Imagining such a system being played by a single performer, the musical result would be thought of as a solo.

• Systems following a player paradigm try to construct an artificial player, a musical presence with a personality and behavior of its own, though it may vary in the degree to which it follows the lead of a human partner. A player paradigm system played by a single human would produce an output more like a duet.

For the moment, a brief example will clarify how the dimensions are used. *Score followers* are a group of programs able to accompany a human instrumental soloist by matching her realization of a particular score against a stored representation of that score, simultaneously performing a stored accompanimental part. Such applications are a perfect example of score-driven systems. The response technique is sequenced, since everything the machine plays has been stored in advance. Finally, score followers can be regarded as player paradigm systems, because they realize a recognizably separate musical voice, assuming the traditional role of accompanist in the performance of instrumental sonatas.

2 Fundamentals

Two basic pillars of interactive systems are MIDI handling and scheduling. The Musical Instrument Digital Interface (MIDI) standard was developed by instrument and synthesizer manufacturers, and it allows controllers, computers, and synthesizers to pass data among themselves (Loy 1985). All of the systems reviewed here deal with the MIDI standard to some extent and therefore require software components to receive, package, and transmit properly formatted MIDI messages. The second imperative of music programs is to be able to perform tasks at specified points in time. Music is a temporal art, and any computer program dealing with music must have sophisticated facilities for representing time and for scheduling processes to occur at particular points in time.

The processing chain of interactive computer music systems can be conceptualized in three stages. The first is the *sensing* stage, when data is collected from controllers reading gestural information from the human performers onstage. Second is the *processing* stage, in which a computer reads and interprets information coming from the sensors and prepares data for the third, or *response* stage, when the computer and some collection of sound-producing devices share in realizing a musical output.

An important reason for dividing the chain into these three links is that there are usually machine boundaries between each successive stage. Commercial manufacturers dominate the sensing and response stages, through MIDI controllers and synthesizers. The sophistication of these devices, which implement several modes of operation and can often themselves be programmed, requires a discussion of sensing and response, rather than simply of a real-time computer program with some input and output. In full-blown interactive music systems, functionality is spread across three clusters of machines, and the designer often can choose to place certain methods within one or another cluster.

The processing stage has commercial entries as well, most notably MIDI sequencers. It is in processing, however, that individual conceptions of interactive music are most readily expressed, in any of a variety of programming languages with temporal and MIDI extensions. In this chapter, we will examine the three phases of interactive processing, looking at the hardware associated with each, the impact of machine boundaries separating each phase, and the nature of communications protocols developed to pass information between them.

2.1 Sensing

The recent fast growth in the development of interactive music systems is due in no small part to the introduction of the MIDI standard. We will begin our examination of the sensing stage with a consideration of MIDI, followed by a look at some of the standard's limitations and the way new sensing technologies have grown up to fill the gaps.

The MIDI Standard

The MIDI standard is a hardware specification and communications protocol that allows computers, controllers, and synthesis gear to pass information among themselves (Loy 1985). MIDI abstracts away from the acoustic signal level of music, up to a representation based on the concept of notes, comprising a pitch and velocity, that go on and off. The MIDI abstraction is eminently well suited to keyboard instruments, such as piano or mallet percussion, which can be represented as a series of switches. In fact, MIDI sensing on such instruments operates by treating each separate key as a switch. When the key is depressed, a Note On message is sent out, indicating which key was struck and with what velocity. When the key is released, a Note Off message (or, equivalently, Note On with a velocity of zero) is transmitted with the key number.

The note concept is the fundamental MIDI paradigm. All MIDI instruments implement it. Following its genesis from commercial keyboard controllers, MIDI represents continuously varying control functions as well. One of these is known as *pitchbend*, usually implemented with a wheel built into the instrument. Each time the wheel is moved, a new pitchbend value is transmitted to the processing stage. Such continuous control messages are transmitted with a controller number and a value. Many instruments allow the user to assign controller numbers to physical devices, remapping the pitchbend wheel, for example, to another control channel. The generation of continuous controls is therefore, in most cases, easily reconfigurable. Moreover, additional layers of remapping and interpretation can be implemented in the processing and response stages.

Although the introduction of the MIDI standard has had the salutary effect of greatly expanding research into and performance with interactive music systems, use of the standard imposes limitations of several kinds (Moore 1988). First, because MIDI communicates on the control level—performance gestural events rather than any representation of the audio signal—the standard cannot be used to describe or control much of the timbral aspect of a musical performance. Control over synthesis and the evolution over time of any particular sound is coded into each synthesizer and may be affected through MIDI only by using an ad hoc collection of triggers, continuous controls, and system exclusive commands, private to each machine and inimical to the very idea of a standard.

That said, several synthesis algorithms have been built into commercial synthesizers that are able to achieve a quite broad and subtly varying range of sounds. The most successful of these offer a small number of fairly powerful control variables, which fit the control situation of a MIDI environment well. In a typical transaction, a Note On message emitted from a computer or controller will trigger a complex reaction from the synthesizer, realizing the attack portion of the sound. Continuous controls can affect variables of the synthesis algorithm during the "steady state" portion of the sound, modifying such things as filter cutoff frequencies or the amplitude of a modulating oscillator. A Note Off message then initiates the sound's decay, again stored as a complex, though relatively constant event in the synthesizer.

A primary cause of this transaction paradigm is the fact that the MIDI standard enforces a transmission bandwidth of 31,250 bits per second. Each eight-bit MIDI byte is surrounded with start and stop bits, making their effective size equal to ten bits. Therefore, a standard MIDI Note On message, which requires three bytes (30 bits) of information, takes approximately 1 millisecond to transmit. As Gareth Loy points out in Loy 1985, the performance through MIDI of a ten-note chord will introduce a delay of 10 milliseconds between the first note of the chord and the last. Though 10 milliseconds is not enough to affect the percept of that event as a single chord, it can have an effect on the timbral quality of the sound. Further, when we consider the impact of a 1-millisecond transmission time on the performance of a ten-note chord sent out simultaneously over ten channels, the 100-millisecond delay between the first note and the last will certainly be heard.

When we consider MIDI as a communications channel not only for note messages but for the state of continuous controllers, the bandwidth problems are even more serious. Though the standard does not provide a good way to control the internal evolution of a sound, such facilities as there are cannot be fed quickly enough at 31,250 bits per second to afford a performer close control over the sounding result (Moore 1988). The result is to accentuate the machine boundary between the computer and its outboard synthesis gear: a user must program the synthesizer with instructions concerning how to evolve a sound in response to triggers sent out from the computer. The limitations of MIDI bandwidth are thus somewhat attenuated, moving some of the musical control over to the sound gear, but at the expense of an integrated and flexible development environment for all aspects of computer performance.

Despite these concerns, the positive influence of the MIDI standard has far outweighed its limitations. Most of the work described in this book could not have been achieved without it. As interactive systems grow in power and application, we can only hope that the standard will grow with them. In any event, the migration of sensing and response capabilities back to the host computer has the potential to obviate the need for such a communications protocol entirely.

Custom Controllers

Information can arrive from sensors in forms other than MIDI. Another important input type is *samples*, the digital representation of a time-varying audio signal. Usually, the sound of some musical instrument is picked up by a microphone, sent through an analog-to-digital converter (ADC), and then on to the computer. Compact-disc-quality sampling rates for digital audio produce (at least) 44,100 16-bit samples per second, so dealing with a raw sample stream demands very high-powered processing. For that reason, interactive systems designed to handle audio have dedicated hardware devices able to process sounds at the requisite speeds. We will return to a discussion of audio input and output in the section on response.

MIDI controllers can be thought of as gestural transducers, providing a representation of human musical performance. Keyboard performances are represented fairly well. Much of the important gestural information from performance on other instruments (strings, winds, voice), however, is not fully captured by MIDI sensors. For that reason, a significant research effort has grown up around the attempt to build controllers better able to capture the range of expression afforded by traditional musical instruments.

Implementing the violoncello interface used for Tod Machover's composition *Begin Again Again . . .*, a team including Neil Gerschenfeld, Joseph Chung, and Andy Hong developed sensors to track five aspects of the cellist's physical performance: (1) bow pressure, (2) bow position (transverse to the strings), (3) bow placement (distance from the bridge), (4) bow wrist orientation, and (5) finger position on the strings (Machover et al. 1991). To sense positions (2) and (3), a drive antenna was mounted on the cello bridge and a receiving antenna on the bow. The capacitance between the two yielded both position of the bow across the strings and position of the bow relative to the bridge. Pressure on the bow was measured from the player's finger, rather than the bow hairs. Again a capacitance measurement was used, by putting a foam capacitor around the part of the bow where finger pressure would be applied. Finger position on the strings was found from the resistance between the metal strings and strips of conductive thermoplastic sheet mounted on the fingerboard beneath them. Finally, wrist angle was read from a sensor mounted on the wrist that measures joint angles from the movement of magnets corresponding to the wrist and the back of the hand. These five traits of the physical gestures were continually tracked by computers during the performance of the piece, and used to change the timbral presentation of computer music associated with each section of the composition (see also section 3.4).

Space-Control Performance

Using gestural control to affect the output of electronic instruments is a principle that was already firmly established in 1919 by the Russian scientist Lev Termen with his "Aetherphone," later called the "Theremin" after the Gallicized version of his name (Glinsky 1992). The instrument produces monophonic music with a quasi–sine wave timbre and is played by moving two hands in the vicinity of antennae controlling pitch and amplitude. The tones come from two heterodyning oscillators, one of fixed frequency, and the other of variable frequency. Both oscillate at frequencies well above the range of human hearing; however, when the variable oscillator's frequency is changed, a difference tone is created between it and the reference oscillator, and this difference tone does fall in the audible range. Moving the right hand toward and away from one antenna changes the variable oscillator frequency, thereby producing eerie portamento effects as the audible beat frequency goes up and down. The amplitude is similarly controlled by the movements of the other hand. Because of this continuous control over pitch and loudness, the instrument is capable of quite expressive performances, though mastery of it requires years of practice. The Theremin was a sensation, and it was played by its inventor and other virtuoso performers to packed houses throughout Europe and the United States. Similar devices existed around the same time but never caught the public imagination the way the Theremin did. An important reason for this was what Termen called "space-control performance": the fact that the instrument was played without anyone actually touching it. Competitors outfitted with more conventional keyboard or other interfaces never aroused the same sense of wonder as the space-control Theremin.

A fascination with the seeming magic of music performed by movement of the hands alone has carried through to the use of hand-based controllers in several recent interactive systems. Stichting STEIM in Amsterdam has devoted a considerable research effort to the development of new gestural controllers, resulting in such devices as The Hands (a pair of proximity-sensitive hand-mounted sensors) and The Web (a weblike device in which manipulations of one part affect other regions) (Krefeld 1990). Similarly, a number of hand controllers have been marketed for various purposes, including the Exos Dextrous Hand Master, the VPL Data Glove, and the Mattel Powerglove, which have subsequently been adapted for experimentation in interactive music. Two composers who have used this technology are Michel Waisvisz of STEIM, who performs the composition *The Hands* with the controller of the same name, and Tod Machover, who adapted the Dextrous Hand Master to control timbral variation through MIDI mixers in his composition *Bug-Mudra*.

The Buchla Lightning Controller is another variation on the same idea: the controller responds to motions made in space with various transmitting devices (Rich 1991). One of these transmitters is a wand, which sends infrared information to a control box. The control box is thereby able to track the motion of the wand within a performance field, which is about as wide as the distance from the transmitter to the control box and whose height is about 60 percent of the width. This performance field is split up into eight cells, and various combinations of the eight cells make up different zones. The controller responds to "strikes" (quick changes of direction made with the transmitter) within a zone, entry or exit from any zone, and combinations of switches built into the transmitters and foot pedals. The control box can be programmed to send out MIDI note, control, or program change commands, as well as MIDI clock messages. Further, one of the Lightning presets allows the controller to talk directly to Max patches. Lightning is thus a general control device, which enables users to make physical gestures in the air and define the functionality of those gestures through MIDI-based programming.

The Radio Drum is a three-dimensional percussion controller, sensitive to the placement of beats on the face of the drum and the position of the drumstick through the air as it approaches the drum face (Mathews 1989). The Radio Drum was designed by Max Mathews and Robert Boie, and Mathews's main conception of the device is to use it to control tempo. In one performance, a singer beats the Radio Drum to cue each successive attack in the performance of an accompanimental part. Of course, the three-dimensional information coming from the drum can be used to trigger much more intricate interactions between the drummer and the computer, an area which has been extensively explored by such composers as Andrew Schloss and Richard Boulanger.

Pitch Detectors

Solutions geared to individual instruments have proliferated because of significant differences among the instruments themselves: critical controls for one family of instruments do not even exist on others. Another obstacle is the fact that reliable real-time pitch tracking from an arbitrary audio signal has not been developed. Commercial devices for the job (pitch-to-MIDI converters) exist, but they have widely variable results for different instruments, even for different performers on the same instrument. General solutions have not been forthcoming because the problem is a difficult one: techniques such as the Fast Fourier Transform (FFT) are often not fast enough or simply fail to find the correct pitch. Consider the case of trying to identify a pitch at 60 hertz: generally, two cycles of the waveform will be required for analysis. At that frequency, a delay of over 30 milliseconds is required in the best case for identification. When we consider, in addition, that the attack portion of an instrumental waveform will be the least regular part of it, the difficulty of quickly and accurately finding the pitch through standard Fourier analysis is readily seen.

One approach to the pitch-tracking problem has been to solve it for other musical instruments as it was solved for keyboards. The keyboard, and mallet percussion, case is simple: each key is treated as a switch, and the pitch played can be read off the switch depressed. Extending this concept to other instruments means fitting them with mechanical sensors to read fingerings or hand position, reducing the problem of pitch detection to one of indexing known fingerings to the pitches they produce. In cases where one fingering produces more than one pitch (overblown wind instruments, for example), minimal additional signal processing can disambiguate between the remaining possibilities.

An early instance of fingering-based pitch detection was built into the IRCAM flute controller. Optical sensors tracked the manipulations made by the player's fingers on the instrument, and the found configurations were used as indices into a table of known pitches for each fingering. Since one flute fingering can potentially produce more than one pitch, additional signal processing on the 4X machine analyzed the audio signal to decide between the remaining possibilities (Baisnee et al. 1986). Other wind instrument devices have been built following similar physical-mapping principles: the Yamaha WX-7 wind controller follows key positions, and in fact extends the traditional range of single-reed instruments with additional octave keys, allowing the player to cover up to seven octaves.

MIDI adaptations for other instruments abound as well. MIDI guitars, for example, have been built by several manufacturers. Entire families of string instruments have been commercialized by Zeta and the RAAD group. Hardly an instrument exists that has not had some work done to allow it to transmit MIDI messages. The underlying message of this trend is clear: the motivation to participate in the expanded possibilities afforded by computer-based instruments is a compelling one for performers and builders alike. The general operating principles of existing orchestral instruments are being maintained, to capitalize on the years of training professional players have had. Because traditional instruments are markedly different, new control adaptations must be made on a highly individual basis. General analysis systems based on the properties of audio signals have not provided a solution, given the inability of techniques such as Fourier analysis to provide accurate results within the demands of real-time performance. Given these constraints, new instrumental controllers combine some interpretation of physical gestures with audio signal processing to provide a wider range of gestural information from instrumental performance. At the same time, controllers divorced from any relation to the orchestral instruments, but which give wider scope to the tracking of expressive gestures, are being developed in growing numbers.

2.2 Processing

The information collected during the sensing stage is passed on to a computer, which begins the processing stage. Communication between the two stages assumes a protocol understood by both sides, and the most widely used protocol is the MIDI standard. Other signals passing between them could include digital audio signals or custom control information. In either case, some form of the procedure for handling MIDI streams would apply.

Early interactive systems always needed to implement a MIDI driver, which was capable of buffering a stream of serial information from a hardware port and then packaging it as a series of MIDI commands. Such a facility still must be included in every program, but for most hardware platforms the problems of MIDI transmission have been solved by a standardized driver and associated software. A good example is the Midi Manager™, written for Apple Macintosh computers. The Midi Manager makes it possible for several MIDI applications to run simultaneously on a single computer. An associated desk accessory called PatchBay allows a user to route MIDI streams between applications and the Apple Midi Driver, and to specify timing relations between all of them (Wyatt 1991).

Beyond the bookkeeping details of receiving and packaging valid MIDI commands, MIDI drivers invariably introduce *time stamps*, a critical extension of the standard. Time stamps are an indication of the time at which some MIDI packet arrived at the computer. In the case of the MIDI Manager, time stamps are notated in one of a number of possible formats, with a resolution of one millisecond. With the addition of time stamps, the timing information critical to music production becomes available. Interpretation processes can use this information to analyze the rhythmic presentation of incoming MIDI streams. Timing information is also needed as the computer prepares data for output through the response stage, and it is here that the function of a real-time scheduler comes into play.

Real-Time Schedulers

Scheduling is the process whereby a specific action of the computer is made to happen at some point in future time. Typically, a programmer can invoke scheduling facilities to delay the execution of a procedure for some number of milliseconds. Arguments to the routine to be executed are saved along with the name of the routine itself. When the scheduler notices that the specified time point has arrived, the scheduled process is called with the saved arguments.

Much of the work on interactive music systems developed at the MIT Media Laboratory, for example, relies on a scheduler adapted from work described in (Boynton 1987). The scheduler allows timed execution of any procedure called with any arbitrary list of arguments. A centisecond clock is maintained in the MIDI driver (also adapted from work by Lee Boynton) and is referenced by the driver to timestamp arriving MIDI data. The clock records the number of centiseconds that have passed since the MIDI driver was opened. Accordingly, incoming MIDI events are marked with the current clock time at interrupt level, when they arrive at the serial port. This same clock is used by the scheduler to time the execution of scheduled tasks.

Tasks are associated with a number of attributes, which control initial and (possible) repeated executions of the scheduled function. We can see these attributes in the argument list to Scheduler_CreateTask, the routine that inserts a function into the scheduler task queue.

```
TaskPtr
Scheduler_CreateTask(time, tol, imp, per, fun, args)
        short imp, tol, per;
        long  time;
        void (*fun)();
        arglist args;
```

The first argument is *time*: the absolute clock time at which the function is to be executed. Absolute clock time means that the time point is expressed in centiseconds since the opening of the MIDI driver. The *tolerance* is an amount of time allowed for startup of the function. If there is a tolerance argument, the function will be called at a clock-time point that is calculated by subtracting *tolerance* from *time*. This accommodates routines whose effect will be noticed some fixed amount of time after their execution. In that case, the function can be scheduled to take place at the time its effect is desired, and the startup time is passed along as a *tolerance* argument.

In figure 2.1, the black bullets represent sounding events produced by some player process. The process needs a fixed amount of time to produce the sound—a *tolerance*—represented by the arrow marking a point some time in advance of the bullet. The call to Scheduler_CreateTask, then, would give the *time* for the desired arrival of a sounding event, with a *tolerance* argument to provide the necessary advance processing.

The scheduler maintains three separate, prioritized queues, and guarantees that all waiting tasks from high-priority queues will be executed before any tasks from lower-priority queues are invoked. The *importance* argument determines which priority the indicated task will receive. If a nonzero *period* argument is included, the task will reschedule itself *period* centiseconds after each execution. Periodicity is a widespread attribute of music production, and the facility of the *period* argument elegantly handles the necessity. Tasks that are periodically rescheduling themselves can be halted by an explicit kill command at any time. In figure 2.1, a *period* argument would continue the sounding events at regular intervals after the first one as shown. The *tolerance* argument remains in force for each invocation, providing the advance processing time required. Finally, a pointer to the *function* to be called, and the *arguments* to be sent the function on execution, are listed. The arguments are evaluated at scheduling time, rather than when the function is eventually invoked.

A similar facility is provided by the CMU MIDI Toolkit, adapted from Doug Collinge's language *Moxie* (Dannenberg 1989): the cause()

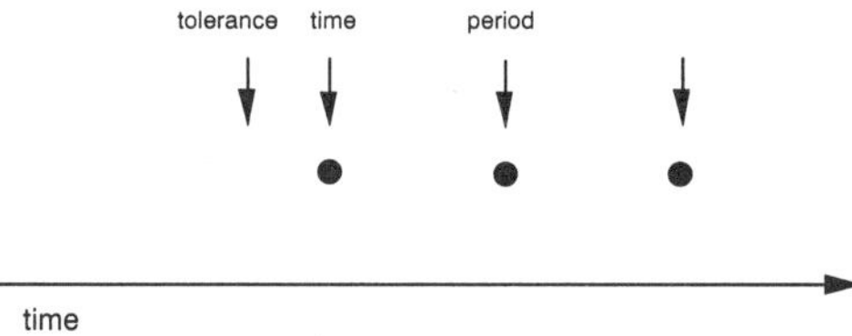

Figure 2.1

routine will invoke a procedure, with the listed arguments, some number of centiseconds in the future. For instance, the call

```
cause(100, midi_note, 1, 60, 0);
```

will induce the scheduler to call the routine midi_note 100 centiseconds after the execution of cause(). The arguments 1, 60, and 0 are specific to midi_note (and correspond to channel, note number, and velocity). Any list of arguments can be presented after the name of the routine to be invoked, as in the Boynton syntax shown above. In fact, one of the most noticeable differences between the two schedulers is that Boynton's expects absolute time points as a reference, whereas Dannenberg's cause() routine requires the execution time of the scheduled routine to be specified relative to the invocation of *cause* itself.

For both versions of this idea (and there are several others), it is important to note that the model assumes that none of the scheduled routines will require a long processing time. Once a procedure is called by the scheduler, it runs until the end, and then relinquishes control to the scheduler again. These routines are not interrupted, except by a strictly limited number of input handlers. If some procedure requires extensive processing, it must reschedule itself at regular intervals to allow the scheduler enough CPU time to keep up with the execution of any other tasks in the queue.

An extensive literature has grown up around the subject of real-time scheduling, particularly as it affects music programming, and several languages have been implemented that address the problem in various ways. The reader is referred to Roger Dannenberg's excellent survey (Dannenberg 1989). Besides the scheduler included in the Midi Manager, extensive possibilities for scheduling events have been built into Max, the graphic programming language for interactive systems that we will examine in some detail.

Building Functionality

Along the sensing/processing/response chain, the differentiation of functionality among systems is accomplished most strongly through processing. Certain classes of hardware can generally be grouped with each link in the chain. Controllers contribute to the sensing stage, and synthesizers and other sound-making gear work in the response stage. The hardware of the processing stage is a digital computer. The programs running in this computer are the subject of this book, and different approaches to the processing stage will be seen repeatedly in the following pages.

We have already reviewed some of the problems surrounding sensing and two of the indispensable components of processing: MIDI handling and scheduling. The rest of the processing component is what distinguishes Michel Waisvisz's *The Hands* from Morton Subotnick's *A Desert Flowers* from Jean-Claude Risset's *Duet*. In describing the sequence of events in an interactive music system, this subsection provides only a placeholder for a discussion of the cornucopia of possible processing approaches. The rest of this book fills the placeholder by describing in detail the processing link in the chain.

2.3 Response

The response stage resembles the sensing stage most strongly in the protocol used to pass information. Again here, the computer and the devices used to actually perform the responses communicate most often through the MIDI standard. The exact nature of the directions sent out by the computer will depend on the synthesis devices in use and the kinds of effects those devices are used to realize. Presently, commercial MIDI gear tends to fall into two large groups: synthesis and sampling. Synthesis modules use an algorithm—for example, frequency modulation—to produce sounds. Sampling gear has stored waveforms, often recordings of traditional acoustic instruments, which are played back at specific pitches in response to MIDI messages. Response commands sent to the devices, then, would include Note On and Off messages and whatever controller values are desired for manipulation of the device's sound production technique.

Real-Time Digital Signal Processing

Before the arrival of MIDI, interactive computer music was often realized using specialized digital signal processing hardware for the sensing and response stages. A prominent example of this approach was the series of realtime processors designed by Giuseppe di Giugno and his team at IRCAM, culminating in the 4X machine (Baisnee et al. 1986). The 4X was used for a range of interactive compositions, including Pierre Boulez's *Repons*, several pieces by Philippe Manoury, such as *Jupiter* and *Pluton*, and my own *Hall of Mirrors*. Sensing involved the intake of audio samples from microphones and reading commands typed at an alphanumeric keyboard. Responses were generated by real-time signal processing of the audio taken in from the microphones, producing a live transformation of sounds already being performed by acoustic instruments. Later, MIDI handling was added to the capabilities of the 4X real-time system, to take advantage of the MIDI controllers which were by then becoming available in large numbers (Favreau et al. 1986).

As MIDI synthesis equipment became more sophisticated and duplicated many of the techniques developed in the leading computer music institutions, much of the work of response generation fell to such devices. Another important reason for the dominance of commercial gear through the late 1980s and early 1990s was the considerable expense involved in acquiring and maintaining a machine like the 4X, a cost prohibitive for most studios and certainly for individuals.

With the introduction of digital signal processing chips such as the Motorola 56000, however, the pendulum began to swing back toward real-time signal processing as a viable choice for generating sound. The efficiencies of mass production, coupled with the installation of these chips on a variety of add-on boards designed for personal systems such as the IBM PC, Apple Macintosh, and NeXT machine, made DSP hardware both inexpensive and relatively widespread. The viability of digital signal processing power in personal workstations is changing the face of response synthesis techniques. Direct-to-disk sampling applications, and specialized hardware/software packages such as the Digidesign SampleCell, now make possible the extensive use in performance of recorded sound, or transformations of live sound, without relying on external MIDI samplers.

IRCAM Signal Processing Workstation

The accelerated use of digital signal processing in live performance is again changing the nature of response capabilities in interactive music systems. The standard for the integration of control- and audio-level programming has moved forward with the commercialization of the IRCAM Signal Processing Workstation (ISPW). The ISPW consists of a NeXT computer equipped with a special accelerator board, on which reside two Intel i860 processors (Lindemann et al. 1991). The i860s are very fast, general-purpose processing devices. Before the ISPW, real-time digital signal processing tasks were accomplished with specialized processors, built particularly for DSP, such as the Motorola 56000. The advantage of using a general-purpose processor such as the i860 is that the machine boundary between signal- and control-level computations is erased.

To take advantage of this flexibility, a new version of Max was written to include signal objects. These objects can be used to build signal-processing programs, just as MIDI Max objects are configured to implement control programs. When the two classes are combined, the conceptualization and implementation of interactive systems using real-time signal processing is considerably eased. First, the response phase of the system is entirely programmable: not the choices of a manufacturer but the demands of a composition can decide the synthesis algorithms used. Second, a single programming environment can be used for both the processing and response phases. Third, since processing and response are realized with the same machine through the same programming environment, the need for communications protocols such as MIDI, with all their bandwidth and conceptual limitations, falls away (Puckette 1991).

The realization on the ISPW of powerful signal analysis techniques can eliminate much of the need for external sensing as well. The workstation is fast enough to perform an FFT and inverse FFT in real time, simultaneously with an extensive network of other signal and control processing. Already pitch- and envelope-tracking objects have been used for compositional sketches. If continuous sensing of pitch, amplitude, and timbral information can be achieved from the audio signal alone, the entire sensing/processing/response chain could be reduced to a single machine, with all the attendant gains in flexibility and implementation power that entails.

2.4 Commercial Interactive Systems

Commercially available interactive systems began to appear in the mid-1980s. Such programs illustrate the processing chain outlined in the previous section and several hallmarks of interaction. Rather than survey the full range of applications, we will briefly consider *M* and *Jam Factory*, two ground-breaking efforts in the field, before moving on to Max, a newer graphic programming environment that allows users to design their own interactive systems.

M and Jam Factory

In December of 1986, Intelligent Music released M and Jam Factory. Intelligent Music is a company founded by composer Joel Chadabe for developing and distributing interactive composing software. Chadabe and three others designed M; one of those collaborators, David Zicarelli, also designed Jam Factory (Zicarelli 1987). Among the breakthroughs implemented by these programs are graphic control panels, which allow access to the values of global variables affecting their musical output. Manipulating the graphic controls has an immediately audible effect. The sensing performed by M and Jam Factory centers around reading manipulations of the control panel and interpreting an incoming stream of MIDI events. Responses are sent out as MIDI.

Each program implements different, though related, compositional algorithms. "The basic idea of M is that a pattern (a pattern in M is a collection of notes and an input method) is manipulated by the various parameters of an algorithm" (Zicarelli 1987, 19). Four patterns are active simultaneously, and variables for each of them can be changed independently. The algorithm allows control over such parameters as *orchestration*, which assigns patterns to MIDI channels; *sound choice*, which selects program changes for the channels of a pattern; *note density*, the percentage of time that notes from a pattern are played; and *transposition*, which offsets pitch material from its original placement. Duration, articulation, and accent are governed by *cyclic distributions*, collections of data used to reset the values of these parameters with each clock tick. Further, the mouse can be used to "conduct" through various settings of these variables.

Jam Factory implements four *players*, whose material is generated using the transition tables characteristic of Markov chains (see section 6.2). Several tables of different orders are maintained, and "an essential part of the Jam Factory algorithm is the probabilistic decision made on every note as to what transition table to use" (Zicarelli 1987, 24). Separate transition tables for pitches and durations are employed, and each player has independent tables for both parameters. The probabilities of different-order transition tables being used affects the degree of variation and relatively straightforward playback of the stored material. For instance, first-order tables depend only on the previous pitch (in the case of melodic generation) to determine the following one. Second-order tables look at the previous two pitches, and so on. "For many applications, 70-80 percent Order 2 with the rest divided between Orders 1 and 3 will blend 'mistakes' with recognizable phrases from the source material in a satisfying manner" (Zicarelli 1987, 25).

Timing is expressed on two levels. First, a master tempo defines the rate of clock ticks. Then a time base, independent for each voice, sets the number of ticks that pass between successive events. This scheme closely follows the MIDI conception of time, which is organized around beats in a tempo. Beats always represent an identical number of ticks: quarter notes, for example, can span 24, 48, or 96 clock ticks. Though the number of ticks is variable for different applications or pieces of hardware, once a resolution is chosen, it remains constant for that notated duration. The speed of quarter-note realization, then, is changed by varying the overall tempo, which defines the duration of one clock tick. The advantage of this scheme is that the relation of events to an underlying meter is kept constant through tempo changes. The disadvantage is that it enforces a conceptualization of musical time in beats and tempi, even in music for which these are not appropriate categories.

M and Jam Factory are clear examples of performance-driven interactive systems. There is no stored score against which input is matched. The performance driving the program is basically a series of gestures with the mouse; an *input control system* allows the same functionality to be transferred to a MIDI keyboard. The response method is generative: stored lists of material are varied through the manipulation of a number of performance parameters. The programs follow a player paradigm in that they realize a distinct musical voice from the human performance. In fact, M and Jam Factory are unusual with respect to later programs in that the human performance itself is not particularly musical: rather, the performer's actions are almost entirely directed to manipulating program variables.

Max

In 1990, Opcode Systems released the commercial version of Max, a graphic programming environment for interactive music systems. Max was first developed at IRCAM by Miller Puckette and prepared for commercial release by David Zicarelli. Max is an object-oriented programming language, in which programs are realized by manipulating graphic objects on a computer screen and making connections between them. The collection of objects provided, the intuitively clear method of programming, and the excellent documentation provided by Opcode make Max a viable development environment for musicians with no prior technical training.

Throughout this book, examples of music programming techniques will be illustrated with Max. From the CD-ROM supplement, working

Max patches can be downloaded and run on an Apple Macintosh computer. Even without a computer, the graphic nature of the language allows us to readily follow the algorithm being discussed. For an in-depth introduction to Max, the reader is referred to the documentation provided by OpCode Systems Inc. with the program (Dobrian and Zicarelli 1990). Enough discussion of the modules used in the illustrations will be provided with each example to make the process under discussion clear to those readers unfamiliar with Max as well.

Object orientation is a programming discipline that isolates computation in *objects*, self-contained processing units that communicate through passing *messages*. Receiving a message will invoke some *method* within an object. Methods are constituent processing elements, which are related to each other, and isolated from other methods, by virtue of their encapsulation in a surrounding object. Depending on the process executed by a method, a message to an object may enclose additional arguments required by that process as well. Full object orientation includes the concept of inheritance, by which objects can be defined as specializations of other objects. Max does not implement inheritance, though the fundamentals of messages and methods will become quite clear from using the language. For an introduction to the concepts of object-orientation and their application to music programming, the reader is referred to Pope 1991.

In the next three sections, we will look at some objects in Max designed to handle the sensing, processing, and response stages of an interactive system. First, we can glimpse the flavor of programming in the environment: using Max, a composer specifies a flow of MIDI or other numerical data among various objects representing such operations as addition, scaling, transposition, delay, etc. A collection of interconnected objects is called a *patch* (in fact, Max has sometimes been called *Patcher*). Objects in a patch can be connected and moved to control data flow easily between them; "monitor" objects can be placed anywhere in a signal path, to inspect the input to or output from other objects; tables and histograms can easily be added to store or display data. Further, patches can be constructed hierarchically: once a working configuration of objects for some process has been found, it can be saved to a file and then included as a subpatch in other, larger programs.

Although Max is designed for making interactive music programs, one should always remember that it is a programming language, and therefore fundamentally different from sequencers and patch editors and similarly specialized commercial software applications. The effort required to achieve the same sequencing sophistication with Max that is available in programs such as Vision or Performer, for example, would be considerable and unjustified if the specialized packages do everything that is needed. Once the limitations of these programs are felt, however, and as soon as ideas of interactive and algorithmic composition arise, the power and flexibility of a programming language is indispensable. Other languages are available, but the documentation, ease of use, and focused optimization of Max for building such systems are compelling recommendations indeed.

Sensing

Sensing in Max includes an extensive collection of objects for handling MIDI messages. These objects access the internal MIDI driver software maintained by the program; according to the preferences of the user, either a self-contained MIDI driver or the Apple MIDI Manager can be selected for this purpose. MIDI sensing objects are distinctive, for one thing, because of the nature of information required by their inlets. On a Max object, the name of the object is found in the middle of the graphic box. Along the top are darkened *inlets*, where messages are sent to the object. Along the bottom, the black strips are *outlets*, where messages are sent out. Each object has inlets and outlets suited to the methods it encapsulates. The *midiin* object, for example, has one inlet and one outlet (see figure 2.2).

Midiin receives a stream of messages from a MIDI port. A port could be one of the Apple serial ports, either printer or modem. It could also be a *virtual port*, associated with a configuration maintained by PatchBay and the Apple MIDI Manager. The inlet to *midiin* is used to indicate the port to which the object should be listening. From the outlet comes MIDI bytes, retrieved from the designated port.

This object is emblematic of one source of power found in the Max environment: behind the simple object lies communication with a resident MIDI driver, or with the Apple Midi Manager, possibly extended by the Opcode Midi System (OMS). Rather than dealing with the intricacies of each standard, a musician has only to understand

midiin

Figure 2.2

midiin to deal with MIDI streams. I will not continue to insist on the value of this level of abstraction, because the point should be clear enough: with environments like Max, musicians are free to concentrate on musical issues. The complications of scheduling and MIDI management, which are, as we have seen, the two indispensable elements of interactive systems, are hidden behind simple and uniform programming elements.

Processing

Like section 2.2 on general processing principles in interactive systems, the following section is little more than a placeholder for the rest of the book. Processing is the heart of any interactive program: the examples scattered through the text, and included on the CD-ROM, illustrate the enormous variety of approaches to processing musical information. Here again, however, we will pause to consider facilities for treating one of the most important aspects of processing: the manipulation of time, and, as a fundamental tool for such manipulation, scheduling of events.

A prototypical Max scheduling object is *delay*. *Delay* receives a bang message at its left inlet and sends it back out after some number of milliseconds, set either by an argument to the object or as a message arriving at *delay*'s right inlet. Bang is the most common Max message. Almost all objects understand bang to mean "do it." In other words, whatever the object does, it will do when a bang arrives at its leftmost inlet. In this case, *delay* delays the transmission of a bang. What allows *delay* to save up the incoming bang and send it back out at some specified point in the future is Max's internal real-time scheduler.

In figure 2.3, the *delay* object at the center of the patch serves to delay the transmission of a bang message from its left inlet to its outlet. A bang can be sent to *delay* by clicking on the button connected to its left inlet. When the patch is first loaded, 1000 milliseconds (1 second) will pass between the time the top button is clicked and the time the button attached to *delay*'s outlet flashes, indicating the transmission of the bang. This is because *delay* was given an initial *argument* of 1000, the number shown immediately following the name of the object. Arguments can be used to set variables within an object to some initial value, as was done here. They are listed after the name of the object when it is first placed on the screen. Besides bang, *delay* also understands the message stop. A stop message can be sent to *delay* by clicking on the

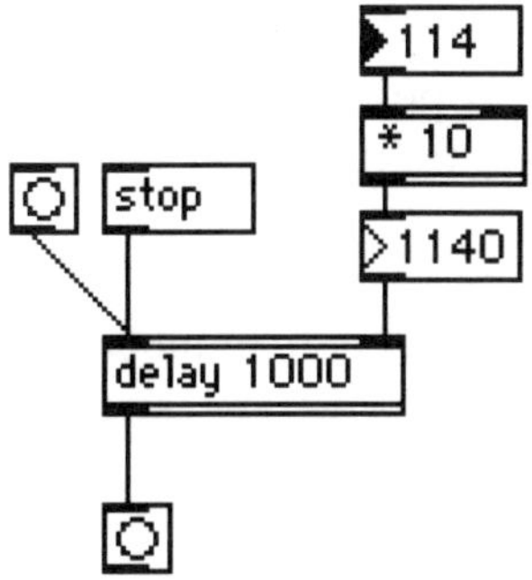

Figure 2.3

message box with stop written in it, connected to *delay*'s left inlet. Stop tells *delay* to abort the transmission of any bangs it may be saving up. Therefore, if stop is clicked after sending a bang to the *delay* inlet, but before a second has gone by, delayed transmission of the bang will be cancelled, and the lower button will not flash.

The amount of time the bang is delayed can be varied using the objects stacked above *delay*'s right inlet. Initially, bangs are delayed by 1 second, because the argument given to the object sets its delay time to be 1000 milliseconds. If the uppermost number box is manipulated, new delay times will be sent to the *delay* object, changing the duration between incoming and outgoing bangs. In the patch pictured, the delay time objects have been changed to set the delay between incoming and outgoing bangs to 1140 milliseconds (1.14 seconds).

Response

The response stage of an interactive system sends the results of processing out to some collection of devices, usually to make sound, and usually through MIDI. Again, Max provides a full range of objects for responding through MIDI, of which the *noteout* object is a good example.

We can see quite clearly from the graphic representation of the object (figure 2.4) that it handles output, or response. Notice that the object has no outlet. This is because the MIDI management tools of Max lurk

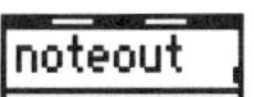

Figure 2.4

behind *noteout*'s facade. Again, programs built with noteout are able to send MIDI messages directly out the serial port, or to use Midi Manager or OMS without the details of such transmission being a matter of concern to the programmer.

The inlets of *noteout* correspond directly to the format of the MIDI Note On message. The leftmost inlet expects a MIDI note number, the middle inlet requires a MIDI velocity between 0 and 127, and the rightmost inlet is used to set the MIDI channel on which the resulting message will be transmitted. What will be sent to these inlets are questions of processing—the musical decisions and methods of the previous phase.

In the patch in figure 2.5, some processing has been added above the *noteout* object. Attached to the right inlet is a message box with the message "1." Clicking on this box will set *noteout* to send messages out on MIDI channel 1. Above the middle inlet are some objects to set the velocity field. Clicking the toggle at the top of the stack on will set the velocity inlet of the *noteout* object to 90 (as we can see from the number box just above it). Clicking the toggle off sets the velocity to zero, turning the note off. Above the leftmost inlet is a keyboard slider, which can be used to set the pitch number of the note message. To produce output, a user would click first on the "1" message box, to set the MIDI channel. Then, clicking on the toggle would set the velocity field to 90. Finally, clicking on a note on the keyboard slider would turn the note on. To turn the sound back off again, first the velocity toggle must be clicked to the off state. Then, clicking on the same note of the keyboard slider will cause the sound to turn off. This is because the *noteout* object will perform its method when new input arrives at the leftmost inlet. Therefore, if the velocity field is changed without reclicking

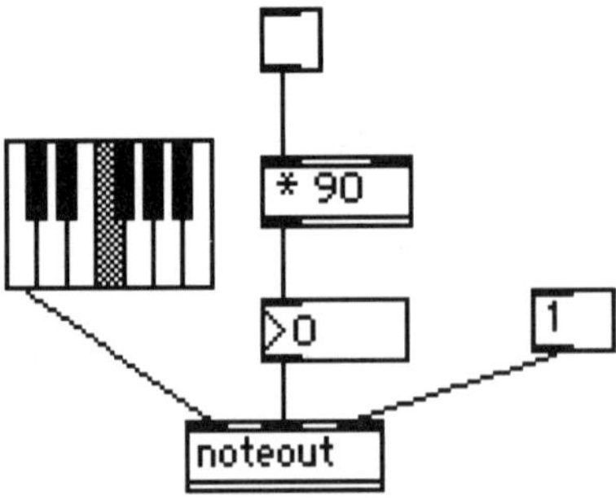

Figure 2.5

on the pitch slider, no effect is heard. This principle is a general one in Max—for most objects, the operation of the object is executed when a message arrives at the leftmost inlet. Patches should be used and constructed with this in mind, to avoid unexpected results from problems with ordering.

The patch in figure 2.6 introduces some additional aspects of Max programming, and begins to show how the language can be used to manage the distribution of functionality across the processing/response boundary. We have seen that Max supports levels of abstraction in which working patches can be encapsulated and included in other, larger configurations. The patch of figure 2.6 is a subpatch, in that it is written to be included in other patches. Across the top of the figure, then, are three *inlets*, marked "pitch," "velocity," and "segment time." When included in an enclosing patch, these three inlets will appear at the top of the box representing this subpatch, just as small blackened inlets appear at the top of standard objects, such as *stripnote* in the figure. Similarly, the boxes with arrows pointing up at the bottom are outlets, and indicate where information will flow out of the subpatch and back into the surrounding program.

As a subpatch, this bit of code does not perform a completely self-contained function, as did the earlier examples. Its job is to take pitch and velocity pairs, and a segment length, and prepare these for the realization of an amplitude envelope segment with a response-phase device. (This example was adapted from programs written by Miller

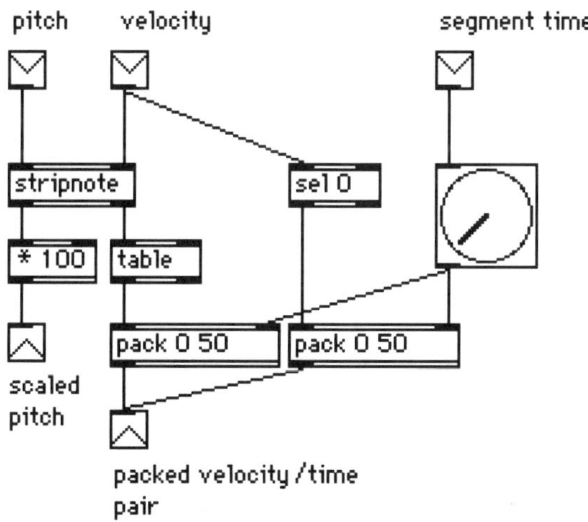

Figure 2.6

Puckette and Cort Lippe for compositions by Philippe Manoury, including *Pluton* and *La partition du ciel et de l'enfer*.) The pitch sent to the subpatch is multiplied by 100, to allow for microtonal inflections between semitones. If a Note On message is being handled, the velocity value will be nonzero. In that case, the incoming velocity is mapped to a new velocity with the *table* object, which we will explore in more detail in the following section. Otherwise the velocity remains zero, indicating a Note Off. In either case, the velocity is packed with a time value, which indicates the duration during which the amplitude setting of the response device should move from its present value, to the one produced by this subpatch. *Packing* numbers puts them into a list, which can be manipulated as a single item—sent into one inlet, for example. *Unpacking* reverses the operation.

2.5 Examples

In this section, I will present two simple examples of music generation methods implemented with Max. They refer to some of the earliest examples of algorithmic thought in Western music composition. The stages of interactive music systems will be shown in the context of simple working programs, and the basics of Max notation as it will be used for the remaining examples in this text are reviewed.

Guido's Method

Several authors have described the theoretic groundwork of compositional formalisms, and their recurrent use throughout the history of Western music (Loy 1989). An early example is Guido's method for composing chant. To set a liturgical text in chant, all of the vowels of the text are extracted. Guido specified a table comprising the tones of the scale and a way to use the derived vowel set as an index into the table. To produce a chant melody, the user looks in the table of tones for the one corresponding to each vowel of the text in turn. The tone found is set against the syllable containing the vowel, and the process continues until the end of the text is reached. The original correspondence was defined as in figure 2.7.

```
vowels  : a e i o u a e i o u a e i o u a
pitches : G A B C D E F G A B C D E F G A
```

Figure 2.7

The pitches are the scale members ranging from the G below middle C, to the A one line above the treble clef. The vowels are arranged above these pitches. To find a pitch for a vowel, the composer located a vowel in the top line, and found a corresponding pitch underneath. Note that there is more than one pitch associated with each vowel. Forming a chant with Guido's method, the composer would rely on more traditional heuristics for choosing between the possibilities: selecting the closest pitch to the previous one, for instance, or favoring certain intervals.

First written down around the year 1026, Guido's method is a perfect example of table lookup as a compositional formalism. The continued usefulness of this idea is evidenced by the presence in Max of the object *table*. Just as Guido employed the concept, *table* in Max is used to store compositional material and read it back out under different orderings for various circumstances. Its appearance on the screen shows the most important features of the structure: a two-dimensional graph of values contains all of the table's information. The x axis of the graph indicates the addresses of values in the table, and the y axis marks the range of potential numerical values to be stored. Each address in the table, then, holds one value within the specified range.

In figure 2.8, the contents of a Max *table* object are shown. Along the bottom of the rectangle representing the table, the addresses are shown. 0 is the lowest available address, and 4 the highest: there are 5 addresses in all. The address 2 is also marked along the x axis, because

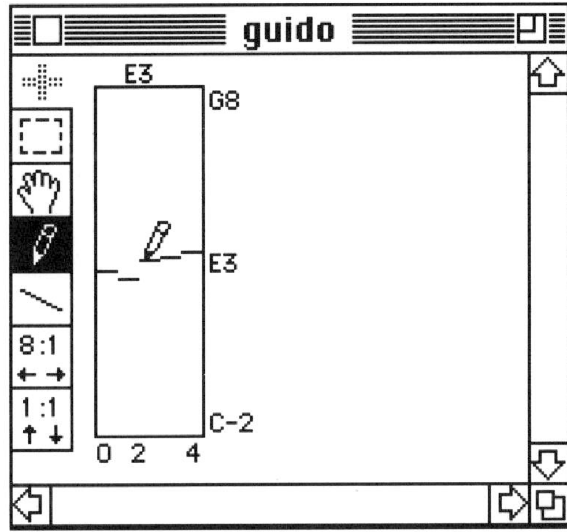

Figure 2.8

the pencil cursor is pointing to the value stored at location 2. Similarly, along the y axis are marked pitch names, corresponding to the values stored. E3 is marked across from the pencil cursor, since that is the value currently stored at address 2.

We can easily implement a version of Guido's method using the Max *table* object. Each vowel is used to generate an address sent to the left inlet of the table, and the pitch found at that address is played out as a MIDI note. This program is inadequate as a full Guidonian chant generator, because we limit the vowels to one pitch each. In the original table, each vowel corresponds to several pitch choices. Precisely this aspect of Guido's method means that it is not strictly algorithmic: each step in the process is not definite, because any vowel (the address) corresponds to more than one possible value. This lack of precision leaves room for artistic judgement to influence the outcome of the method. Such "trapdoors" can often be found in compositional formalisms, down to the programs in use today. To bring the method to a point where it can play chant melodies interactively as the text is typed, however, a decision must be made.

A variety of strategies are possible, any of which can easily be implemented in Max. In the second interactive Guidonian chant generator, shown in figure 2.10, the full vowel/pitch correspondence table

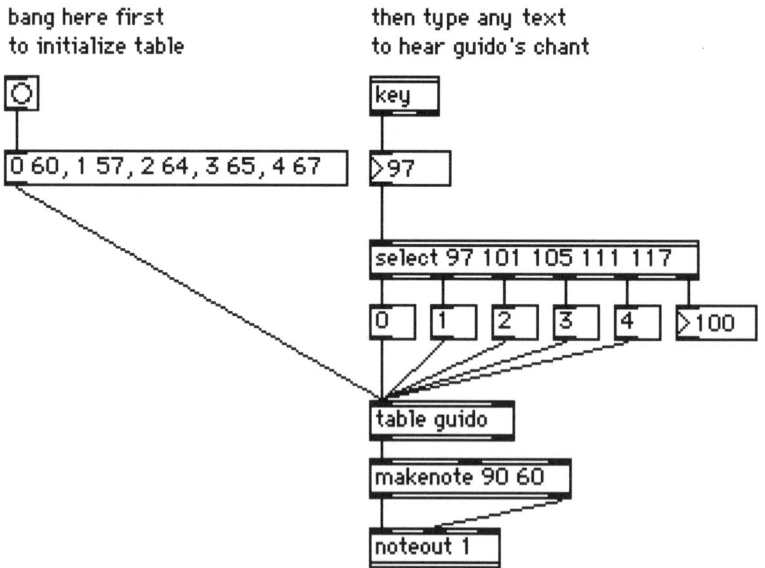

Figure 2.9

is used. Each vowel typed can produce several indices into the table: the vowel "a" addresses four places, and every other vowel, three.

The strategy implemented in figure 2.10 for choosing a particular address at any given vowel is to cycle through the possibilities: each successive occurrence of a vowel will index the next possible pitch for that vowel in the table. When the end of the table is reached, the cycle begins again at the beginning of the list. Each vowel cycles through the table independently of the others—in other words, one vowel could be accessing its last possible entry at the same time that another is still pointing to its first.

Now, typing any text on the computer's keyboard will simultaneously produce a Guidonian chant melody. As the text is typed, the vowels are selected and used as an index into a table of possible pitches, and each vowel cycles through its entries independently. The rhythmic

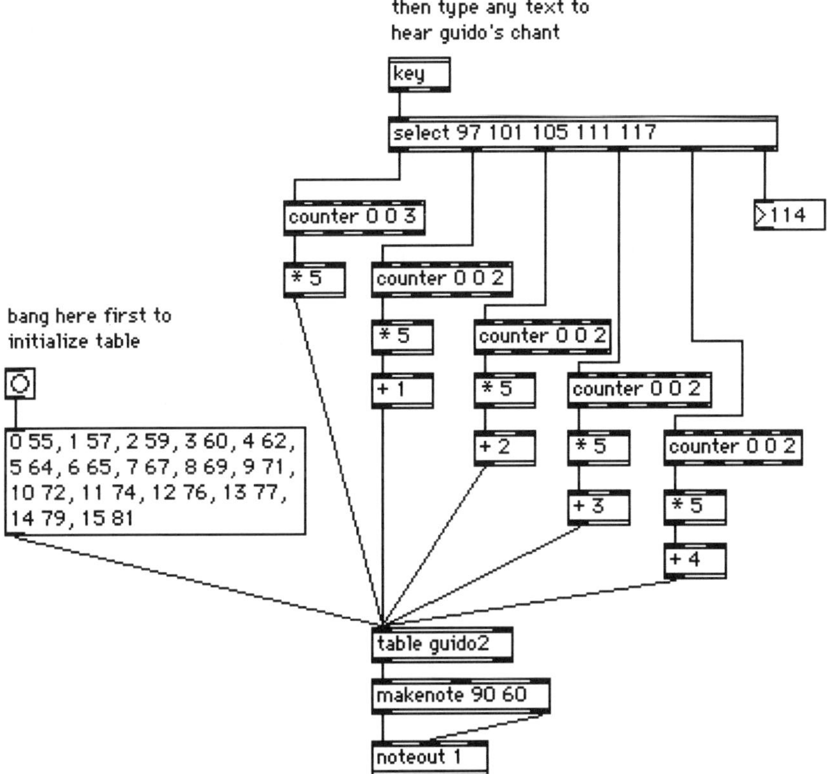

Figure 2.10

presentation is purely a function of typing speed; each successive tone is produced as soon as the corresponding vowel is typed.

Isorhythm

As can be said of many currents in compositional thought, exploration of formalisms in the generation of music has waxed and waned over the centuries. Periods of intense interest are followed by relative neglect, until stylistic circumstances bring formalistic procedures to the fore once again. After Guido's method, another important algorithmic school grew in the fourteenth century with the rise of the isorhythmic motet (Reese 1959). An isorhythm is a repetition of some pattern of durations, usually in the tenor, coupled to the pitches of a liturgical chant. Interesting variations arise when the length of the chant melody and the length of the duration pattern are unequal: as the two are repeated, different parts of the chant come to be associated with different durations.

Here again, the formalism can be modeled as a form of table lookup. Let us store an isorhythm in a Max table as a succession of durations held at adjacent addresses. In the traditional usage, the table would be

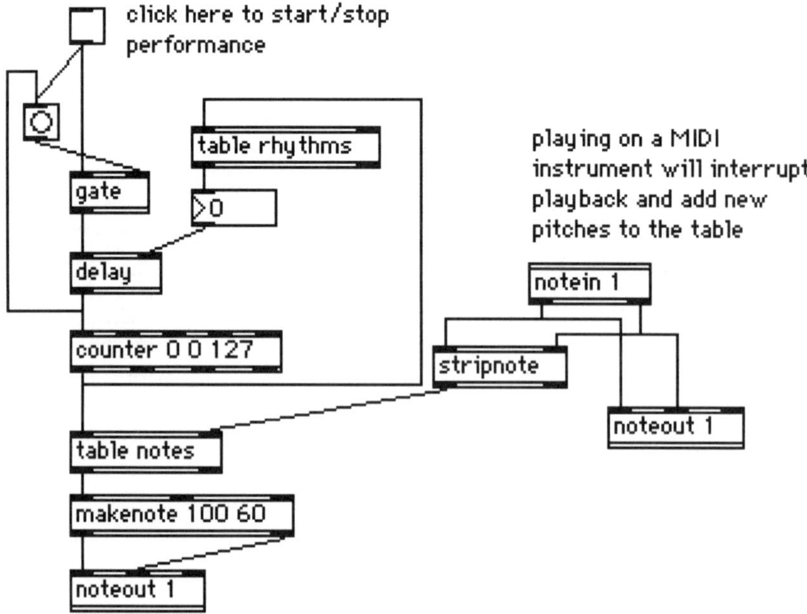

Figure 2.11

read in order from the beginning until the last address is reached. Then, the address counter would be reset to the first position, and the table read through again. A second table can be used to hold the successive pitches of the chant melody, and these paired up with the durations found in the isorhythm table. The Max patch shown in figure 2.11 contains two such tables, marked *pitches* and *durations*. Clicking the start toggle on will cause the resulting melody to play through, looping back to the beginning at the end of each complete presentation. The power afforded us by the interactive implementation of this idea, however, allows experimentation with several variations, some explored in the fourteenth century, and some not.

First, we have made this algorithm interactive by specifying that input coming from a MIDI keyboard will replace pitches in the note list. The *table* object will output the value stored at some address, unless a new value is presented to the right inlet. In that case, the new value is stored and nothing sent out. Therefore, if we connect the pitch information coming from a MIDI source to the data inlet of the pitch table, notes played through MIDI will be fed into the table at whichever address is currently chosen by the *counter*.

Now we can affect the computer's performance by our playing: if we do nothing, the output will sound as before. If we play new notes, the result will become less repetitive, as fresh pitches are added to the basic material. If we play quickly enough, notes will not be repeated at all, since they will be replaced before they are performed a second time.

Another possibility would be to make the effective lengths of the two tables unequal. If we added a second *counter* object to step through the durations table, we could set its upper limit to a value lower than that in the notes counter, for example. Then, setting the whole process in motion would cause different parts of the pitch table to be matched with different parts of the duration pattern each time through, until eventually they realign at the beginning of both tables and the process begins anew. The *counter* object allows us a number of other variations on this idea: we could make one counter read through the table from beginning to end, then turn around and read back from end to beginning, oscillating back and forth through the data instead of looping around. The other could read every other element, always moving backward.

How may we evaluate this system? First, we can categorize it according to our previously introduced dimensions: the technique is, first of all, performance driven. There is no stored score or concept of beat or tempo employed here, only time offsets. Second, it is essentially generative. Although external data feed the algorithm, the basic operation uses stored elemental material to generate the output, as opposed to transformations performed on the input as a musical whole. The system follows the player paradigm: the machine's music is recognizable as a voice separate from the human player.

The compositional method, in this form, is not particularly interesting. The output shows some readily perceptible relation to a human performance but does nothing more than repeat it with a constant, rudimentary style of variation. There are no control variables to allow changes in the variation technique. Many isorhythmic motets, however, are very beautiful pieces of music. This is because the formalism was again replete with "trapdoors": the isorhythmic method was used as a structural device, serving to unify and organize a much more complex and varied musical whole.

Often such formalisms have served a similar role—as a basic structure, a stimulant for the composer's imagination, or even an "in joke" between the composer and generations of analysts to come. As computers have been enlisted to realize such processes, however, more and more responsibility is given over to the process. Certainly, many programs are used collaboratively by the composer, who is free to override, interpret, or elaborate the output of the compositional formalism in any way, just as the users of isorhythmic techniques did. But as experience and a realization of the power of such processes grow, a great many programs have been implemented, with a sophisticated and highly developed sense of musicianship, for the automated, and unassisted, composition of music.

3 Live Computer Music

This chapter reviews a broad spectrum of existing interactive systems, elaborating and refining a framework for discussion of these programs in the process. Many of the fundamental issues surrounding interactive systems will be sharpened as they are considered in connection with working examples. Further, a range of compositional concerns and motivations come to light through a careful consideration of the music actually made.

3.1 Cypher

Cypher is an interactive computer music system that I wrote for composition and performance. The program has two main components: a listener and a player. The listener (or analysis section) characterizes performances represented by streams of MIDI data, which could be coming from a human performer, another computer program, or even Cypher itself. The player (or composition section) generates and plays musical material. There are no stored scores associated with the program; the listener analyzes, groups, and classifies input events as they arrive in real time without matching them against any preregistered representation of any particular piece of music. The player uses various algorithmic styles to produce a musical response. Some of these styles may use small sequenced fragments, but there is never any playback of complete musical sections that have been stored in advance for retrieval in performance.

In the course of putting together a piece of music, most composers will move through various stages of work—from sketches and fragments, to combinations of these, to scores that may range from carefully notated performance instructions to more indeterminate descriptions of desired musical behavior. Particularly in the case of pieces that include improvisation, the work of forming the composition does not end with the production of a score. Sensitivity to the direction and balance of the music will lead performers to make critical decisions about shaping the piece as it is being played. Cypher is a software tool that can contribute to each of these various stages of the compositional and performance process. In particular, it supports a style of work in which a composer can try out general ideas in a studio setting, and continually refine these toward a more precise specification suitable for use in stage performance. Such a specification need not be a completely notated score: decisions can be deferred until performance, to the point of using the program for improvisation. The most fundamental design criterion is that at any time one should be able to play music to the system and have it do something reasonable; in other words, the program should always be able to generate a plausible complement to what it is hearing.

Connections between Listener and Player

Let us sketch the architecture of the program: The listener is set to track events arriving on some MIDI channel. Several perceptual features of each event are analyzed and classified. These features are density, speed, loudness, register, duration, and harmony. On this lowest level of analysis, the program asserts that all input events occupy one point in a *featurespace* of possible classifications. The dimensions of this conceptual space correspond to the features extracted: one point in the featurespace, for example, would be occupied by high, fast, loud, staccato, C major chords. Higher levels look at the behavior of these features over time. The listener continually analyzes incoming data, and sends messages to the player describing what it hears.

The user's task in working with Cypher is to configure the ways in which the player will respond to those messages. The player has a number of methods of response, such as playing sequences or initiating compositional algorithms. The most commonly used method generates output by applying transformations to the input events. These transformations are usually small, simple operations such as acceleration, inversion, delay, or transposition. Although any single operation produces a clearly and simply related change in the input, combinations of them result in more complicated musical consequences.

Specific series of operations are performed on any given input event according to connections made by the user between features and transformations. Establishing such a connection indicates that whenever a feature is noticed in an event, the transformation to which it is connected should be applied to the event, and the result of the operation sent to the synthesizers. Similarly, connections can be made on higher levels between listener reports of phrase-length behavior, and player methods that affect the generation of material through groups of several events.

The preceding description provides a rough sketch of the way Cypher works. Much more detail will be provided in later chapters: from the theoretical underpinnings in chapter 4 through an exposition of the analytical engine in chapter 5, to a review of composition methods in chapter 6. Already, however, we can relate the program to the descriptive framework for interactive systems.

Considered along the first dimension, Cypher is clearly a performance-driven system. The program does not rely on stored representations of musical scores to guide its interaction with human performers. A cue sheet of score orientation points is used in performances of notated compositions, but this level of interaction is distinct from the more rigorous following techniques of score-driven programs. Further, the facilities for playing back stored scores in response are quite attenuated in Cypher. Although stored fragments can be played back in a limited way, I have never used any sequences in compositions using Cypher.

The indistinct nature of the classification metrics I propose can be clearly seen by the position of Cypher with respect to the second dimension: the program uses all three techniques, though with varying degrees of emphasis, to produce responses. Of these three classes, Cypher performs transformations most often, algorithmic generation somewhat, and sequencing hardly at all.

Finally, Cypher is a player paradigm system. Performing with the program is like playing a duet or improvising with another performer. The program has a distinctive style and a voice quite recognizably different from the music presented at its input. The player/instrument paradigm dimension is again a continuum, not a set of two mutually exclusive extremes. We can place Cypher at the player paradigm end of the scale, however, because a musician performing with it will experience the output of the program as a complement, rather than as an extension or elaboration, of her playing.

Tutorial 1—Input and Output

In the following collection of four tutorials, the operation of Cypher from its graphic interface will be explained. Cypher itself can be downloaded from the companion CD-ROM; these tutorials will make the most sense if they are followed while working with the program. First, we need to establish the program's channels of communication to the outside world. The upper right section of the interface, shown in figure 3.1, is used to establish output channels and program changes for the responses of Cypher.

The *Bank* and *Timbre* radio buttons together determine the sounds used to play the output of the composition section. Following normal Macintosh interface practice, exactly one radio button can be active for both functions—there will be one bank and one timbre chosen at any given time. The meaning of these buttons is established in a text file, called *cypher.voices*, which is read by the program on startup. This allows users to change the effect of the *Bank* and *Timbre* buttons simply by editing *cypher.voices* to match any local configuration of synthesis gear.

A listing of a typical *cypher.voices* file is shown in figure 3.2. The first specification recorded, as we see, is the number of MIDI channels available for output. In this configuration, there are ten MIDI output channels. Next, the file indicates which channel numbers are associated with the ten outputs. Then a series of program changes are listed. Here, the meaning of the *Bank* buttons is established. When it is selected, each *Bank* button sends out a set of program changes, one for each output channel. Which program changes are sent is specified as shown in the listing; there are eight sets of program changes, one for each button on the interface. Using this configuration file, we see that when a user clicks on *Bank* button 0, MIDI channels 1, 2, 3, 4, 5, 6, 7, 8, 10, and 11 will receive the program change messages 16, 11, 8, 29, 3, 9, 1, 3, 1, and 21 respectively.

The *Timbre* buttons choose subsets of the ten possible channels, which will all receive copies of the MIDI Note On and Note Off

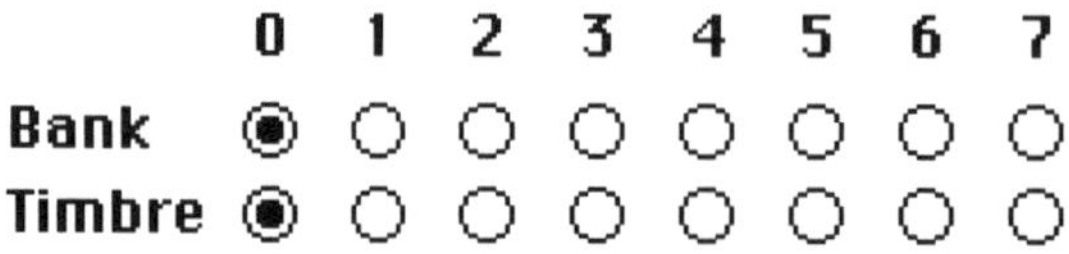

	0	1	2	3	4	5	6	7
Bank	◉	○	○	○	○	○	○	○
Timbre	◉	○	○	○	○	○	○	○

Figure 3.1

```
10                                  ; number of output channels

1 2 3 4 5 6 7 8 10 11               ; output channels to use

16 11  8 29  3  9  1  3  1 21       ; bank0 programs
18 11 17  2 28 13 30  2 12  2       ; bank1 programs
24  8 15 26 16 30  6 12  4 20       ; bank2 programs
 8  1 12 19  1 24  9 14  6 16       ; bank3 programs
 1  5 26 32 30 19 14 16  7 18       ; bank4 programs
 7  9 12  1 31  9 30 11 14  3       ; bank5 programs
 7  3  8  1 16  7  8 18  5 19       ; bank6 programs
23  4 17 14 31  9  9 24 17 15       ; bank7 programs

3 2 3 4 4 3 4 5                     ; # of channels per timbre

3  8 10                             ; output channels of timbre 0
8 10                                ; output channels of timbre 1
2  6 11                             ; output channels of timbre 2
1  3  4 11                          ; output channels of timbre 3
1  2  3 10                          ; output channels of timbre 4
4 10 11                             ; output channels of timbre 5
5  6 10 11                          ; output channels of timbre 6
1  5  6  7 10                       ; output channels of timbre 7

1 2                                 ; input channels
```

Figure 3.2

messages coming from the composition section. The entries in *cypher.voices* shown in figure 3.2 after the specification of the *Bank* buttons deal with the meaning of the *Timbre* buttons. First, the number of channels across which output will be sent is listed, one entry for each *Timbre* button. Thus, following this specification, *Timbre* button 0 will instruct the program to send out on three channels, *Timbre* button 1 on only two channels, and so on. Next, the configuration file lists precisely which output channels those are. So, for *Timbre* button 0, we know that it will limit output to three channels. In the line followed by the comment "`output channels of timbre 0`" we see that those three will be channels 3, 8, and 10.

Finally, two entries indicate which input channels will be monitored by the program when either the *Kbd* or *Ivl* selections are chosen from the interface. *Kbd* and *Ivl* refer to the two most commonly used source of MIDI input signals: either some kind of MIDI keyboard controller; or an IVL pitchrider, a commercially available device that converts

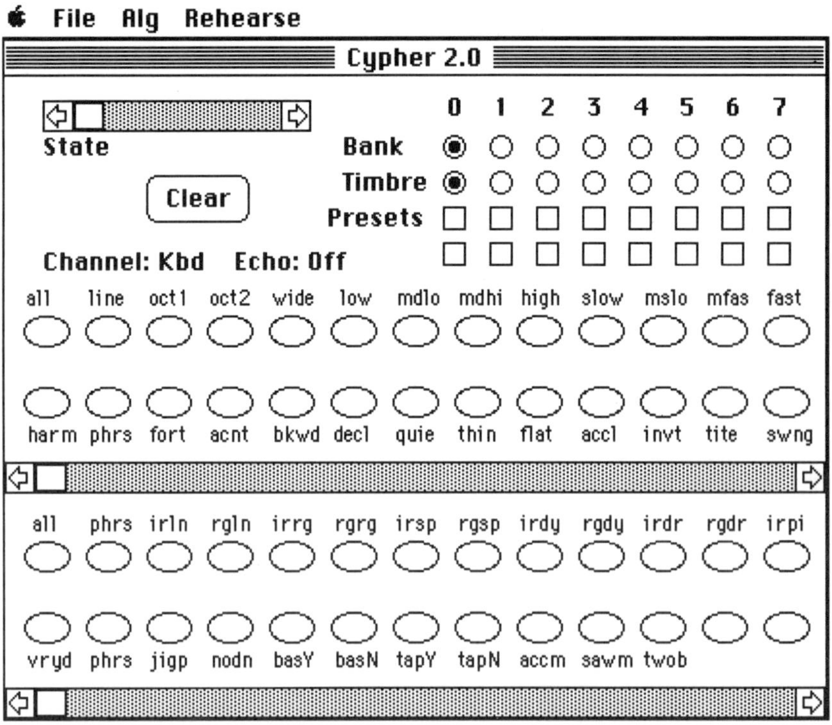

Figure 3.3

audio signals to streams of MIDI data. On the interface, there is an entry marked **Channel:** followed by either *Kbd, Ivl,* or *Nobody.* By clicking on the current selection, users will cycle through the three possibilities. When the **Channel:** selection reads *Kbd,* Cypher will listen to events arriving from the channel listed as the next-to-last entry in *cypher.voices* (channel 1 in figure 3.2). When **Channel:** selects *Ivl,* Cypher listens to MIDI coming from the channel listed in the last *cypher.voices* entry (channel 2 in figure 3.2), and when **Channel:** selects *Nobody,* Cypher will not respond to MIDI events arriving from any channel.

Tutorial 2—Making Connections

Cypher is equipped with a graphic interface to allow the connection of features to transformation modules, the selection of timbres, and the preservation and restoration of states. A reproduction of the control panel is shown in figure 3.3. The ovals occupying the lower third of the interface are used to configure connections between analysis messages emanating from the listener and composition methods executed in response. The upper two rows of ovals correspond to level 1 of both the listener and player; the lower ovals are used to configure level 2. We can see the various featural classifications indicated under the highest row of ovals; from left to right they are marked *all* (connecting a composition method to this will cause the method to be invoked for all listener messages); *line* (density classifications of single-note activity will cause a trigger to be sent out from this oval); *oct1* (density classifications of chords contained within an octave will send a trigger from here) and so on. The scroll bar underneath the pair of level-1 ovals can be used to bring the rest of the messages and methods into view. Shown in figure 3.4 are some of the additional ovals available on level 1.

When a listener message and player method are connected, that method will be called every time the listener produces the correspond-

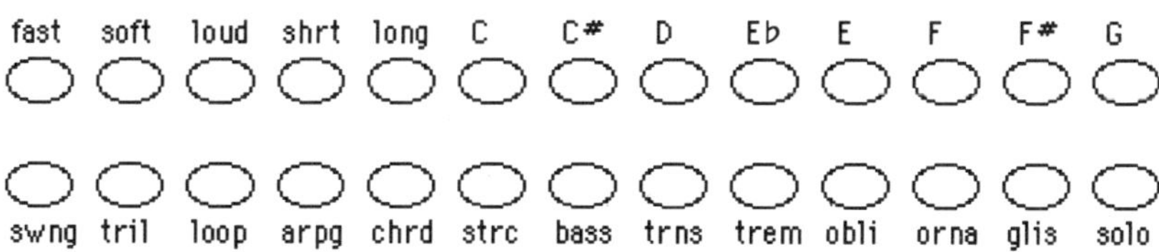

Figure 3.4

ing classification. To make a connection, a user simply draws a line from a message to a method, or vice versa. In the following example, I will assume that the reader has access to the companion CD-ROM and has installed Cypher on the hard disk of a Macintosh/MIDI computer system. Once the program is running, click and hold down the mouse button inside the listener oval marked *line*. Then, while continuing to hold down the button, draw a line to the player method marked *invt*. Inside the method oval, release the mouse button. A line should continue to appear between the two ends of the connection.

Now, whenever single notes (as opposed to chords) are played to the program, Cypher will respond with a pitch which is the inversion of the pitch played, around an axis of symmetry located on the E above middle C (MIDI note number 64). For example, if the performer plays the F above middle C (MIDI note number 65), Cypher will play E♭ (MIDI 63). The performer plays G (MIDI 67), Cypher plays D♭ (61), and so on. Direction is reversed—as the performer plays upward, Cypher goes down; the performer goes down, Cypher, up. Playing a chord will not provoke a response, however: Cypher is silent. This is because there are no composition methods associated with the density classifications for chords.

Let us make a second connection, between the listener message *oct1* and the player method *arpg*. *Oct1* indicates that a chord has been heard, with all of its constituent pitches contained within a single octave. The *arpg* transformation method will take all of the pitches given to it in a chord and play them back out as an arpeggio, that is to say, one after another. Now, Cypher has two different responses, which change according to the nature of the music being played by the performer. Single notes will still trigger the inversion behavior, and chords within an octave will be arpeggiated. Chords wider than an octave will still provoke no response, because again there is no associated player method.

In figure 3.6, the listener ovals at one end of the connection have gone off the left of the screen. When the user draws a connection to ovals

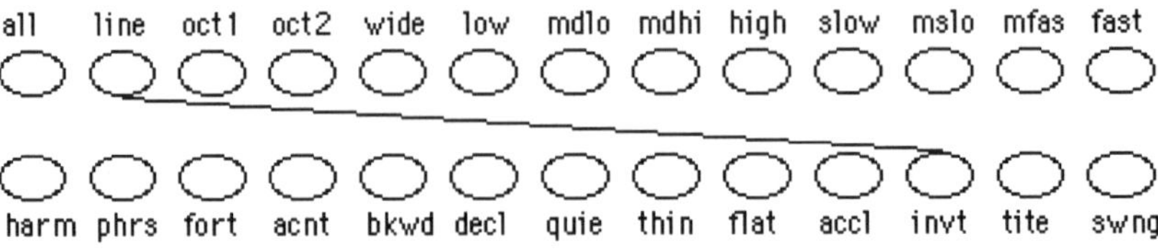

Figure 3.5

off either end of the interface, the ovals showing will scroll automatically to bring others into view, as the user continues to draw either left or right. The end of the connection is made normally, and the screen will be left with the origin of the connection somewhere off the end of the display, as in figure 3.6.

Now draw a third connection between the listener message oval marked *loud*, and the transformation method *tril*. The first two connections we made concerned the same feature (density). Either one or the other was active. The third connection is based on a different feature, loudness. This can be present or absent at the same time as either of the other two. The connection indicates that whenever the performer plays loudly, the trill transformation will be invoked. Now, quiet single notes will provoke the same response as before: they are inverted around the middle of the keyboard. Loud single notes, however, will be inverted, and have a trill attached to them. Similarly, quiet chords within an octave will be arpeggiated. Loud chords will be arpeggiated, and each note of the arpeggio will be trilled. Even chords wider than an octave now will be played back with a trill, if they are performed loudly. Only wide chords played quietly have no response at all.

Any feature/filter connection may be broken again by clicking once in an oval at either end of the line. In fact, clicking on an oval will disconnect all the lines arriving at that oval, so that if several transformations are all connected to a single feature, clicking on that feature

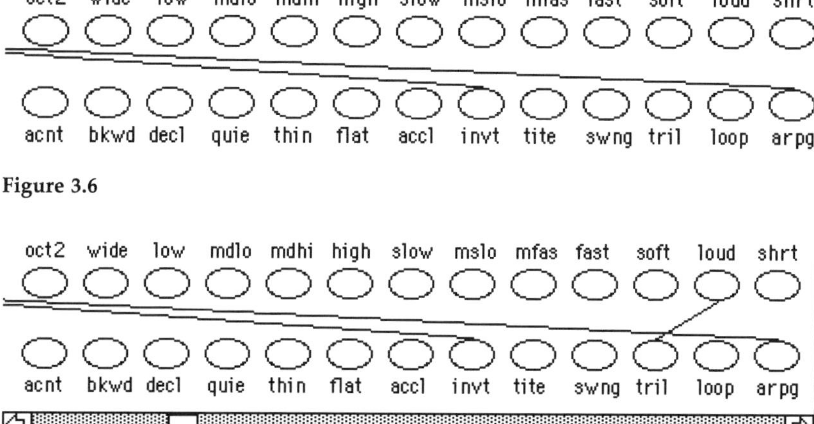

Figure 3.6

Figure 3.7

will disconnect all the transformations. Clicking on the transformation end of the line of that connection, however, will disable only the link between the feature and that single transformation. Any other links to the same transformation will likewise be severed. The *Presets* check boxes are simply collections of connections; they are toggles, which alternate between making and breaking certain sets of connections. As many as desired can be turned on at any one time.

A feature may be connected to any number of transformation modules; similarly, a transformation module may be connected to any number of features. If a configuration indicates that several methods are to be invoked, the transformations are applied in series, with the output of one being fed through to the input of the next. This is why, when a loud chord is played in the example configuration, a series of trills results. The first transformation applied is *arpg,* which splits the chord into separate notes. Then, this result is passed to *tril,* adding trills to each one of the individual chord members.

Because it is invoked in series, the same collection of transformations will produce different outputs depending on the order of their execution. The priorities of the transformations are reflected and established by their appearance on the interface. When several modules are to be applied to an input event, they are invoked from right to left as they appear on the screen. To reorder the priorities, a module can be "picked up" with the mouse and moved right or left, giving it a lower or higher priority relative to the other transformations. This new ordering of transformation priorities will be stored in the program's long-term memory, so that the next invocation of the program will still reflect the most recent ordering.

Tutorial 3—Level-2 Connections

The third and fourth rows of ovals on the interface represent the listener and player on the second level. The listener ovals (again, those higher on the panel) refer to the regularity and irregularity of the first-level features: *irrg,* for instance, stands for *irregular register,* meaning that the registers of incoming events are changing within phrases. The complementary analysis is indicated by *rgrg,* which stands for *regular register,* and means that the events in the current phrase are staying in a constant register more often than not. From left to right, the features that are tracked for regularity are density (ln), register (rg), speed (sp),

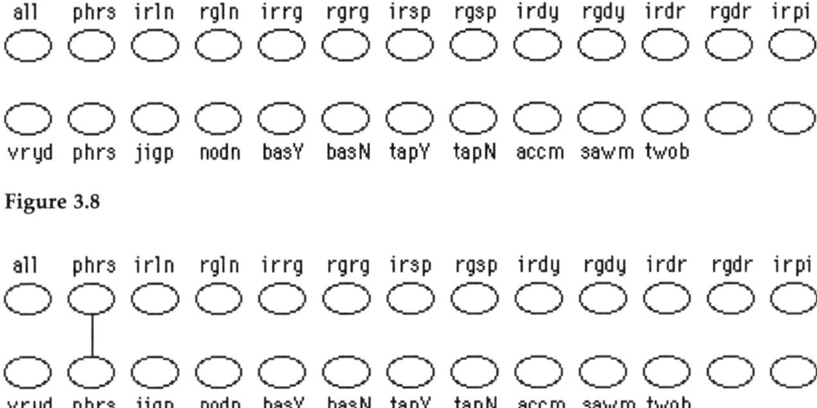

Figure 3.8

Figure 3.9

dynamic (dy), duration (dr), and pitch (pi). The classification of regularity and irregularity is explained in chapter 5.

There are some other level-2 listener messages than the ones dealing with regularity and irregularity. As on level 1, the first oval is marked *all,* which will invoke a connected player method on every incoming event. The second oval is *phrs,* which sends out a message on every event that Cypher takes to be the beginning of a new phrase. After the regularity/irregularity pairs, twelve key roots are listed: the oval marked *C,* for example, will send out a message for every event when the listener believes the current key harmonically is C major or minor.

The lowest row of ovals represents the level-2 player methods. Connections between listener messages and player methods are accomplished in the same way as for level 1. Let us make a connection between the listener oval marked *phrs,* and the player oval with the same marking (figure 3.9).

The *phrs* player method makes a thumping sound. The *phrs* listener message is sent out whenever Cypher thinks a new phrase has begun. Therefore, by connecting the two, we will hear the thump at all of the phrase boundaries identified by the program. You will notice that while Cypher's choices are not entirely accurate, neither are they entirely arbitrary. Again, chapter 5 covers in some depth how phrase boundaries are located.

Now we will add two more connections: from *rgln* to *vryd* and from *irln* to *nodn* (figure 3.10). With these connections we are calling up player methods from the regularity/irregularity reports concerning

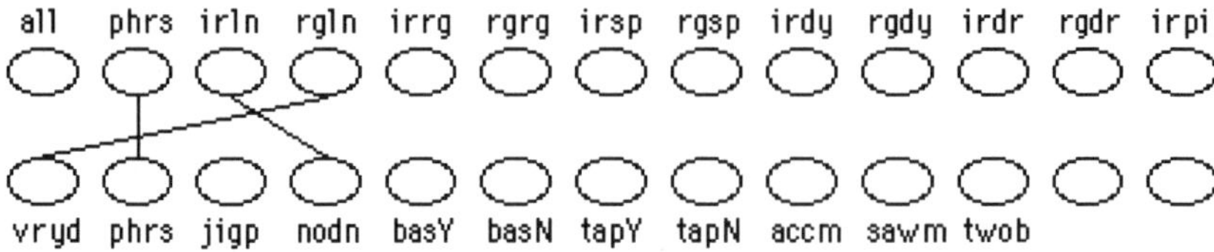

Figure 3.10

density. *Rgln* is an abbreviation of "regular line" (using "line" to indicate vertical density). *Irln*, then, is an abbreviation of "irregular line."

The regularity message is connected to the *VaryDensity* method: this process looks to see whether lines or chords are currently being played and instructs the player to do the opposite. That is, if the performer is playing lines, these will be transformed into chords, and chords will be changed into lines through arpeggiation. The complementary message, indicating irregular density behavior, is connected to the *NoDensity* method. This disconnects any of the methods used by *VaryDensity*, negating that operation. The regularity classification is done across the current phrase. Assuming the *phrs/phrs* connection is still active, at each new phrase boundary Cypher will play a thump. Then depending on whether predominantly chords or lines are played (regular behavior) or a mixture of the two (irregular behavior), the program will either play with the opposite density or not respond at all.

Tutorial 4—Menus

The *File* menu provides a number of commands concerning the state save-and-restore mechanism, and the execution of Cypher itself. The first three menu items have to do with opening and closing state files. A *state* captures all of the current program settings; saving a state means storing all of the connections, timbre and bank settings, and other control variables active at the time of the save. Restoring a state returns the program to some given collection of settings.

The state file menu items follow the layout of the usual Macintosh application *File* menu: *New*, *Open*, and *Close*. A state *file* contains many individual state *records*. With one file open, a user can save up to 100 different records. When a user opens a different file, the state records contained in it (again up to 100) become available. The *New* command opens a new state file, which will then be ready to receive and retrieve state records. *Open* is similar, but will present a dialog box with the names of all currently available state files, from which the user may choose. Finally, *Close* will close any currently open state file, clearing the way for a different one to be used (only one state file may be open at a time).

The next set of entries saves and restores individual states from the file collections opened with the previous section. *Save* will save the current program settings to a file, and *Restore* will restore a state from an open file. The record number for the *Save* and *Restore* commands is indicated with the state slider. If the slider is positioned on zero, a *Save* command will put the current program settings in an open file at record zero. The *Restore* command would retrieve the settings from record zero. The state slider must be moved to a new position before executing either the *Save* or *Restore* commands, which will then use the new record position in the file to perform their operation. The *Dump* command instructs the program to save each state, when passing through states with the score-orientation process. When *Dump* is turned on, a complete state file for a given composition will be saved automatically. The final *File* menu entry is *Quit*, which exits the program.

The second available menu is the *Alg* (for *Algorithm*) menu. The entries each invoke one of the compositional algorithms described in chapter 6. The performance parameters for these invocations are compiled into the program; relatively inflexible, this menu is primarily provided as a means of testing and demonstrating the basic texture implemented by each algorithm.

The remaining menu is *Rehearse*. The *Single* and *Free* commands will be covered in the section on score orientation. *Hung* is a MIDI panic button, used to terminate hung notes. Anyone who has used MIDI will be familiar with the phenomenon of the stuck note, which occurs when a Note On command somehow gets sent out without the corresponding Note Off command. When that happens, the sound simply goes on interminably. The *Hung* menu item will silence any hung notes, by the rather direct device of sending out a Note Off command to every note number on every channel. The rudely named command *ShutUp* will also terminate any stuck notes, with the further effect of preventing the program from producing any more sound. Sound will again issue from the program when the *Clear* button is clicked; *Clear* will also disconnect all level-1 and level-2 listener and player agents.

The text controller *Echo* cycles through the possibilities On and Off. When *Echo* is on, the MIDI data arriving from the device indicated by the channel input controller will be copied and sent out to the synthesizers selected by the *Bank* and *Timbre* buttons. This provides a convenient way to work on the *cypher.voices* file, trying out different voice combinations by directly playing them from the keyboard, for instance, rather than hearing them only as an expression of program output.

3.2 Score Following and Score Orientation

Now that we have seen how Cypher is used, we will review music that has been made with it. Before doing so, let us set the stage for that review, and the examination of other interactive systems following it, by looking at ways to coordinate machine and human performances. Two divergent means to the same end are considered: score following allows a tight synchronization between a solo part and a computer accompaniment; score orientation refers to a range of applications that coordinate human and computer players by lining them up at certain cue points in a composition.

Score Followers

The first dimension in our interactive system classification scheme distinguishes between score-driven and performance-driven programs. The paradigmatic case of score-driven systems is the class of applications known as *score followers*. These are programs able to track the performance of a human player and extract the tempo of that performance on a moment-to-moment basis. The best theory of the current tempo is then used to drive a realization of an accompaniment (Vercoe 1984; Dannenberg 1989).

A pattern-matching process directs the search of a space of tempo theories. The derived tempo is used to schedule events for an accompanying part, played by the computer, whose rhythmic presentation follows the live performer—adapting its tempo to that of its human partner. A comparison of the time offsets between real events and the time offsets between stored events (to which the matching process has decided that the real events correspond), yields an estimate of the tempo of the real performance and allows the machine performer to adjust its speed of scheduling the accompaniment accordingly.

The classic example of score following uses a computer to accompany a human soloist in the performance of a traditional instrumental sonata. As the human soloist plays, the computer matches that rendition against its representation of the solo part, derives a tempo, and plays the appropriate accompaniment. The human can speed up or slow down, scramble the order of notes, play wrong notes, or even skip notes entirely without having the computer accompanist get lost or play at the wrong speed. Such applications are unique in that they anticipate what a human player will do: the derivation of tempo is in fact a prediction of the future spacing of events in a human performance based on an analysis of the immediate past.

Score followers are score-driven, sequenced, player-paradigm systems. The pattern matching must be reliably fault tolerant in the face of wrong notes, skewed tempi, or otherwise "imperfect" performances rendered by the human player. Barry Vercoe's program is able to optimize response to such performance deviations by remembering the interpretation of a particular player from rehearsal. Successive iterations of rehearsal between machine and human results in a stored soloist's score which matches more precisely a particular player's rendering of the piece (Vercoe 1984).

The application described in Dannenberg and Mont-Reynaud 1987 is able to perform real-time beat tracking on music that is not represented internally by the program. The beat-tracking part develops a theory of a probable eighth-note pulse, and modifies the tempo of this pulse as additional timing information arrives. At the same time, the harmonic section of the program navigates its way through a chord progression by matching incoming pitches from a monophonic solo against sets of the most probable pitches for each successive chord. Here, the principles of score following are expanded to implement a similar functionality—performing an accompanimental part against an improvisation. Some things about the improvisation are known in advance—for example, the chord progression—however, the precise sequence of notes to be played, and their timing relations, are not known. Here we can see the essence of score following, comparing a performance against a stored representation of some expected features of that performance, carried out on a level other than note-to-note matching. Such a program moves over toward the performance-driven end of the scale and demonstrates one potential application area for these techniques that goes beyond the classic case.

The musical implications of score following in its simplest form are modest: they are essentially tempo-sensitive music-minus-one machines, where the computer is able to follow the human performer rather than the other way around. In most compositional settings, however, score following is used to coordinate a number of other techniques rather than to derive the tempo of a fixed accompaniment. In many of the compositions recently produced at IRCAM, for example, the computer part realizes a sophisticated network of real-time signal processing and algorithmic composition, guided throughout the performance by a basic score-following synchronization system. In his paper "Amplifying Musical Nuance," Miller Puckette describes this technique of controlling hidden parameters as a human player advances through the performance of a score (Puckette 1990). The hidden parameters are adjusted, and sets of global actions executed, as each successive note of the stored score is matched.

> The notes, and more especially the global actions, need not merely select synthesizer parameters. In practice, much use is also made in this context of live "processes" which may generate a stream of notes or controls over time; global actions can be used to start, stop, and/or parameterize them. Notes may themselves be used to instantiate processes, as an alternative to sending them straight to the synthesizer. If a "process" involves time delays (such as in the timing of execution of a sequence), this timing may be predetermined or may be made dependent on a measure of tempo derived from the live input. (Puckette 1990, 3)

The following section describes some of the basic tools in Max used to accomplish the kinds of score synchronization previously described.

Follow, Explode, and Qlist

In Max, several objects support score following, including *follow*, *explode*, and *qlist*. The *follow* object works like a sequencer, with the added functionality that a follow message will cause the object to match incoming Note On messages against the stored sequence. Matches between the stored and incoming pitches will cause *follow* to output the index number of the matched pitch. *Explode* is similar to *follow*, with a graphic editor for manipulating events. *Qlist* is a generalized method for saving and sending out lists of values at controlled times.

In the patch in figure 3.11, the outlets of *notein* are connected to *stripnote*, yielding only the pitch numbers of Note On messages. These are sent to a *makenote/noteout* pair, allowing audition of the performance (albeit a rather clumsy one, since all the velocities and durations are made equal by the arguments to *makenote*). Further, the incoming pitch numbers are sent to a *follow* object, to which are connected a

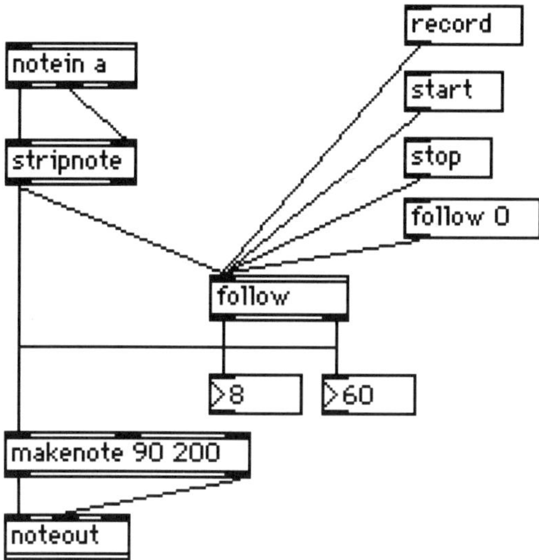

Figure 3.11

number of message boxes, lined up in the upper right corner of the patch. Clicking on the `record` message will cause *follow* to start recording the pitches arriving from *stripnote*. Then, clicking on `start` will make *follow* play the pitches back. The note numbers are sent out *follow*'s right outlet, where we can see them in the number box and hear them through *makenote/noteout*. Clicking `stop` will halt either recording or playback. Finally, once a sequence of note numbers is stored in the *follow* object, clicking on `follow 0` will start the object looking for the pitches of the sequence to be played again from the beginning. Each match between the stored sequence and new performance causes the index number of the matched pitch in the sequence to be sent out the left outlet; we can track the progress of the match with the number box attached to that outlet. Users can experiment with the leniency of the matching algorithm: playing some extra notes will not affect the match of the sequence when it is resumed. Skipping a note or two will cause the matcher to jump ahead as well. More radical deviations from the stored version, however, will eventually make the machine lose its place.

Explode is a graphic score editor built on top of the basic functionality of *follow*. Figure 3.12 shows an *explode* window: the black dashes in the main grid represent MIDI note events, where the x axis represents time, and the y axis note number. The chart above the grid makes it possible

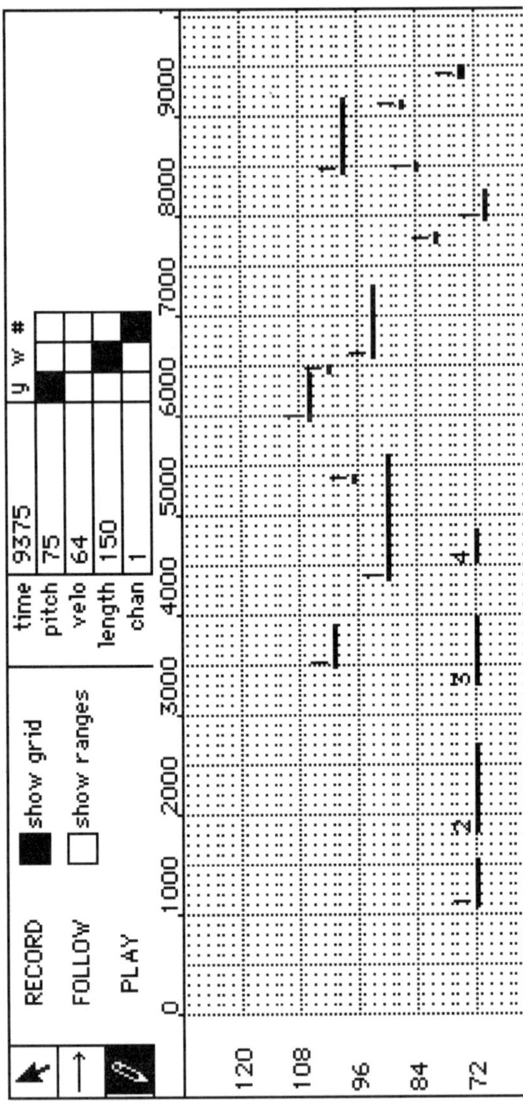
RECORD
FOLLOW
PLAY
show grid
show ranges
time 9375
pitch 75
velo 64
length 150
chan 1
y w #
0 1000 2000 3000 4000 5000 6000 7000 8000 9000
120
108
96
84
72
1
2
3
4

Figure 3.12

to change the quantities being represented by the *y* axis (y), the width of the dashes (w), or the numerical legends shown above each dash (#). The way the graph in figure 3.12 is set up, y shows pitch, w represents the duration of each event, and # shows the associated channel number. Further, the elongated rectangles next to the five parameter names (time, pitch, velo, length, chan) can be used to edit events directly. Whenever a single event, or group of events (selected with the shift key down), is selected, typing numbers in these parameter boxes will set all selected events to have the entered parameter value.

With the three icons in the upper left corner, the user can choose tools to move existing events (the arrow), stretch events in time (the horizontal arrow), or draw completely new ones (the pencil). Once a sequence has been specified, it can enter into the same relations with other messages and objects as *follow*: that is, it can play back the material, or follow another MIDI stream as it performs the sequence, sending out the index numbers of matched events.

A *qlist* is an object that manages lists of values, sending them out in response to messages. Lists in a *qlist* are separated by semicolons, which distinguish them one from another. The lists themselves can be

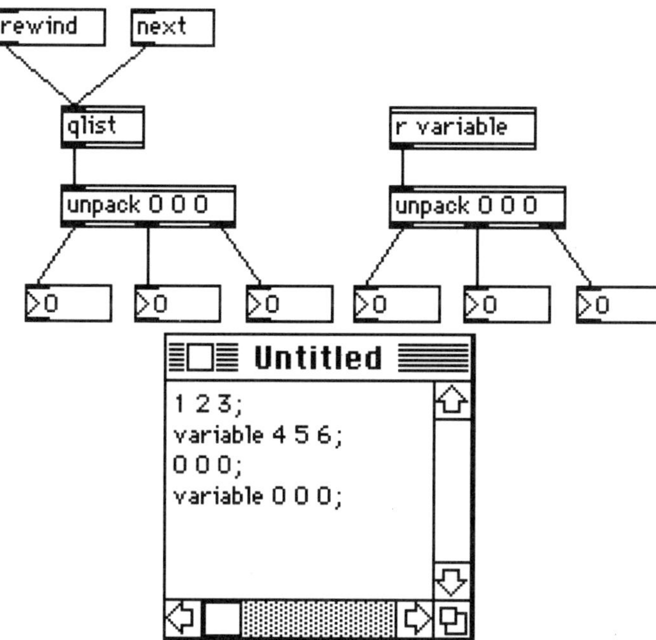

Figure 3.13

either simple lists of numbers or lists with a designated receiver. In figure 3.13, the window labeled **Untitled** was obtained by double-clicking on the *qlist* object. Within this window, lists of numbers are indicated, separated by semicolons. When the *qlist* receives a rewind message, it will reset its pointer to the beginning of the list. Next messages then will step through the lists, sending the stored values either through the outlet of the *qlist* object (for unlabeled lists) or to the receiver of a named variable. Successive next messages sent to the *qlist* in figure 3.13, then, will set the first three number boxes to read 1, 2, 3, and the number boxes below the variable receiver to read 4, 5, 6. All number boxes will then be reset to zero, as the qlist continues.

Explode and *qlist* can be used together as a general framework for score following. The score to be matched can be entered and tracked using the *explode* object. Event markers are attached to the *explode* score, to signal when the player arrives at points requiring a response. When a marker is found, a next message is sent to the *qlist*, which will forward the next record of values and messages to objects connected to its outlet or mentioned as receivers. See the **score_following.demo** prepared by Cort Lippe, on the companion CD-ROM, for an example of these objects working together.

Score Orientation

Score following is a powerful technique for tracking completely stored scores. Several programs have implemented related mechanisms for finding cues at specified points in a composition: rather than matching every incoming event against a score, these systems are concerned with synchronizing human and machine performances on a much coarser scale. Because such mechanisms are designed not to follow note-by-note performance but to find certain landmarks, I refer to them generically under the rubric of *score orientation*.

During a musical performance, an interactive program must be able to advance from one type of behavior to another. One way to advance it is through user manipulation of some interface, be it an alphanumeric keyboard, foot pedals, or graphic control panel. Score following can similarly drive a sequence of program states, for example when used in conjunction with a *qlist*. Score orientation is essentially the same idea. The goal of the technique is to advance the computer program from one state to another as the performance of some composition progresses. In contrast to score following, however, score orientation examines the incoming performance only at certain times, looking for some cue that marks the point at which the next program configuration should be introduced.

An important part of score-following applications is that they maintain a representation of the expected performance such that it can be efficiently be matched in real time. Another critical component is the pattern matcher itself, which must accept performances containing unforeseeable deviations from the stored version and be able to find the correct point in the score after a period of instability in the match. Score orientation, therefore, differs from score following in those two critical areas. In score orientation, the program is following the human performance to find those points in the composition where it is to advance from one state to the next. The technique does not follow a complete representation of the human player's part but is only scanning its input for cues at those moments when it expects to perform a state change. Further, score orientation can be accomplished with much less sophisticated pattern matching. Cues can usually be found that will be unambiguous enough inside a given time frame for the orienter simply to search for that single event.

Daniel Oppenheim's Dmix system implements score facilities that straddle the following/orientation distinction outlined here. He notes a difference between *horizontal* and *vertical* tracking, in which horizontal tracking corresponds to the classic score-following case. Vertical tracking allows a more spontaneous connection between a live performer and computer response, in which improvisations or interpretations by a performer would control variables of ongoing compositional algorithms, affecting a much broader range of parameters within the musical context than tempo alone. Dmix is an object-oriented, integrated system for composition and performance; within it, the SHADOW mechanism can treat collections of events as scores for either horizontal or vertical tracking. Moreover, such scores can be treated by other parts of Dmix (an extension of Smalltalk-80) for simulating a performance, editing, or transfer to disk (Oppenheim 1991).

Windowing

Cypher's score-orientation process uses a technique called *windowing*. A window is a designated span of time. During the duration identified by a window, the program is searching for a particular configuration of events; when that configuration is found, the program state is updated and, if necessary, the opening of another window is scheduled. If the desired configuration has not been found by the end of a window, the state change and scheduling of the next window are done anyway. This ensures that the program will never remain in a given state indefinitely waiting for any single cue.

Cues can be missed for a variety of reasons; in practice, one missed target will not throw off the orientation. Usually, the next window successfully finds a match near its leading edge. If two or three windows in a row pass without a match, however, the orienter is irretrievably lost, and must be righted through external intervention. But even if nothing were ever played to the score orienter, the program would eventually make it to the end of the piece—it would just no longer be synchronized with an external performer. The graphic interface provides mechanisms for beginning execution at any given state and for recovering from missed cues, if this should be necessary in performance.

There are six parameters associated with a score-orientation window: (1) the time offset between the identification of the preceding orientation cue and the expected arrival of the next one; (2) the leading edge of the window, or time in advance of the expected arrival of the target event, at which to begin looking for it; (3) the trailing edge of the window, the duration after the expected arrival of the target event during which to continue looking for it; (4) the type of event being targeted (pitch, attack, pattern, etc.); (5) the specific event of that type to be located (pitch number, attack point, pattern description, etc.); and (6) the routine to be invoked when a target has been found. All of these parameters are coded by the user into a cue sheet, which the score orientation process will use to schedule and execute polling for the designated events during performance.

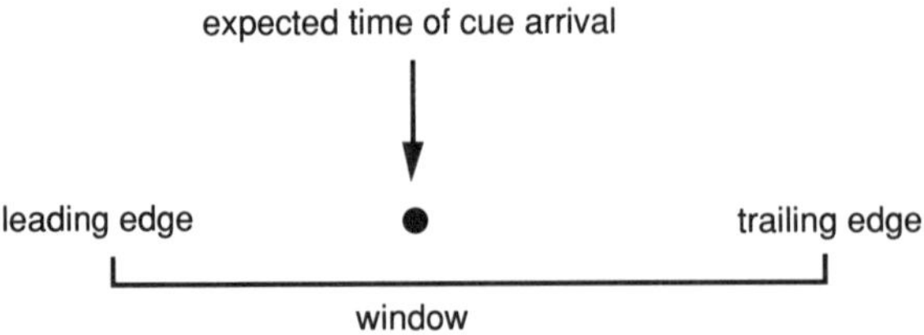

Figure 3.14

The following is a typical entry for the cue sheet of a Cypher composition: `{ 7080L, 2500L, 4000L, PITCH, 59 }`. There are five fields in the structure, which correspond to the expected arrival time of the cue (7080 milliseconds after the previous cue); the time in advance of the expected arrival to open the search window (2500 milliseconds); the time after the expected arrival to continue the search (4000 milliseconds); the type of cue to look for (PITCH); and which pitch to notice (59, or the B below middle C). With these settings, the duration of the search window is 6.5 seconds, with the arrival of the cue expected close to the beginning of the window.

There are six different cue types for events targeted by the score orientation routine. These are

- **Pitch** Any MIDI pitch number can be specified as the target event.
- **Attack** At the opening of the window, a pointer is set to the most recent incoming MIDI event; the next event past this pointer—that is, the next event played—will trigger the state change.
- **Root** A chord root, expressed in absolute terms (C, F, Ab, etc.) as opposed to relative terms (I, IV, V, etc.) can used as a target event.
- **Function** Chord roots described as functions—that is, in relative terms (I, IV, V, etc.)—can be used as targets with this event type.
- **Time** This option essentially bypasses the windowing mechanism. The state change will be executed when the duration indicated has elapsed, regardless of other conditions.
- **No Attack** This type uses the Boredom parameter; when no MIDI input has come for a duration exceeding the Boredom limit, *no-attack*-type state changes will be executed.

This collection of cue types reflects the demands of the compositions learned by this implementation of Cypher. They have the virtue of simplicity and are quite robust; however, they are by no means an exhaustive list of the types of cues one might want, or even of the cue types the program could easily accommodate. In essence, any of the messages coming from a listener could be used as a cue; a certain register identification, or a phrase boundary, for example, could be recognized by the score-orientation process and used to trigger a state change. This list should be regarded as an example, motivated by the circumstance of a few compositions; the complete list would be simply an inventory of all possible listener messages.

Once a cue has been found, any routine can be called with any number of arguments. A pointer to the routine and its arguments are saved when the specifications for the window are first introduced. In Cypher compositions, the arrival of a cue triggers the invocation of a *score point,* a typical example of which is illustrated in figure 3.15.

In this bit of code, the sounds used by the composition section are changed with the `SynthManager()` and `TimbreManager()` calls, which install program changes and channel configurations. The rest of the score point makes connections between listener messages and player methods on level 1. The same effect could be achieved by calling up states saved in a state file; in fact, a parallel state file does exist for each piece, containing all the information laboriously written out here. Using this text encoding of the state changes is largely a convenience, as it allows examination of the state in a relatively succinct and easily editable form.

Score orientation has some attractive features, among them the fact that search is performed only around those moments where something needs to be found and that it continues to be useful in the face of scores that change from performance to performance; if anything about the context in an indeterminate section is constant, it can still be used to cue the score orienter. The technique has, however, some equally obvious problems. First among them is the fact that when a window ends without locating the target, the system has no way to tell whether the target event was not found because it was played before the window opened, or because it has yet to be played, or because an error in the performance means that it will never be played. Therefore, the program itself cannot adjust the positioning of the following window,

```
/* m 33 */
void
ScorePt7()
{
	SynthManager( SET, 1);
	TimbreManager(SET, 3);
	HookupLink(0, Grac, OR, Lin);
	HookupLink(0, Trns, OR, Low);
	HookupLink(0, Trns, OR, Midhi);
	HookupLink(0, Glis, OR, High);
	HookupLink(0, Accl, OR, Slow);
	HookupLink(0, Phrs, OR, Fast);
	HookupLink(0, Acnt, OR, Short);
}
```

Figure 3.15

because it does not know if its schedule of cues is running early or late. The cure for this problem would be to provide the orienter with better targets—not single pitches or attacks, but small local contexts. If most of the recognizable information from a whole measure is provided, for instance, missing one note within the measure would have no effect on the orienter.

Rehearsal Mechanisms

One of the most critical components of an interactive system is a rehearsal mechanism. Artificial performers should be able to integrate with normal rehearsal techniques as seamlessly as possible. This demands two things of the program: that it be able to start anywhere in the score, and that it be able to get there quickly. Musicians tend to start at structural breaks in the music and may start at a certain bar several times in rapid succession. Or they may rehearse a section of the piece repeatedly. If it takes the computer markedly longer to be prepared to start playing from any point in the score, human players' patience with their neophyte performance partner may flag at the most critical juncture, during rehearsal.

In Cypher, a performance file is made up of complete state records for every change of state in a composition. A *state* is the set of variables whose values uniquely determine the behavior of the program. These variables include the connections between input features and transformation modules, output channel configurations, and the like. Each state comprises about 2000 bytes of data and so can easily be saved in great numbers without taxing the storage capacity of personal computers. Advancing from one state to the next is accomplished through the windowing score-orientation technique.

The *Rehearse* menu and state slider in the upper left on the control panel make up the state save-and-restore mechanism. The slider is used to select a state record number; these range from zero to sixty, though the upper limit is completely arbitrary and easy to change. To record a state to memory, the user first positions the slider so that the state number showing beneath it corresponds to the desired state record in the file. Then the item *Save* is selected from the *File* menu. This will record the current state shown on the interface to the currently open file, at the given state record number. If no state file is open, a dialog box will first appear asking which file is meant to receive the new record. The complementary operation is performed in response to the *Restore* item in the *File* menu. Again the record number is accessed from the slider, and then the requested state is retrieved from the open file. If no state file is open, a dialog box asks for the specification of one. If no such record is present in the open file, an error message is generated.

The interface accesses two modes of rehearsal: *Single* and *Free*. Both these options reference a state slider to find out what the initial state number for the rehearsed material should be. *Single* will return the program to that state and stay there. This mode allows rehearsal of small sections of the score for as long as is desired, without advancing to subsequent score states. In contrast, *Free* will revert to the state number given by the slider and commence performance of the piece from that point. In this mode, the succession of state changes will be executed as in a complete performance of the work, allowing rehearsals to start at any given point and continue from there.

An Example

The example in figure 3.16 is taken from *Flood Gate*, a composition for violin, piano, and Cypher. In this example, we will examine a score-orientation state change associated with a pitch cue. In figure 3.16, at the beginning of measure 6, the A circled in the piano part is the target of the window associated with state 1. The opening of the window arrives some seconds before measure 6, approximately one measure earlier. The circled A is chosen as a target for two reasons: first, because it is an important event in the context of measure 6, one likely to be treated carefully by the pianist in any event; and, second, because there are no other appearances of that pitch in the immediate vicinity—particularly, none in measure 5, when the window opens.

The expected arrival time of the A is the focal point of the score-orientation window for state 1. The estimate of when this cue will arrive is made at the time of the previous state change, that associated with state 0. When state 0 is activated, the current absolute clock time is noted. The ideal temporal offset of the next cue, that associated with state 1 from the time of activation of state 0, is added to the current time. The result is used as the estimated time of arrival of the following event. When the cue for state 1 arrives, again an ideal offset preceding state 2 is added to the current clock time.

Ideal cue arrival times are initially calculated from an examination of the score. Using the notated metronome marks as a guide, one can

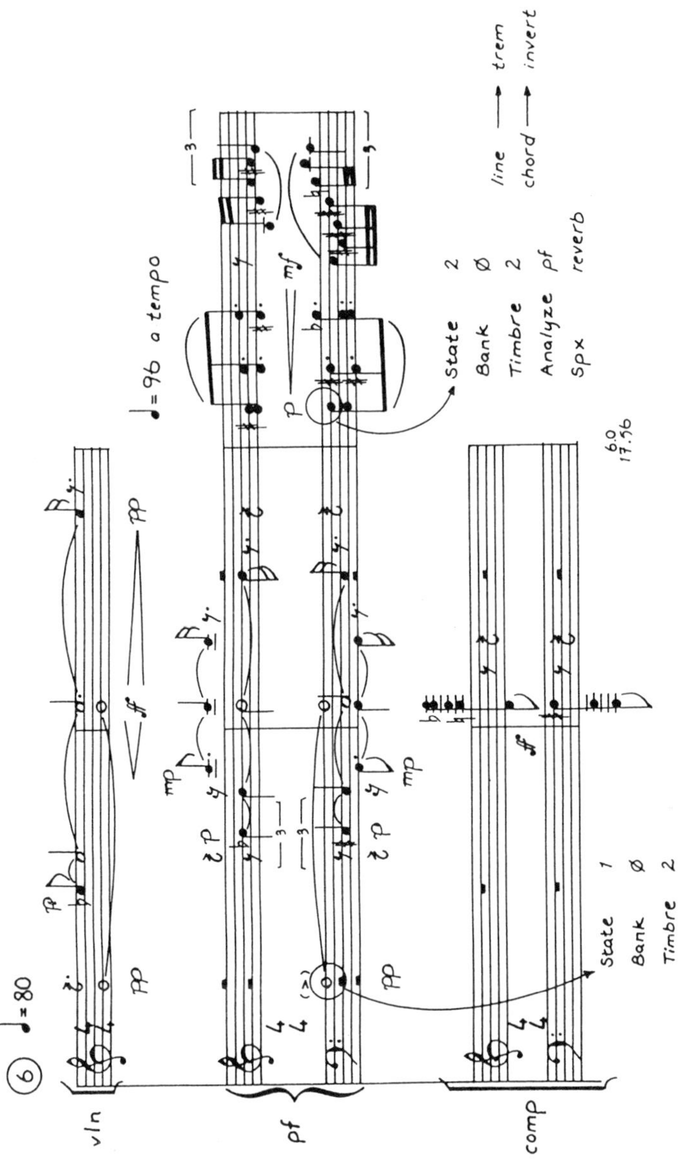

6
♩= 80
♩= 96 a tempo
vln
pf
comp
State 1
Bank Ø
Timbre 2
State 2
Bank Ø
Timbre 2
Analyze pf
Spx reverb
line ⟶ trem
chord ⟶ invert
6.0
17.56

Figure 3.16

determine the temporal offset between one point in the score and another from the number of beats at a given tempo separating the two points. The rehearsal process will serve to bring these ideal estimates in line with the actual performance practice of a particular human ensemble. The offsets between cue points, and the window sizes surrounding each cue will typically be tuned during rehearsal to find a comfortable fit between Cypher's score orienter and the other players.

Returning to our example, the window associated with state change 1 remains open until approximately the beginning of measure 7. When the expected A is found, the chord shown in the computer part at the beginning of measure 7 is scheduled, as is the opening of the next window, associated with state 2, targeted for the F at the start of measure 8. The chord, which is notated in the score at the downbeat of measure 7, will be scheduled as an ideal offset from the arrival of the cue pitch A; in other words, if measure 6 is played exactly in tempo, the chord will arrive exactly on the downbeat of measure 7. The gesture is composed to allow for the arrival of the computer's chord somewhere other than exactly on the beat, however; the musical idea is a swell in the violin and piano leading to a dynamic climax accentuated by the computer part. In some cases, even with score orientation, the computer takes the lead: this is a natural example, in that the arrival of the chord marks the high point of the crescendo. The human players quite naturally adjust their performance to accommodate their machine partner's timing.

If the end of the window associated with state 1 is reached without finding the A, that is, if we reach measure 7 without seeing the target, the chord and state-2 window opening are scheduled anyway. In that case, the chord opening measure 7 will be quite late, which is usually a very telling signal to the human players that Cypher is confused. The F of state 2 will then probably be found close to the start of the window for state 2, however, (since the window scheduling was initiated a little late), and the computer and human performers are then once again synchronized.

3.3 Cypher Performances

Several compositions were written during the development of Cypher. These works fell into two broad categories: largely notated pieces, and completely improvised performances. There are four notated works (which themselves all include some forms of improvisation), using human ensembles ranging from one to eight players. Musicians were constantly improvising with the program, usually on an informal basis, but on several occasions Cypher contributed to a more or less completely improvised performance in concert. In the notated works, human players are asked to perform at various times through either of two means of musical expression: interpretation of a written part, or improvisation. Interpretation comes into play during the performance of completely notated sections, in which case the players behave as the interpreters of Western concert music normally do: reading the music to be performed from the page, and rendering it with their own trained musical judgment. In other sections, the players are given the freedom to improvise, in keeping with the spirit of the composition. Usually, some constraints or indications of basic material are given to the players in the improvised sections; ideally, however, the improvisations are rehearsed and honed through the collective rehearsals of composer, performer, and computer.

During the evolution of Cypher, developments in my musical thinking have often been spurred by new formal possibilities the program provides. I have long been interested in developing ways to involve the player in shaping a composition during performance. The improvisational segments of pieces written with Cypher show an organic relation to the rest of the composition because the program knits together notated and improvised material in a consistent way. Responses to both sorts of material are generated identically, but the improvisational sections show great variation from performance to performance, while the notated parts stay relatively constant. Sharing material between the two styles of performance and weaving improvisational elaboration into an ongoing presentation of notated music, however, seem to make a coherent whole out of performances that might easily fall into irreconcilable pieces.

Notated Works

The first notated work I wrote with Cypher was *Flood Gate* (1989), a trio for violin, piano, and computer. The score includes conventionally notated music and some partially or completely improvisatory sections. The software development for this work concentrated on a number of the system's fundamental performance tools: score orientation, studio to stage compositional refinement, and algorithmic responses to improvisation.

Whether the music is notated or improvised, the computer characterizes what it is hearing and uses that information to generate a musical response. In the completely notated sections, the output of the computer part is virtually identical from performance to performance, since the same material is being played into the same highly deterministic processes. There are some random numbers in these processes, but they are used in tightly constrained ways. For example, the ornamentation filter will add two pitches in close proximity to the input pitch. Although the ornamental pitches are chosen at random within a small ambitus, the effect of a small flourish around a target pitch is the perceived result; in other words, the use of random numbers is so tightly restricted that the relation of input to output is virtually deterministic. In the improvised sections, the output of the computer part is also a transformation of the human performer's input: the transformations are a function of the features extracted from the music played to the computer. Each performance of the improvised sections is different; one goal of the composition was to marry composed and improvised elements in the same piece, using similar algorithmic techniques. Score orientation guided Cypher through sixty-one state changes in the course of a ten-minute piece, with no operator intervention.

Most of the processing used in this piece took place on level 1 of both the listener and player. This being the first essay, the most immediate forms of analysis and reaction were used. The work succeeds as an example of interaction on a featural level but points out the advantage of being able to guide processing on higher musical levels as well: phrase length effects such as crescendo and accelerando are largely missing from the computer output. Figure 3.17 is a page from the score, illustrating the material with which the pianist was presented for her improvisation.

The next composition to use Cypher was a work for solo piano and computer, called *Banff Sketches* (1989–91). This piece was, appropriately enough, begun during my residency at the Banff Centre in Alberta, Canada, during the summer of 1989, in collaboration with the pianist Barbara Pritchard. Subsequent performances, including those at the SIG-CHI '90 conference, the MIT Media Laboratory, a *Collage* concert of Media Laboratory works at Symphony Hall in Boston, and the ICMC 1991 in Montreal provided opportunities to refine and expand the composition.

138
accel. ♩=76
vln
pf
comp
5.1
6.22.68
State 35
Bank 2
Timbre 1
Shadow pf
Spx reverb
7.1
6.29.78

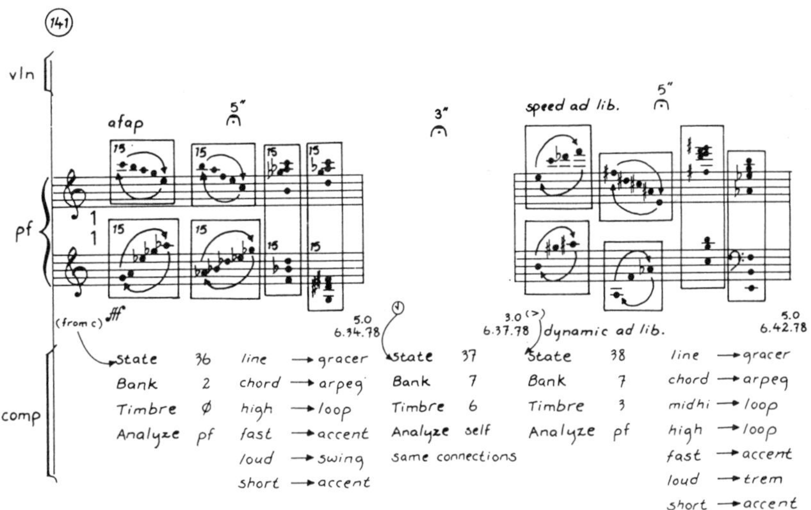
141
vln
pf
comp
afap
5"
3"
speed ad lib.
5"
(from c)
5.0
6.34.78
3.0
6.37.78
dynamic ad lib.
5.0
6.42.78
State 36
Bank 2
Timbre Ø
Analyze pf
line → gracer
chord → arpeg
high → loop
fast → accent
loud → swing
short → accent
State 37
Bank 7
Timbre 6
Analyze self
same connections
State 38
Bank 7
Timbre 3
Analyze pf
line → gracer
chord → arpeg
midhi → loop
high → loop
fast → accent
loud → trem
short → accent

Figure 3.17

One of the main extensions added to the program for *Banff Sketches* was *alternation*. This is a mode designed to emulate the well-known compositional and performance practice of taking turns to elaborate some common material; in jazz a typical application of the idea is "trading eights," where two performers will alternate improvisations of eight bars each, commenting and expanding on ideas introduced by the other. For such an idea to work with Cypher, the program had to know when to store material from the human player and when to compose an elaboration of that material in an unaccompanied presentation. In *Banff Sketches*, alternation patterns were stored as part of the score-orientation cue list, which informed the program whose turn it was to perform. During the human part of an alternation, Cypher stored what was being played, unanalyzed. When the program was due to treat the same material, it was sent through to the listener and transformed through message/method connections in the same way that composition is usually performed simultaneously.

Further, *Banff Sketches* provided the most extensive opportunity for improvisation of any of the principally notated works. In contrast to the organization of *Flood Gate*, improvisations are scattered throughout the composition, as commentaries and extensions to most of the musical ideas presented in the work. Computer solos often follow human/computer improvisatory collaborations, continuing to develop the material just played. Cypher's performance in these sections included the first extensive use of the composition critic; modifications to the behavior of the program were not only a function of state changes coupled to score orientation, as in the case of *Flood Gate* or *Sun and Ice*, but also were effected by metalevel rules incorporated in the critic watching the composition section's output.

An example of these ideas can be seen on page 12 of the score (figure 3.18); the first measure shown is a graphic representation of improvisational possibilities for the performer. The human performer may rely on these indications almost literally; a possible mapping of the graphic symbols to performance is provided with the score. If the player is more comfortable with improvisation, the symbols may be taken as little more than a suggestion. In all of the performances to date, the composer has had the luxury of working together with the performer to arrive at appropriate kinds of improvisation for each section.

Sun and Ice (1990) is a composition for four human performers and Cypher. The human ensemble performs on flute, oboe, clarinet, and a

Figure 3.18

MIDI percussion controller. The percussion controller is directly connected to the program; the three wind players are tracked through a pitch-to-MIDI converter that takes an acoustic signal (all three wind instruments are played into microphones) and returns a MIDI representation of the pitches being played. Only one of the human players is ever being tracked by Cypher at a time; therefore, an important formal decision in the composition of the piece was mapping out which human performer would be interacting with the program when. The main software advance involved the use of compositional algorithms as seed material for introspective improvisation by the program. Structurally, the piece falls out into four big sections; at the end of the second of these, there is an extended improvisation section for the three wind players, followed by a computer solo. Here again we see the principle of a collaborative improvisation coupled with an elaboration of that material by Cypher.

The most extensive notated work was *Rant* (1991), a piece for flute, oboe, horn, trumpet, trombone, piano, double bass, soprano voice, and Cypher, based on a poem by Diane Di Prima. This piece was premiered on April 19, 1991, with soloist Jane Manning and conductor Tod Machover. The piece contrasted several sections for parts of the ensemble against other material presented by the group as a whole. One of the most challenging compositional problems presented by Cypher is the question of how to integrate it with a large ensemble. Full musical textures tend to integrate the contributions of many instruments into unified gestures or sets of voices. Adding an active computer complement to such a context can easily produce a muddled, unfocused result. In *Rant*, the solution adopted to the ensemble integration problem was to put the activity of the computer part in an inverse relation with the performance of the human ensemble. When the rest of the ensemble was performing together, Cypher adopted a strictly subsidiary role. In the numerous sections for smaller forces, the program came to the fore. In particular, two parts of the piece were written for soprano and computer alone, highlighting the interaction between the vocal material and Cypher's transformations.

Improvisations

The following works used Cypher as a performer in a completely improvised setting: little if anything was agreed upon about the nature of the performance in advance, and the program had to contribute to the texture through its analysis capabilities and composition methods, which were either specified live, using the interface, or generated by the critic-driven composition rules.

Concerto Grosso #2 was the public debut of Cypher. This performance, part of the Hyperinstruments concert given at the Media Laboratory in June 1988, combined the improvisations of Richard Teitelbaum on piano, his improvisational software *The Digital Piano*, George Lewis on trombone, Robert Dick on flute, and Cypher. Routing of MIDI signals among the acoustic instruments (which were initially sent through pitch-to-MIDI converters) and computers was done onstage by Richard Teitelbaum. A subsequent, reduced performance was given by Richard Teitelbaum and Robert Rowe at the Concertgebouw in Amsterdam in the fall of 1988.

At the Banff Centre in the summer of 1989, a completely improvised musical performance, *Universe III,* was given by human and machine improvisers. The human players were Steve Coleman on saxophone and synthophone, and Muhal Richard Abrams on MIDI piano. The machine players were Coleman's improvisation program and Cypher. Configuration of the MIDI streams was done onstage, so that the input to Cypher changed continually between the other human and machine performers and itself. The most intriguing result of this performance and the rehearsals leading up to it was the speed with which the jazz players were able to pick up on the transformations tied to features of their playing and to trigger them at will. Connections between the Cypher listener and player were made onstage: a human operator (myself) performed state changes and other major modifications to program behavior.

On a concert given at the MIT Media Laboratory on April 19, 1991, another collaboration combined the live synthophone playing of Steve Coleman with additional voices supplied by his own improvisation software and Cypher. The synthophone's MIDI output was connected to three computers: one running Coleman's software, a second running Cypher, and a third playing alto saxophone samples. Since the Banff Centre performance, Coleman's software improviser has been extended to track live playing and find harmonic structure in it. The harmonies found are then used to direct the pitch selection of the melodic improvisation part. In this performance, Cypher was run to a large extent by an internal software critic. The normal production rules, adjusting the output of the composition section just before performance, remained in force. Additional rules examined the analysis of Coleman's playing and made or broke connections maintained in the connections manager between listener reports and compositional methods. Further, extensive use was made of the harmonic and rhythmic adjustment transformations, tracking the behavior of the synthophone performance to pick up the harmonic context and beat period, then aligning the output of Cypher's composition section to accord with it. The performance of the beat alignment transformation was particularly noticeable; once the beat tracker locked onto Coleman's pulse, the composition section achieved an effective rhythmic coordination with the live playing.

3.4 Hyperinstruments

The *hyperinstruments* project, led by Tod Machover and Joseph Chung, has been carried out in the Music and Cognition group of the MIT Media Laboratory. "Our approach emphasizes the concept of 'instrument,' and pays close attention to the learnability, perfectibility, and repeatability of redefined playing technique, as well as to the conceptual simplicity of performing models in an attempt to optimize the learning curve for professional musicians" (Machover and Chung 1989, 186). Hyperinstruments are used in notated compositions, where an important structural element is the changing pattern of relationships between acoustic and computer instruments. As the preceding quote indicates, a focal point in developing hyperinstruments for any particular composition has been to provide virtuoso performers with controllable means of amplifying their gestures. Amplification is here used not in the sense of providing greater volume, but in suggesting a coherent extension of instrumental playing technique, such that a trained concert musician can learn sophisticated ways of controlling a computerized counterpart to his acoustic sound. One important expression of this concept has been to provide sophisticated control over a continuous modification of the synthetic timbres used to articulate hyperinstrument output.

Hyperinstruments are realized with the Hyperlisp programming environment, developed by Joseph Chung. Hyperlisp is available on the companion CD-ROM. Based on Macintosh Common Lisp Second Edition and the Common Lisp Object System (CLOS), Hyperlisp combines the power and flexibility of Lisp with a number of extensions designed to accommodate the scheduling and hardware interfacing needs of musical applications. Most of this functionality is built into an extensive library of objects, which have proved general enough to realize several quite different compositions, as we shall see shortly.

As the name would suggest, hyperinstruments follow an instrument paradigm. Applications are usually score driven, and the generation technique can best be described as a hybrid of generative and sequenced styles. Hyperinstrument compositions can be thought of as score driven, even though full-blown score following is generally not employed. The music to be played by the human performers is notated quite precisely, allowing latitude in expressive performance but not, generally, in the improvisation of notes and rhythms. Coordination with the computer is accomplished through a cueing system, where cues are sometimes taken from the MIDI representation of a performance and sometimes from the intervention of a computer operator.

Valis

The first composition to make use of the Hyperlisp/hyperinstruments model is *Valis*, an opera based on the novel of the same name by Phillip K. Dick. The music of the opera, beyond the vocal parts, is realized by two hyperinstrument performers, one playing piano, the other mallet percussion, where both instruments send MIDI streams to the computer for further elaboration. Several instruments were developed for different sections of the composition; here much of the groundwork was laid for the kinds of interaction that were to be developed in later compositions.

For example, one instrument animates chords performed on the keyboard with quickly changing rhythmic sequences applied to an arpeggiation of the notes of the chord. The performer controls movement from one chord to the next by playing through the score, and, in an extension of normal technique, can affect the timbral presentation of the arpeggios by applying and releasing pressure on the held notes of the chord. Moreover, the program is continually searching through a database of chords to find one matching what is being played on the keyboard; successful matches are used to move from one rhythmic sequence to another. In that way, the example is score-driven: an internal score is matched against performer input, and successful matches move the computer performance from one rhythmic sequence to the next. The generation is a hybrid of sequenced and generative techniques, since the stored rhythmic score is a sequence, but one that is generatively modified, in timbral presentation and rate of change from one sequence to the next, by the performance of the human.

Towards the Center

Towards the Center (1988–89) is scored for flute, clarinet, violin, violoncello, keyboard, percussion, and computer system. Of these, the strings and woodwinds are miked and slightly processed, while the keyboard and percussion parts are full-blown hyperinstruments. In this piece, the hyperinstruments sometimes form "double instruments," in which control over the sounding result is shared between the two performers.

> The instruments are designed so that each musician can influence certain aspects of the music, but both players are required to perform in ensemble to create the entire musical result. In one variation, the notes on the percussionist's instrument are re-mapped to the pitches which are currently being played on the keyboard. Each octave on the percussion controller sounds the same notes but with different timbres. In addition, the keyboard player uses polyphonic afterpressure to weight the mapping so that certain notes appear more frequently than others. (Machover and Chung 1989, 189)

Hyperlisp maintains a running *time grid*, which allows various kinds of synchronization between performers and the computer part. For example, sequenced scores triggered from the live performance can each be synchronized with the grid, and thereby to each other, without requiring a perfectly timed trigger from the player. Similarly, the performance of the two human players can be pulled into synchronization by aligning incoming attacks with beats of the grid. Tolerances for the strength of attraction to the grid points, and for the speed with which misaligned events are pulled into synch, allow flexible modification of the temporal performance in a variety of situations.

Bug-Mudra

The composition *Bug-Mudra* is scored for two guitars, one acoustic and one electric (both outfitted with MIDI transmission systems), MIDI percussion, and hyperinstrument system. A tape part for the piece is a recording of a sequence, mixed to tape in a single pass and striped with a SMPTE time code track, allowing the subsequent live computer treatment to be able to coordinate with the score in performance with complete accuracy and within 1/100 of a second. A transformation of the SMPTE information to Midi Time Code format is used as the clock driving a Hyperlisp application, enforcing the synchronization between the tape and live hyperinstrument processing. This synchronization is further expressed through the generation of an inaudible time grid, a reference point that is used to coordinate live performance, the tape, and much of the computer output. For example, the time grid is used to quantize the performance of the MIDI percussion player. Subtly shifting attacks coming from the percussion controller to fall exactly on a time point from the grid allow the performer to concentrate on timbral and gestural shaping of the performance rather than on the precise placement of each note in an extremely fast and demanding part.

A performer as yet unmentioned in *Bug-Mudra* is the conductor, whose left hand is outfitted with a Dextrous Hand Master (DHM) able to track the angle of three joints on each finger, as well as the angle of each finger relative to the back of the hand. The DHM is used to extend the traditional function of a conductor's left hand, which generally imparts expressive shaping to the performance, in contrast to the more strictly time-keeping function of the right hand. The DHM in *Bug-Mudra* shapes and mixes timbres in the course of live performance, through an interpretation of the conductor's hand gestures that serves to operate a bank of MIDI-controllable mixer channels.

The tape part of *Bug-Mudra* enforces a particular temporal synchrony not found in the other hyperinstrument compositions. Restrictive in the sense of possible performance tempi, the tape is actually liberating in terms of the precision with which computer and human rhythmic interaction can be realized. Rapidly shifting metric structures underpinning a highly energetic ensemble texture are a hallmark of the piece. SMPTE synchrony permits score following between the tape and computer to take place with centisecond resolution. Gestures from the conductor and electric guitar player, in particular, spawn expressive variation in the realization of the electronic part. The environment of *Bug-Mudra* can be thought of as an instrument, but one that is played by the coordinated action of all three performers plus conductor.

Begin Again Again . . .

The composition *Begin Again Again . . .* (1991) was written for hypercello and computer, on a commission from Yo-Yo Ma. For this work, a great deal of work was done to improve the acquisition of information about the live cello performance (see section 2.1 for a description of the hardware enhancements). MIDI is oriented toward a note paradigm, which represents essentially discrete events. The extension of the standard to continuous control parameters covers level settings, in essence, since each new value is used to change the level of some synthesis parameter directly, for example, pitchbend. Therefore, only the current value of the continuous control is of interest—there is no reason to try to characterize the shape of change over time.

Tracking performance gestures on a stringed instrument, however, does require the interpretation of parameters varying continuously. Identifying bowing styles from instantaneous levels, for example, is not possible: the system must be sampling and integrating readings taken over time. A number of objects were added to Hyperlisp to interpret various kinds of performance gestures, such as note attacks, tremoli, and bowing styles. These objects can be "mixed in" to hyperinstrument modes active at different parts of the piece; rather than having all gestures tracked at all times, gestures with significance for particular sections of the composition can be interpreted as needed. Because of the powerful tracking techniques developed for continuous control and the previously mentioned difficulties of determining the pitch of an audio signal in real time, the gestural information available from a performance of *Begin Again Again . . .* is virtually the inverse of the normal MIDI situation: continuous controls are well represented, whereas pitch and velocity are more approximate.

Necessity became a virtue as the piece was composed to take advantage of the depth and variety of continuous gestural information available. For example, one section of the piece uses an "articulation mapping" in which different signal processing techniques are applied to the live cello sound, according to the playing style being performed. Tremolo thus is coupled to flanging, pizzicato to echo, and bounced bows to spatialization and delays. Further, once a processing technique has been selected, parameters of the processing algorithm can be varied by other continuous controls. Once tremolo playing has called up the flanger, for instance, the depth of chorusing is controlled with finger pressure on the bow (Machover et al. 1991, 29–30).

3.5 Improvisation and Composition

Interactive systems have attracted the attention of several musicians because of their potential for improvisation. Improvised performances allow a computer performer (as well as the human performers) broad scope for autonomous activity. Indeed, the relative independence of interactive improvisational programs is one of their most notable distinguishing characteristics. The composer Daniel Scheidt articulates his interest in incorporating improvised performances thus: "In making the decision to allow the performer to improvise, I have relinquished aspects of compositional control in exchange for a more personal contribution by each musician. An improvising performer works within his or her own set of skills and abilities (rather than those defined by a score), and is able to offer the best of his or her musicianship. Once having become familiar with [an interactive] system's behavior, the performer is free to investigate its musical capabilities from a uniquely personal perspective" (Scheidt 1991, 13).

Further, improvisation demands highly developed capacities for making sense of the music, either by a human operator onstage or by the program itself. If a human is to coordinate the responses of the machine with an evolving musical context, a sophisticated interface is required to allow easy access to the appropriate controls. If the machine organizes its own response, the musical understanding of the program must be relatively advanced.

George Lewis

A strong example of the extended kinds of performance interactive systems make possible is found in the work of George Lewis, improviser, trombonist, and software developer. His systems can be regarded as compositions in their own right; they are able to play with no outside assistance. When collaboration is forthcoming, human or otherwise, Lewis's aesthetic requires that the program be influenced, rather than controlled, by the material arriving from outside. The system is purely generative, performance driven, and follows a player paradigm. There are no sequences or other precomposed fragments involved, and all output is derived from operations on stored elemental material, including scales and durations. Interaction arises from the system's use of information arriving at the program from outside sources, such as a pitch-to-MIDI converter tracking Lewis's trombone. A listening section parses and observes the MIDI input and posts the results of its observations in a place accessible to the routines in the generation section. The generation routines, using the scales and other raw material stored in memory, have access to, but may or may not make use of, the publicly broadcast output of the listening section (Lewis 1989). Probabilities play a large role in the generation section; various routines are always available to contribute to the calculations, but are only invoked some percentage of the time—this probability is set by the composer or changes according to analysis of the input. The probability of durational change, for example, is related to an ongoing rhythmic complexity measure, so as to encourage the performance of uneven but easily followed sequences of durations.

George Lewis's software performers are designed to play in the context of improvised music. The intent is to build a separate, recognizable personality that participates in the musical discourse on an equal footing with the human players. The program has its own behavior, which is sometimes influenced by the performance of the humans. The system's success in realizing Lewis's musical goals, then, follows from these implementation strategies: the generative nature of the algorithm ensures that the program has its own harmonic and rhythmic style, since these are part of the program, not adopted from the input. Further, the stylistic elements recognized by the listening section are made available to the generation routines in a way that elicits responsiveness but not subordination from the artificial performer.

Richard Teitelbaum

Richard Teitelbaum's *Digital Piano* collection is an influential example of a transformative, performance-driven, instrument paradigm interactive system. The setup includes an acoustic piano fitted with a MIDI interface, a computer equipped with several physical controllers, such as sliders and buttons, and some number of output devices, often including one or more solenoid-driven acoustic pianos. This particular configuration of devices arose from Teitelbaum's long experience with live electronic music, beginning with the improvisation ensemble Musica Elettronica Viva in 1967. Two motivations in particular stand out: (1) to maintain the unpredictable presence of human performers, and (2) to use an acoustic instrument as a controller, to contrast with the relatively static nature of much synthesized sound (Teitelbaum 1991).

Using the *Patch Control Language*, developed in collaboration with Mark Bernard (Teitelbaum 1984) (or, more recently, a reimplementation in Max of the same design), Teitelbaum is able to route musical data through a combination of transformations, including delays, transpositions, and repetitions. Before performance, the composer specifies which transformation modules he intends to use, and their interconnections. During performance, material he plays on the input piano forms the initial signal for the transformations. Further, he is able to manipulate the sliders to change the modules's parameter values and to use buttons or an alphanumeric keyboard to break or establish routing between modules. In this case, the musical intelligence employed during performance is Teitelbaum's: the computer system is a wonderful generator of complex, tightly knit musical worlds, but the decision to change the system from one configuration to another is the composer's. The computer does not decide on the basis of any input analysis to change its behavior; rather, the composer/performer sitting at the controls actively determines which kinds of processing will be best suited to the material he is playing.

A new version of Patch Control Language, written in Max by Christopher Dobrian, has extended Teitelbaum's design. The *transposer* subpatch is shown in figure 3.19. Across the top are three inlets, which will receive pitch, velocity, and transposition values from the main patch. When the velocity value is nonzero (that is, the message is a Note On), the transposed pitch corresponding to the pitch played is saved in the *funbuff* array. Notes with a velocity of zero are not passed through the *gate* object and so call up the stored transposition: in this way, even if the transposition level changes between a Note On and Note Off, the correct pitch will be turned off.

Another module, the *excerpter*, is shown in figure 3.20. The *excerpter* is built around the sequencer object visible on the right-hand side of the patch, between *midiformat* and *midiparse*. The rightmost inlet, at the top of the patch, sends packed pitch and velocity pairs from MIDI Note On and Off messages to the sequencer for recording. The next inlet from the right, marked "playback tempo," supplies exactly that: scaled through the *split* and *expr* objects, this inlet eventually sets the argument of a start message. The next inlet to the left sets a transposition level for pitches played out of the sequencer and simultaneously fires the start message, which begins playback from the sequencer at the

This patch transposes notes and makes sure that Note Offs get the same transposition as Note Ons, even if the interval of transposition changes while the note is being played.

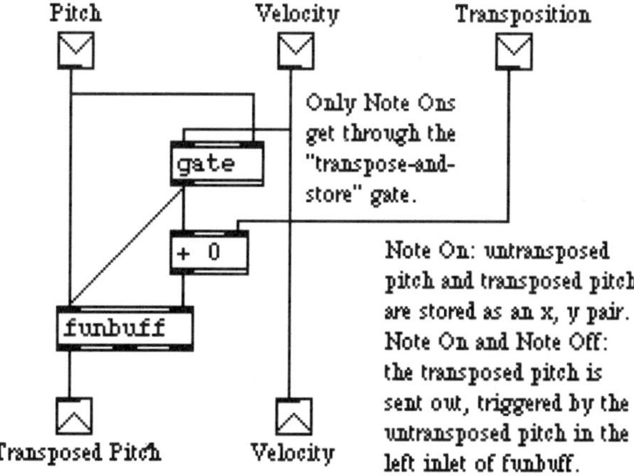
Pitch
Velocity
Transposition
Only Note Ons get through the "transpose-and-store" gate.
gate
+ 0
funbuff
Note On: untransposed pitch and transposed pitch are stored as an x, y pair. Note On and Note Off: the transposed pitch is sent out, triggered by the untransposed pitch in the left inlet of funbuff.
Transposed Pitch
Velocity

Figure 3.19

specified tempo. Finally, the leftmost inlet is used to start and stop recording into the *seq* object.

This again is indicative of the transformative approach embodied by Richard Teitelbaum's improvisation software: the *excerpter* takes in music played during performance, which can then be played back out under a variety of transformations, including tempo change and transposition. Added to this is the elaboration that up to four identically functioning tracks can be operating simultaneously, yielding several layers of differently varied material.

Richard Teitelbaum's software, like George Lewis's, is designed to function in an improvisational context. The musical intent is to establish a dynamic, expressive field of related material. Expressivity is transmitted through the system by maintaining the performer's input, subject to elaborative variations. The technique of chaining together relatively simple transformation modules allows the composer to produce variations along a continuum of complexity, where the number and type of transformations chained together directly affect the degree and kind of complexity in the output. Similarly, the output is more or less recognizably related to the input as a function of the number of processes applied to it. The system tends to resemble a musical instrument more than a separate player, since the decision to change its behavior is made by the composer during performance, rather than by the program itself.

Jean-Claude Risset

Jean-Claude Risset's *Duet for One Pianist* uses an interactive system programmed with Max and is written for the Yamaha Disklavier played as if by four hands. That is to say that a human performer plays two hands' worth of the piece, and MIDI data from that performance is transmitted to a computer running Max, which applies various operations to the human-performed data and then sends out MIDI commands to play two more hands' worth on the same piano. For example, the section "Double" plays sequences in response to notes found in the score, and "Fractals" adds several notes in a quasi-octave relationship to each note played (Risset 1990).

The Max patch was written by Scott Van Duyne at the MIT Media Laboratory; the subpatch in figure 3.21 is from the "Mirrors" section of the work, which casts notes played by the human back around a point of symmetry to another part of the piano ("Mirrors" can be heard

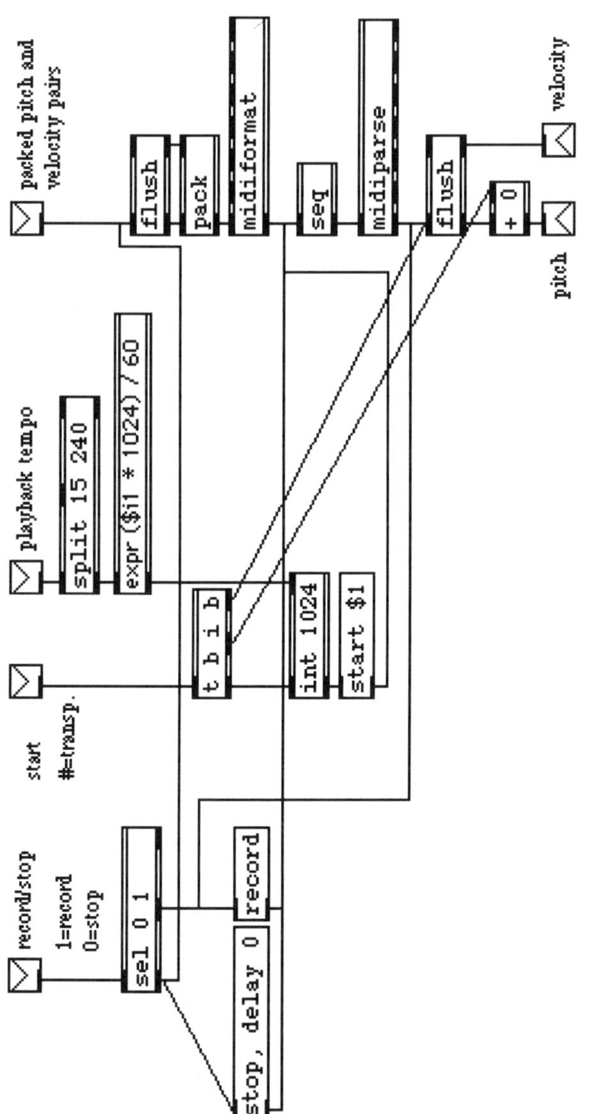
packed pitch and velocity pairs
flush
pack
midiformat
seq
midiparse
flush
+ 0
pitch
velocity
playback tempo
split 15 240
expr ($i1 * 1024) / 60
t b i b
int 1024
start $1
start
#=transp.
record/stop
1=record
0=stop
sel 0 1
record
stop, delay 0

Figure 3.20

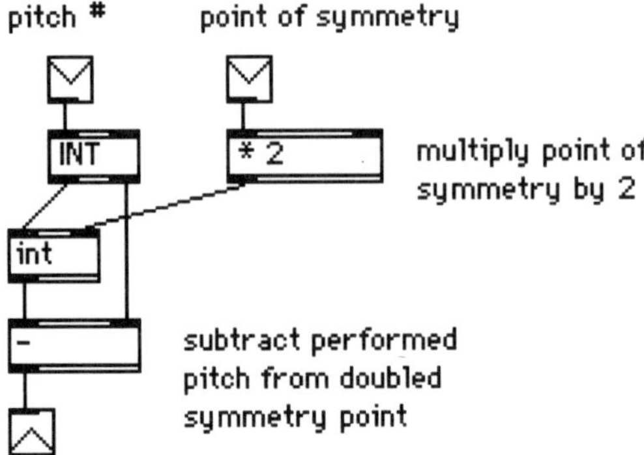

Figure 3.21

on the companion CD-ROM; the subpatch resides there as well). The opening is a quotation from the second movement of Webern's Op. 27, which uses the same principle. We can see from the patch that the basic algorithm is quite simple: the right inlet receives a point of symmetry (expressed as a MIDI note number), and the left inlet the performed MIDI notes. The point of symmetry is multiplied by 2, and incoming pitches subtracted from that product. The result moves the new pitch an equal interval away from the symmetry point as the original note, in the opposite direction.

The subpatch of Figure 3.22, called *transpup*, is at the heart of the "Fractals" section. Five of these subpatches are active simultaneously, casting pitches played by the human up the piano in differing intervallic relationships. The resulting structures are fractal in their self-similarity but also related to Shepard tones in their seeming combination of motion and stasis. The transposition and delay inlets to transpup are simply passed through to the first two outlets, allowing the outside patch to monitor what has been passed through. A simple *pipe* object delays transmission of the pitch and velocity inlets by the same duration, set by the "delay." "Fractals" can be heard on the companion CD-ROM.

Risset's work forms an interesting contrast with the systems of Teitelbaum and Lewis; although an extensive network of interactive relations is explored, the piece is a completely notated piece of concert music, rather than an improvisation. The *Duet* is usually performance driven but sometimes tracks portions of the human part more closely, in a score-driven style. In the performance-driven sections, particular pitches on the piano often advance the behavior of the Max patch from

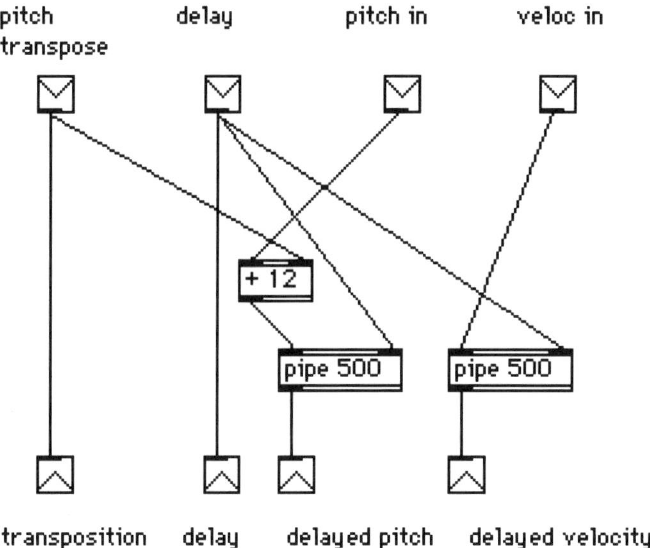

Figure 3.22

one state to the next. The piece clearly follows a player paradigm; the title alone is evidence of as much. All three types of response method are in use.

David Jaffe and Andrew Schloss

David Jaffe and Andrew Schloss have explored several styles of interaction in live computer music, as composers, players, and in duet performances with each other. Their piece *Wildlife* is an ensemble interaction for four participants, "two biological and two synthetic" (Jaffe and Schloss 1991). Two computers, a NeXTstation and a Macintosh IIci, are running separate interactive programs. David Jaffe performs on a Zeta electric MIDI violin, and Andrew Schloss on the Boie Radio Drum (see section 2.1). The Macintosh tracks and processes MIDI coming from the violin and drum and passes MIDI commands to an on-board SampleCell and to the NeXT computer. The NeXT performs further processing of the MIDI stream coming from the Macintosh, executes some compositional algorithms, and controls synthesis on a built-in DSP 56001 and a Yamaha TG-77 synthesizer.

Each of the five movements of the work implements a different kind of interaction. In the first, the violin triggers piano sounds through a chord-mapping scheme, in which certain pitch classes are coupled with chords and octave information is used to control the chords' registral placement. The chord maps are chosen by the drum, producing a double instrument between the two players: each is responsible for some part of the sounding result. Further, the drum has its own performance possibilities, and the violinist can choose to step out of the chord-mapping mode and play single notes or send pitchbend controls to the drum sounds. This situation is indicative of the musical environments of *Wildlife*—all four ensemble members are responsible for part of the resulting texture, and several combinations of interaction are possible. Part of the performance, then, becomes the choice of interaction mode and the way ensemble members choose to affect each other's action.

The second movement is again built on a subtle interaction between the violin and drum players. The violin triggers sustained organ sounds when a foot pedal is depressed. Over the drone, the violin can play additional acoustic sounds without triggering more organ sounds until the foot pedal is pressed again. Meanwhile, the drum has access to the material played by the violin and can color it timbrally. Either single notes from the violin performance can be chosen and played with various timbres, or a continuous mode will play back a series of notes from the violin material, with the tempo determined by the drummer holding a stick above the surface of the drum, like a conductor. Similarly, in the fourth movement pizzicato playing by the violin sparks no computer response itself, but the material is sent on to the drum, where it will be elaborated by the percussionist. In the last movement, the radio drum's x and y coordinates are mapped onto a continuous DSP vowel interpolation space, whereas the z dimension is mapped to loudness. At the close, all four ensemble members contribute to a bluegrass fantasy.

Wildlife is a performance-driven interactive system. A hybrid generation method including transformative and generative algorithms is ingeniously distributed between the two human players and two computers. The system seems close to the instrument paradigm: the computer programs become an elaborate instrument played jointly by the violin and percussion. In that respect, some modes of interaction in *Wildlife* seem close to the "double instrument" techniques of Tod Machover's *Towards the Center*. Unlike that piece, the primary style of interaction is improvisation, in which various strategies of collaboration and sabotage play a guiding role in the formation of the work.

David Wessel

David Wessel has worked extensively in improvisational settings, using custom software written in Max (Wessel 1991). The software is a collection of listening assistants, composing assistants, and performing assistants. It has usually been used in duo improvisation settings, where one player improvises on an acoustic instrument and Wessel affects the interactive environment with some MIDI controller, such as the Buchla Thunder. Both acoustic and MIDI signals are captured from the acoustic player; the computer performer is able, with the help of the listening assistants, to record and analyze the acoustic performance in real time. Then, the composing and performing parts are used to formulate a response and adjust it to the demands of the concert situation.

One of the fundamental ideas of the interaction is that the computer performer is able to record phrases from the acoustic performer onstage. In early versions, a MIDI keyboard "was configured so that the lowest octave functioned as a phrase recorder. Recording was initiated when a key in this octave was depressed and stopped when it was released. The stored fragment was associated with that key and the corresponding keys in the other octaves of the keyboard were used to play back transformations of the recorded phrase" (Wessel 1991, 345).

One complication with this model is that the computer operator is not able to indicate that a phrase should be saved until it has already begun to be played. To be able to transform appropriate phrases, the software must be able to store ongoing musical information and "reach back" to the beginning of phrases when they are called for. For this, Wessel divides the program's memory into short-term and long-term stores. The short-term memory holds MIDI-level information, whereas the long-term memory uses higher-level abstractions. With the short-term store, listening assistants perform phrase boundary detection, to notice those structural points that will demarcate the onset of saved phrases. Following the grouping mechanisms of (Lerdahl and Jackendoff 1983), Wessel uses a time-gap detector to indicate phrase boundaries.

From this we can already see that Wessel's system is a performance-driven one. Transformation is an important response type: one method generates chords from melodic material by maintaining a weighted histogram of performed pitches and favoring those related to an estimated tonal context. In other words, notes from a melodic line are run through the histogram, and the pitches with most resonance in the harmonic field are employed to generate accompanying chords. Pitches extraneous to the current harmony are discarded.

Clearly, this approach represents a performer paradigm system. In (Wessel 1991), however, the composer articulates a vision of interactive performance similar to the "dual instrument" models of Jaffe and Schloss, or Machover's *Towards the Center*: following the example of Stockhausen's *Microphonie I*, David Wessel envisages new computer environments where the performers and computer are jointly involved in the generation of sound. Rather than an additive superimposition of individual sound sources, one source collectively controlled, in Wessel's view, could offer new possibilities of interaction on both technical and musical levels.

Cort Lippe

The composer Cort Lippe has been involved in many of the projects realized at IRCAM using Max's score-following and signal-processing capabilities. His own composition, *Music for Clarinet and ISPW* (1992), exemplifies that experience. In the signal flow chart shown in figure 3.23, we see the various levels of processing involved in the realization of the piece. First of all, the clarinet is sampled through an ADC and routed through the pitch tracker resident on an IRCAM i860 DSP board (ISPW) mounted on the NeXT computer (see section 2.3). The output of the pitch tracker goes on to a score following stage, accomplished with the *explode* object. Index numbers output from *explode* then advance through an event list, managed in a *qlist* object, which sets signal-processing variables and governs the evolution of a set of compositional algorithms.

The signal processing accomplished with the ISPW is quite extensive and includes modules for reverberation, frequency shifting, harmonization, noise modulation, sampling, filtering, and spatialization. In fact, all of the sounds heard from the computer part during the course of the piece are transformations of the live clarinet performance. The processing routines listed above can pass signals through a fully connected crossbar, such that the output of any module can be sent to the input of any other. These routines are receiving control information from the *qlist* and from a set of compositional algorithms, which "are themselves controlled by every aspect of the clarinet input: the raw clarinet signal, its envelope, the pitch tracker's continuous control

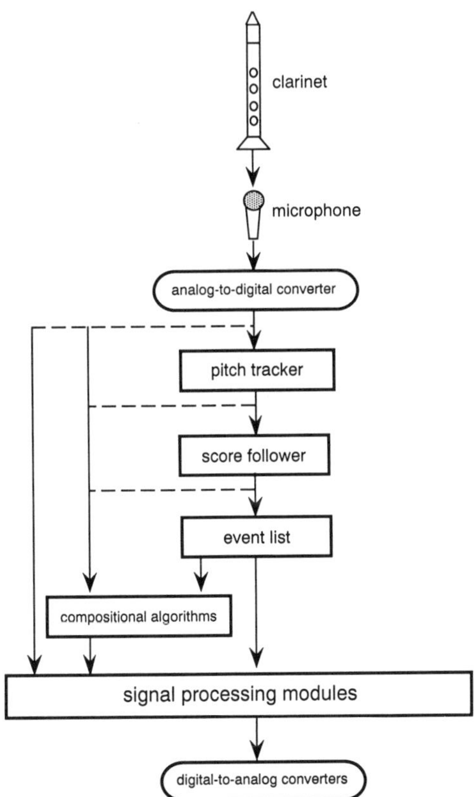

Figure 3.23

information, the direct output of the score follower, and the electronic score's event list all contribute to [their] control" (Lippe 1991b, 2).

Cort Lippe's *Music for Clarinet and ISPW* is a score-driven interactive music system. The explode/qlist score-following combination described in section 3.2 is used to track the clarinet player's progress through a notated score. The signal-processing facilities in the extended version of Max written for the ISPW allow extensive timbral transformations of the live clarinet performance, as well as pitch and envelope tracking to feed the score-following mechanism. The response methods are transformative and generative, but in the extended sense of using timbral transformations and synthesis rather than the note-based MIDI routines usually found. Finally, the piece embodies a performer paradigm, in that the clarinet is engaged in an expansive dialog with a second musical voice; a voice, moreover, that is a regeneration and reinterpretation of her own sound.

3.6 Multimedia Extensions

To this point we have examined an array of interactive systems, moving from improvisation through notated works to extended forms of interaction based on real-time signal processing. A number of developers have moved beyond the design of systems for music only, to building environments capable of integrating visual with musical effects. We will look at three of those endeavors here: two involved with synchronizing musical improvisation and real-time animation, and the other coupling lighting effects to interactive music analysis.

Don Ritter

Orpheus is an interactive animation system designed by the visual artist Don Ritter. The program accesses stored digital video frames, and can display these in any order, combined with one of over 70 cinematic transitions, including fades, flashing, and the like. Images and transitions are linked to and synchronized with real-time input from a MIDI source. Correspondences stem from a user-defined control file, which indicates relations between various musical parameters, and the visual effects that will appear in response. "For example, a control file may define that an increasing musical interval in the third octave will cause the display of a bouncing ball in a forward motion; a decreasing interval, however, will display the ball in a backward motion" (Ritter 1991, 1). Orpheus analyzes several features of the musical performance, including register, dynamic, pitch, note density, duration (of notes or rests), chord type, and timbre. Performances often include two instances of Orpheus, one producing background imagery, and the other foreground. Both use distinct images and control files.

The analysis performed relies on a comparison of incoming MIDI values with a collection of thresholds, which may be defined by the user. For example, MIDI pitches are classified as high or low according to their position relative to a pitch threshold. Loudness is decided the same way. The program keeps track of timing information, including when notes go on and off, to determine a note density per unit time. A control file can define correspondences between the results of these three classifications and sets of images and transitions. We may think of the three analyses as three binary switches; each classification takes one of two values. Therefore, the three taken together form a featurespace with eight locations. Each point in the featurespace can be associated with an "action list": these are scripts specifying image frames and transitions, which will be applied when the corresponding group of classifications is found in the input.

> Additional Actions become active when note and rest durations become greater than their associated threshold values. This situation will cause a change in cinematic transitions, but not in frame selection. For example, if the rest threshold is set at two seconds and the long rest Action is set at "drop screen," when a rest greater than two seconds is encountered, the currently displayed frame will slide to the bottom of the screen and display only the top 10% of the image. Imagery will stay in this "dropped" position until the next note occurs after which the screen will jump back to its normal full screen position. (Ritter 1991, 8)

Don Ritter's animation system has been used in collaboration with such improvisers as George Lewis, Richard Teitelbaum, Trevor Tureski, and David Rokeby. Because it is capable of characterizing some salient features of an ongoing musical performance, Orpheus can change its behavior in ways that are not known in advance but that nonetheless demonstrate correspondences which are immediately apparent to an audience.

Roger Dannenberg

Roger Dannenberg has carried out a number of important developments in interactive systems design, including compositions exploring the combination of algorithmic composition and interactive animation. In his piece *Ritual of the Science Makers*, scored for flute, violin, cello, and computer, Dannenberg uses MIDI representations of the human performances to launch and guide processes generating both musical textures, and accompanying images. These are often related; in the heraldic opening of the work, for example, crashing sounds in the computer part are tied to graphic plots of the amplitude of the crashes, using images akin to trumpet bells (Dannenberg 1991).

The piece illustrates the complexity of combining processes controlling several media, or even several uses of the same medium, simultaneously. In section 2.2, we reviewed the cause() routine, a basic scheduling facility in Moxie and the CMU Midi Toolkit. *Ritual of the Science Makers* relies on cause(), within a Moxc/C programming environment, to govern the scheduling of processes for music and animation. Certain operations of sequencing, performance capture, and interactive parameter adjustment, however, were better handled with the Adagio score language. To benefit from the advantages of process design and temporal sequences, the program for *Ritual* allowed Adagio scores to call C routines and set variables and allowed C to invoke Adagio scores. Adagio scores are interpreted and so can be quickly changed and reinserted into the performance situation, allowing a much more flexible and effective environment for the adjustment of parameter settings than would be the case if they had to be recompiled in the C program at each change.

Most music-scheduling regimes require that the processes invoked not be interrupted except by a limited number of hardware-servicing routines. This nonpreemption requirement simplifies numerous control flow and data consistency problems. In a mixed animation/music environment, however, Dannenberg found that the combination of relatively slow graphics routines and music processes requiring a much greater degree of responsiveness was best handled by introducing a limited interrupt capability: "the solution I have adopted is to divide computations into two groups: (1) time-critical, low-computation music event generation, and (2) less critical graphical music computations. The graphical computations are off-loaded to a separate, low-priority "graphics" process that is preempted whenever a time-critical event becomes ready to run in the primary "music" process. To coordinate graphical and music events, messages are sent from the music process to the graphics process to request operations" (Dannenberg 1991, 153).

Ritual of the Science Makers is a completely notated score, though the interaction would work with improvised material as well. In fact, the ensemble's parts are simply transcriptions of studio improvisations recorded by the composer. Roger Dannenberg suggests that as multimedia applications are extended into real-time interaction, some of the relatively stable techniques used for purely musical systems, such as nonpreemptive scheduling, may have to be reconsidered. These problems become even more acute when signal processing and large-scale analytical processes are thrown into the mix.

Louis-Philippe Demers

The programmer and lighting designer Louis-Philippe Demers has created an interactive system that follows musical contexts as it changes lighting patterns during performance. The standard method for real-time lighting control saves collections of settings among which automated cross-fades can effect a gradual change. Demers's system, @FL, instead describes lighting as a series of behaviors; moreover, these behaviors can be tied to musical contexts in production-style rules. For example, a lighting behavior in @FL could be "*A* happens quickly when *B* and *C* occur simultaneously, otherwise *A* happens slowly" (Demers 1991). @FL is a graphic programming language, quite similar in style to Max: objects are represented as boxes with inlets and outlets, and hierarchical patches can be programmed by describing the data flow between them.

Several performances have been realized through @FL. The earliest was a realization of Stravinsky's *Rite of Spring*, played on two computer-controlled pianos in an arrangement by Michael Century. The lighting program changed the intensity of light on either piano as a function of the density of the music being performed on that instrument. In a collaboration with me, listener messages from Cypher were used to control lighting behaviors described with @FL in a performance of *Banff Sketches*. Zack Settel's composition *Eschroadepipel* for clarinet and interactive music system similarly used ongoing information about the state of the musical score to direct changes in lighting behavior controlled through Louis-Philippe Demers's system.

4 Music Theory, Music Cognition

The centuries-old field of music theory and the field of music cognition, whose lifespan is measured in decades, are becoming more and more explicitly connected, in both their research goals and methodology. Cognitive science is a collection of disciplines concerned with human information processing (Posner 1989), and music cognition is the branch of that field devoted specifically to aspects of human intelligence as they apply to music (Sloboda 1985). A telling indication of their convergence with music theory was the appearance of the first volume of Eugene Narmour's book *The Analysis and Cognition of Basic Melodic Structures: The Implication-Realization Model* (Narmour 1990), the final chapter of which includes specifications of cognition experiments that could be conducted to confirm or deny hypotheses advanced in the theory.

With or without music cognition, music theory has always addressed the question of how humans experience music. When building computer programs to emulate aspects of musical skills, we do well to profit from the guidance that tradition can lend. Computer emulations represent an applied music theory, implementing ideas from classic or more recent theories and testing their function in the context of live performance. Similarly, music cognition is concerned at once with investigating the music information-processing capabilities of the mind and building computer models able to recreate some of those capabilities. Here again, perhaps even more directly, the construction of interactive music systems can be guided by research carried out in a related discipline.

In this chapter, we will examine issues in music theory and cognition as they relate to the construction of interactive music systems. Our interest extends to both theoretical correlations and some resulting practical implications for the engineering of working interactive programs.

4.1 Music Listening

Probably the skill on which all musical disciplines rely more than any other is listening: "having a good ear" describes skilled musicians of any specialty. The contrast between listening and music analysis should be drawn here: analysis is related to listening, as are all musical skills, but differs in two ways relevant to this discussion. First, music analysis has random access to the material; the analyst proceeds with the text of a written score, which he can consult in any order regardless of the temporal presentation of the piece in performance. Second, the analyst is often concerned with learning the compositional methods used in constructing the work; depending on the method, these may have anywhere from a great deal to almost no perceptual salience for the uninitiated listener. The listener, by contrast, is constrained to hear the piece from left to right, as it were, in real time. There is no random access; rather, the music must be processed as it arrives. The groupings and relations the listener forms can only arise from cognitively available perceptual events and the interaction of these events with short- and long-term memory. Seen in this light, the problems of music listening are simply part of the larger problem of human cognition.

A primary goal in the development of Cypher has been to fashion a computer program able to listen to music. The inspiration and touchstone for successful music listening is, naturally, human performance of the task, and Cypher implements what I take to be a method with plausible relations to human music processing. Still, I do not make the stronger claim that this program is a simulation of what goes on in the mind. For one thing, we simply do not yet know how humans process music. Because of the elusive nature of the thought processes the theories of cognitive psychology seek to explain, we remain unable to verify these theories. It is irrelevant to this work, however, whether the processes implemented in it correspond directly to those at work in the human mind. At best, the program offers an existence proof that the tasks it accomplishes can be done this way. The point, in any case, is not to "reverse engineer" human listening but rather to capture enough musicianship, and enough ways of learning more complete musical knowledge to allow a computer performer to interact with human players on their terms, instead of forcing an ensemble to adapt to the more limited capabilities of an unstructured mechanical rendition.

Music Cognition

Work in music cognition with implications for interactive music systems investigates the elicitation of structure from an ongoing musical flow, and the ways such structuring affects the comprehension, performance, and composition of music. Examples include the schemata theory of musical expectation (McAdams 1987), the influence of structural understanding on expressive performance (Clarke 1988), and various formal representations of pitch and rhythmic information (Krumhansl 1990).

The field of music cognition is relatively new, particularly in comparison with music theory, which is a centuries-old collection of techniques for describing the construction of musical works and the ways they are experienced. Music theory has long dealt with the tendency of Western music to exhibit directed motion, or dramatic form, in its progression through time. Observers including Wallace Berry and Leonard Meyer have discussed goal-oriented patterns of tensions and relaxation (Berry 1976), and the way these arouse expectations, which are then confirmed or denied, in the mind of the listener (Meyer 1956). A perspective that describes musical discourse as movements of progression and recession around points of culmination and fulfillment is but one way of characterizing the experience of music; several studies, for example Kramer 1988, note many others. Still, the idea that enculturation and gradually acquired expectations of typical continuation play a major role in music listening has spurred several research efforts in interactive systems, including Cypher.

Expectation is, to be sure, only a part of what goes on during listening —for many kinds of music, it is not even the most important part. I am convinced that listening to music fully engages our cognitive capacity in a deep, significant way and that this stimulation is what makes music a universal and lasting interest for every human culture. Cypher does not, of course, capture all of that richness. Rather, the focus is on developing a computer program that can learn to recognize some facets of Western musical style and incorporate that knowledge in an evolving strategy for participating in live musical contexts.

In the remainder of this book, I will use words such as "understanding" "intelligence," "learning," and "recognition" to speak of program function. It is not the point of this usage to further fan the flames of debate raging around the aptness of these words to describe the behavior of a computer program (Winograd and Flores 1986). The work described here actually exists and has been used with human musicians in a wide variety of settings over a period of several years. Programs are said to "understand" or exhibit "intelligence" in the sense that musicians interacting with them feel that the programs are behaving musically, that they can understand what the systems do, and that they can see a musically commonsense relation between their performance and the program's. The word "understanding" is used to describe a quality of this interaction as it is experienced by musicians performing with a program.

4.2 Hierarchies and Music Theory

In this section I present some structural perspectives developed in the field of music theory, particularly those related to questions of hierarchy and progression. The point of the discussion is to gauge the descriptive power of each organizational scheme, whether this power can be amplified in combination with other structures, and what consequences the adoption of multiple perspectives has for the coherence and versatility of theories of music.

Heinrich Schenker

In the early part of this century the Galician music theorist Heinrich Schenker developed an analytic technique with significant implications for the questions we are considering here. In particular, his work explored the combination of a strong concept of structural levels, with the idea of progression from event to event within levels. The hierarchical nature at the basis of Schenker's thought is readily apparent: "[Schenker] demonstrated that musical structure can be understood on three levels: foreground–middleground–background. . . . Analysis is a continuous process of connecting and integrating these three levels of musical perception" (Felix Salzer, in Schenker 1933, 14).

In the Schenkerian analysis shown in figure 4.1, notice the reduction of musical surface structures to a series of nested levels, with directed motion between certain events within each level. Such a graph portrays a double perspective on the musical flow: hierarchical in its layered organization and progressive in the implications between events within levels.

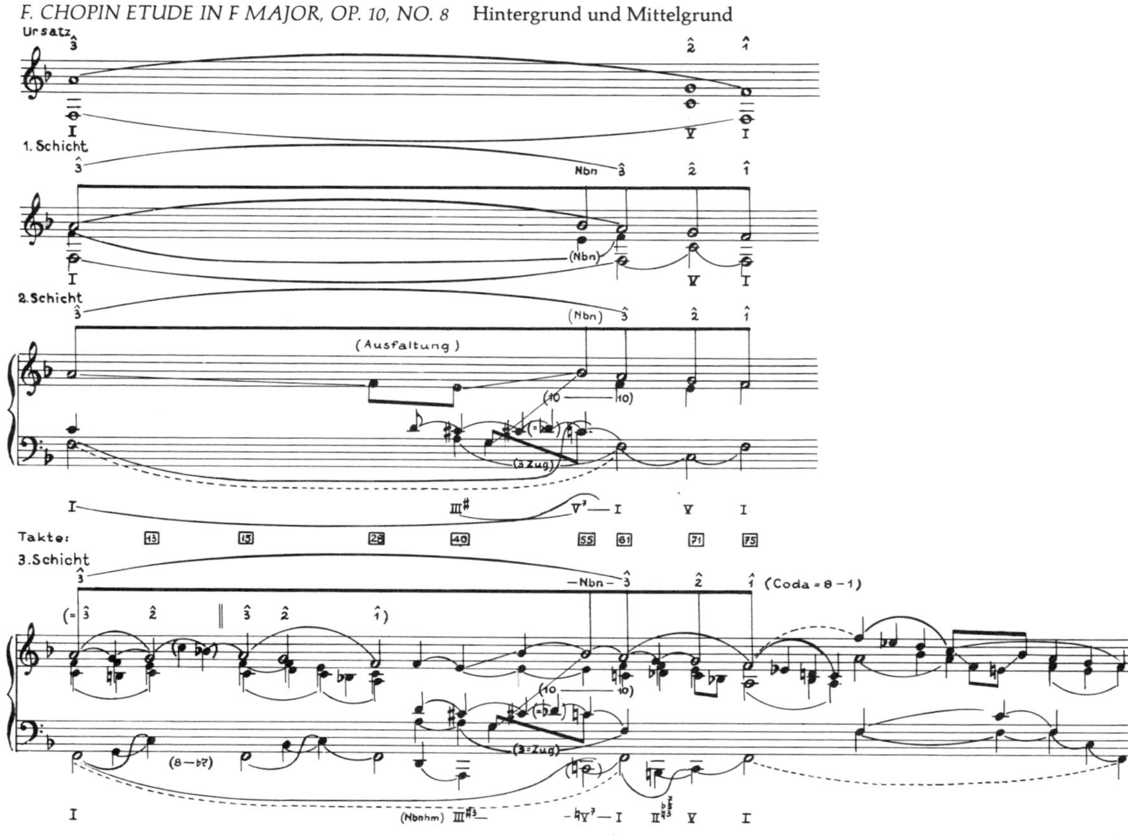

Figure 4.1 Reprinted from Heinrich Schenker, *Five Graphic Music Analyses*, p. 47. © 1969 Dover Publications, Inc.

Beyond the use of hierarchy and progression, another contribution from Schenker's theory is his use of *recursion*. Recursive techniques use the same process on distinct levels of a problem, telescoping up or down to find similar structures on varying scales. "Schenkerian analysis is in fact a kind of metaphor according to which a composition is seen as the large-scale embellishment of a simple underlying harmonic progression, or even as a massively-expanded cadence; a metaphor according to which the same analytical principles that apply to cadences in strict counterpoint can be applied, *mutatis mutandis*, to the large-scale structures of complete pieces" (Cook 1987, 36).

These three ideas—hierarchy, directed motion, and recursion—form a major part of the Schenkerian legacy to musical analysis; however, the application of the whole of Schenker's thought runs up against a rigidity of structure, which unnecessarily restricts the music it can successfully treat. The *Ursatz*, one of the foremost concepts associated with Schenker's name, is a background structure that Schenker claims is present in every well-composed piece of music—even though, as Schenker was aware, the Ursatz clearly does not underlie a great percentage of the world's musical styles. The nonconformance of most non-Western music, indeed, of many centuries' worth of Western music, to the Ursatz, was a sign to Schenker that such music had not reached the summit of musical thought, dictated by the forces of nature, which he believed was achieved by Western tonal music in the classical style. "If, as I have demonstrated, all systems and scale formations which have been and are taught in the music and theories of various peoples were and are merely self-deceptions, why should I take seriously the Greeks' belief in the correctness of their prosody?" (Schenker 1979, 162; see also Narmour 1977, 38).

Schenker's rejection of music that did not fit his structural perspective is an extreme case, but not an isolated one. I find it to be emblematic of a recurring tendency in music theory to embrace a particular structural perspective so strongly that the theorist becomes blinded to the considerable power of a listener's mind to organize and make sense of music in ways unforeseen by any single theoretic account.

We may conclude by reiterating some relevant contributions of Schenkerian analysis—structural levels, progressive motion within levels, and recursion—and the cautionary tale of its inventor's application of them: trying to enforce a particular perspective in describing musical thought can end by discarding a significant part of the phenomena the theory could well be used to illuminate.

Lerdahl and Jackendoff

The music theory of Heinrich Schenker and the linguistic theory of Noam Chomsky are two major influences on the work of composer Fred Lerdahl and linguist Ray Jackendoff, set forth in their book *A Generative Theory of Tonal Music* (Lerdahl and Jackendoff 1983). The combination of Chomsky and Schenker is certainly not incidental: as noted by John Sloboda, "their theories have some striking similarities. They both argue, for their own subject matter, that human behaviour *must* be supported by the ability to form abstract underlying representations" (Sloboda 1985, 11).

Lerdahl and Jackendoff's theory is designed to produce representations of pieces of tonal music that correspond to the cognitive structure present in an experienced listener's mind after hearing a piece. "[The theory] is not intended to enumerate what pieces are possible, but to specify a *structural description* for any tonal piece; that is, the structure that the experienced listener infers in his hearing of the piece" (Lerdahl and Jackendoff 1983, 6).

They focus on those parts of music cognition they consider to be hierarchical in nature.

> We propose four such components, all of which enter into the structural description of a piece. As an initial overview we may say that *grouping structure* expresses a hierarchical segmentation of the piece into motives, phrases, and section. *Metrical structure* expresses the intuition that the events of the piece are related to a regular alternation of strong and weak beats at a number of hierarchical levels. *Time-span reduction* assigns to the pitches of the piece a hierarchy of "structural importance" with respect to their position in grouping and metrical structure. *Prolongational reduction* assigns to the pitches a hierarchy that expresses harmonic and melodic tension and relaxation, continuity and progression. (Lerdahl and Jackendoff 1983, 8–9)

There are two kinds of rules in the theory: well-formedness rules and preference rules. The first rule set generates a number of possible interpretations. The second rule set will choose, from among those possibilities, the interpretation most likely to be selected by an experienced listener.

One of the attractions of Lerdahl and Jackendoff's work is that it treats musical rhythm much more explicitly than do many music theories, Schenker's being an example. In fact, they regard their theory as a foundation for Schenker's work: where his graphs highlight the relative importance of different pitches in a composition, Lerdahl and

Figure 4.2 Reprinted from Fred Lerdahl and Ray Jackendoff, *A Generative Theory of Tonal Music*, p. 144. © 1983 The Massachusetts Institute of Technology.

Jackendoff point to segmentation and rhythmic structuring as the cognitive principles underlying that sense of importance. Another strength of their approach is that it coordinates the contributions of several musical features, including meter, harmony, and rhythm. Further, predictions of phrase boundaries made by their model correspond well to reports from listeners under some test conditions (Palmer and Krumhansl 1987).

The output of the well-formedness rules is hierarchic and recursive, as figure 4.2 shows. The tree structure at the top of the figure can be divided into hierarchic levels according to the branching structure; the rules generating branches and their relative dominance at each level are the same and are applied recursively. The progressive perspective, indicating directed motion within levels, is attenuated in the Lerdahl and Jackendoff version. The successive levels of the rhythmic interpretation shown in figure 4.2 are related in an exacting tree structure; the only deviation from formal trees is that leaf nodes sometimes are linked to two adjacent nodes on the next highest level. The construction of these trees through application of the rule set makes possible comprehensive predictions of the strong/weak beat relationships experienced in a given musical context.

Again in the case of Lerdahl and Jackendoff's theory, however, an exaggerated reliance on one perspective leads both to uncomfortable accounts of cognition, and finally to a devaluation of music not conforming to the structure. First of all, their theory does not say anything about how the representations they describe are actually formed by a listener during audition: "Instead of describing the listener's real-time mental processes, we will be concerned only with the final state of his understanding. In our view it would be fruitless to theorize about mental processing before understanding the organization to which the processing leads" (Lerdahl and Jackendoff 1983, 3–4). This stance arises from a Chomskian desire to identify what a listener knows when she knows a work of music—what mental representations could account for the kinds of behavior we recognize as musical.

Another potential problem has to do with the cognitive reality of the upper reaches of the full tree structure they propose: "Evidence for the highest level in this structure is rather sparse, and is confined to statements by a number of composers (Mozart, Beethoven, Hindemith) which indicate that they were able to hear (or imagine) their own compositions in a single 'glance'" (Clarke 1988, 2–3).

The reality of this proposed representation can be questioned in connection with the first problem: given what is known about human memory systems and their capacity, how can such a complete image of a piece of music be built up and remain present after a single audition or, for that matter, even after repeated listenings? Perhaps this question reduces to a chicken-and-egg problem: Lerdahl and Jackendoff maintain that it makes no sense to consider the experience of listening until a plausible model of the resulting structure has been built; others find it hard to imagine a representation without a plausible model of how it might be constructed. The fact that Lerdahl and Jackendoff have not come up with an account of how listening produces the structure they propose suggests that there is no easy solution.

Fred Lerdahl, in his essay "Cognitive Constraints on Compositional Systems" (1988), gives the following motivation for relating the theory elaborated in Lerdahl and Jackendoff 1983 to compositional technique: "Cognitive psychology has shown in recent decades that humans structure stimuli in certain ways rather than others. Comprehension takes place when the perceiver is able to assign a precise mental representation to what is perceived. Not all stimuli, however, facilitate the formation of a mental representation. Comprehension requires a degree of ecological fit between the stimulus and the mental capabilities of the perceiver" (Lerdahl 1988, 232).

Lerdahl complains that modern music composition has discarded any connection between what he refers to as the compositional grammar used in constructing a piece and the grammar listeners use to form a mental representation of it. This argument leads to his "*Aesthetic Claim 2*: The best music arises from an alliance of a compositional grammar with the listening grammar" (Lerdahl 1988, 256). A recurring example in Lerdahl's essay is Boulez's composition *Le Marteau Sans Maître*, which does have, if one accepts Lerdahl's decomposition of the composing/performing/listening complex, a singularly striking decoupling of compositional and listening grammars. But, as Lerdahl points out, "this account is complicated by the fact that, as noted above, Boulez created *Le Marteau* not only through serial procedures but through his own inner listening. In the process he followed constraints that, while operating on the sequence of events produced by the compositional grammar, utilized principles from the listening grammar" (Lerdahl 1988, 234).

In my view, Fred Lerdahl should not be so surprised that Boulez's serial technique, his "compositional grammar," is often treated as if it were irrelevant, particularly when he himself notes that much of the interest of the piece comes from the workings of a musical mind operating beyond the scope of the purely formal rules. He cannot have it both ways: he cannot maintain that what makes *Le Marteau* a great piece of music is Boulez's musicianship, his "intuitive constraints," and maintain at the same time that music cannot be great unless cognition is explicitly coded into the formal system. To say that "the best music arises from an alliance of a compositional grammar with the listening grammar" and at the same time to recognize *Le Marteau* as a "remarkable" work when no such alliance occurs must mean that the *Aesthetic Claim 2* carries little force indeed.

What is important is the way listeners make sense of music, a sense employed by composers, performers, and listeners alike—the very point so emphatically put forward by Lerdahl himself. Lerdahl and Jackendoff are the first to point out, however, that though their theory may well explain parts of that sense, it is not by any means complete. Basing aesthetic claims, and establishing constraints on composition, on an incomplete account again amounts to overestimating the theory and shortchanging the mind's capacity to deal with many different kinds of music.

Eugene Narmour

A forceful statement against an overreliance on tree structures in music theory can be found in Narmour 1977:

> If, however, as has been implied, the normal state of affairs in tonal music is *non*congruence of parameters between levels instead of congruence, it follows that analytical reductions should be conceptualized not as trees—except perhaps in the most simplistic kinds of music where each unit (form, prolongation, whatever) is highly closed—but as *networks*. That is, musical structures should not be analyzed as consisting of levels systematically stacked like blocks . . . but rather as intertwined, reticulated complexes—as integrated, nonuniform hierarchies.
>
> Unity would then be a result of the interlocking connections that occur when implications are realized between parts rather than as a result of relationships determined by the assumption of a preexisting whole. (Narmour 1977, 97–98)

He observes in his article "Some Major Theoretical Problems Concerning the Concept of Hierarchy in the Analysis of Tonal Music" (1984) that in fact much of what passes for hierarchical structuring in music theory is not hierarchic at all, but rather "systemic," by which he refers to "musical relationships which are conceived in Gestaltist fashion as parts of a completely integrated whole" (Narmour 1984, 138). These structures, he states, are not hierarchic because differentiations of material on lower levels are not reflected in their representation on levels higher up. Because of the loss of information as we travel up the tree, all individual characteristics of a particular piece of music are subordinated to a priori style traits; such analysis "reduces an idiostructural event to a default case of the style" (Narmour 1984, 135).

Narmour's own theory, the implication-realization model, has as a structural consequence the postulation of an extensive, multifaceted network of connections among musical events on various levels of a composition. Following the work of Leonard Meyer and others, Narmour emphasizes the impact of listeners' expectations on their experience of a piece of music. Further, he recognizes the operation of multiple perspectives in music cognition: "What makes the theory and analysis of music exceptionally difficult, I believe, is that pieces display both systematic and hierarchical tendencies *simultaneously*. And, as we shall see, this suggests that both 'tree' and 'network' structures may be present in the same patterning" (Narmour 1977, 102).

Eugene Narmour's theory tends to assume the goal-directed, expectation-based model of music cognition. It relies heavily on the ideas of hierarchy and progression; in fact, it is the most consistently progression-oriented theory of the three reviewed here. Because Narmour sees progressions operating between noncongruent elements, however, his analytical structures tend not to resemble trees; for much the same reason, they are not recursive.

4.3 Cypher Hierarchies

Cypher's listener and player are organized hierarchically, though these hierarchies tend toward Narmour's network ideas rather than the more strictly structured trees of Lerdahl and Jackendoff. Further, the music representations adopted are expressed in a computer program, where processes realize the thrust of the theory. "To understand how memory and process merge in 'listening,' we will have to learn to use much more 'procedural' descriptions, such as programs that describe how processes proceed" (Minsky 1989, 646). The program has been deeply influenced by several strands of thought in music theory, among them the ones we have just reviewed. Moreover, Cypher does not describe many aspects of musical experience as well as do these predecessors. Its virtues, I would venture, are that Cypher concentrates on building a working procedural implementation of its theory, which can be tried out with music as it is performed, and that Cypher builds up its musical competence through several perspectives and the interaction of many simple, cross-connected processes.

The levels of Cypher's hierarchies are distinguished in three ways. First, higher levels refer to collections of the objects treated by lower levels. For example, on the listening side, the lowest level examines individual events, while the next highest level looks at the behavior within a group of such events. Second, higher levels use the abstractions produced by lower levels in their processing. So, the second-level listening agents, which describe groups of events, will use the classifications of those events made by a lower-level analysis to generate a description. Third, because of the temporal nature of music, groups of events will be extended through time; therefore, higher levels in the hierarchy will describe structures that span longer durations of time.

Figure 4.3 shows some important ways relations are drawn between the events analyzed and generated by the program; however, this way of looking at the information is only one of many perspectives Cypher adopts in the course of carrying out various tasks. This first perspective is so strictly hierarchical that we can best depict it as a tree structure; subevents are connected to only one superevent, and not to each other. Other perspectives do not relate things in such an orderly way. The underlying idea is to provide several different ways of regarding and manipulating the parts of a musical context: "A thing or idea seems meaningful only when we have several different ways to represent it —different perspectives and different associations" (Minsky 1989, 640). This section will review the organizations suggested by different perspectives on the data under consideration and by the kinds of connections and communication linking the agents that process that data.

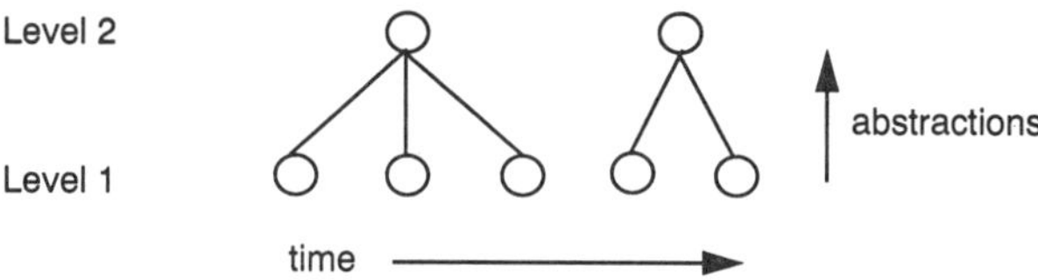

Figure 4.3

The Progressive Perspective

We are considering various perspectives on the operation of Cypher. One important axis around which to organize these perspectives separates the raw material from the processing. Some structures concern the way the sounding events, which make up the fabric of the analyzed or generated textures, are grouped and related. The processes that perform the analysis and generation are themselves operative on different levels, and have their own connections of communication and grouping. We have already seen one perspective on the musical events, captured by the tree structure drawn above. Another perspective places more emphasis on their progression through time and the associated relations of succession and precedence.

Figure 4.4 illustrates the progressive perspective. The objects shown represent the same sounding events pictured on level 1 of the previous figure. There the emphasis was on their subsumption in metaevents; here we see that pointers connect events to their neighbors in both temporal directions. By traversing the pointers, we can arrive at proximate events either earlier or later in time. The progressive perspective is adopted on other structures as well; harmonic progressions, patterns of rhythm or melody, and higher level groups of Cypher events all are related, at times, by the operations of succession and precedence.

Already we can see that multiple perspectives tangle the depiction of relations between sounding objects; we can perhaps combine progression and hierarchy into a single visual representation that makes sense (figure 4.5).

All events are connected in a hierarchy and simultaneously tied together in relations of succession and precedence. The addition of the progressive perspective takes our example far from the usual definition of a tree structure, however. Although it is clear enough to follow the combination of two relations, the effect of multiplying perspectives can be easily recognized as well: universal laws of relation between

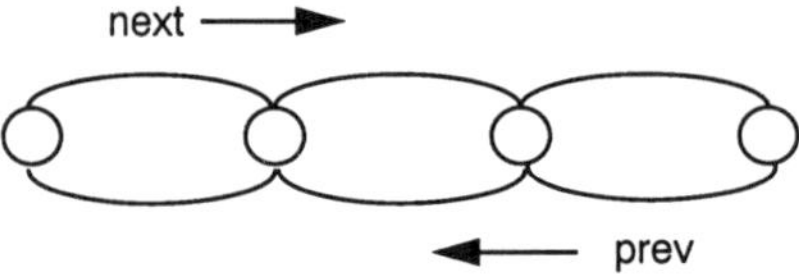

Figure 4.4

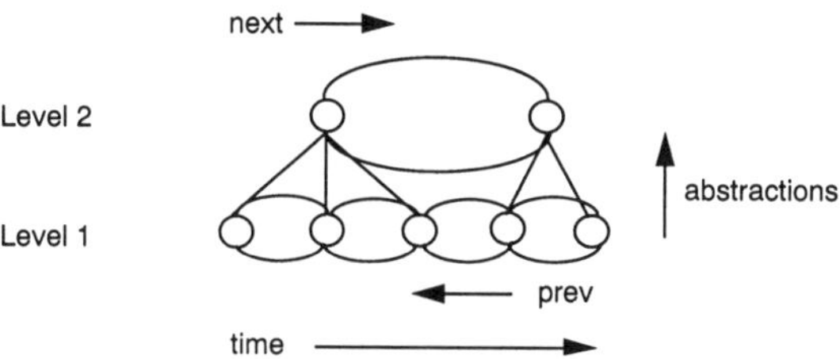

Figure 4.5

objects become obscured and complicated when there are several ways to connect and relate them.

In Cypher, a single, simple, universal form for relating objects, such as a tree structure, has been abandoned in favor of collections of ways to relate things. Our structures may become difficult to draw, but we will not be constrained by the representation to adopt a complicated solution to a problem that can be simply treated by a more appropriate perspective. Such pragmatism may seem straightforward, but as our review of other structural approaches has shown, it is in fact an exception to common practice. Many prominent music theories devise a single structural perspective within which to describe musical behavior and continue to adhere to that perspective no matter what difficulties are encountered in trying to deal with the fullness of musical experience.

Message Routes

On the other side of the events/processing axis, Cypher includes two large collections of interacting agents: those associated with the listener and those associated with the player. The processes within each collection communicate with each other; different kinds of messages are passed between the two collections. The hierarchical perspective on these processes is largely a function of the level of the events they treat: level-1 processes deal with the individual sounding objects; level-2 processes deal with groups of these events.

Processes communicate by passing messages. These communication links form another perspective through which the ongoing musical information is regarded; the pattern of links and the messages passing across them give an indication of which features of the music are important for which tasks, and how the agents carrying out various tasks collaborate in their execution. Figure 4.6 shows some typical communication links within and between the two sides.

Although the lines of communication are hierarchical, in the sense that there is a meaningful distinction to be made between levels of processing, we see that they resemble a network of relations rather than a more strictly formed tree structure. There are many processes on each side dealing with any single sounding event. Further, some general directions of the information flow can be noted: first, information tends to go up from the sounding events to analytical processes on the listening side, and on the playing side, generation methods are sending increasingly precise information down to the level of individual events, which, when complete, are sent on to the response devices at the specified time. Another important regularity is that information passes only from the listener to the player and not in the other direction. The only communication passing from the player back to the listener involves queries for additional data.

4.4 Expressive Performance

The most noticeable difference between the musical performances of human and machine players is the expressive variation human musicians invariably add. Expression is performed across several parameters, among them onset timing, dynamic, and duration (articulation). Studies in performance practice such as Palmer 1988 are beginning to give us good data about the strategies humans use to play expressively, which is critical information if machine players are to learn to incorporate such expression in their own performances. Such work is of

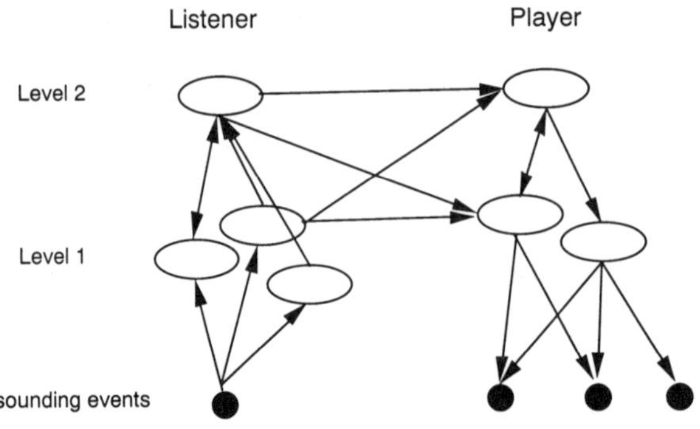

Figure 4.6

central importance to the development of interactive systems for two reasons: first, the cognitive faculties these studies highlight are an important part of human musical understanding, and second, to the extent that they can uncover operative performance strategies, these strategies can be implemented and made part of the arsenal of performance techniques available to interactive programs.

Cypher is one of the interactive systems beginning to use the findings of music cognition to implement the program's performance mechanisms. Human performers accomplish expressive variation through many musical parameters, including pitch inflections and timbral change. Cypher ignores timbral information and does not include continuous controls such as pitch variation. Therefore, those parameters, though highly desirable candidates for manipulation by a computer performer, are left untreated by the program. Rather, the problem of expressivity is explored through two parameters currently available to the system: variations of timing and loudness.

Expressive Timing

A sense of time is one of the most critical musical faculties. In human performance, we may separate structural from expressive timing considerations, as is done by most listeners (Clarke 1987). For example, listeners will usually interpret a series of gradually lengthening durations as a pattern of equally spaced notes undergoing a ritardando. In such a case, the structural rhythm perceived is the string of equally spaced note values. The expressive component of the percept is the ritard.

The separation of rhythmic experience into structural and expressive components is a form of *categorical perception*. As evidence of this, Eric Clarke discusses experiments in which two easily structured rhythmic presentations are chosen. A series of test rhythmic patterns is generated, with the two simple cases at the extremes. Intermediate steps form an interpolation between them, continuously varying durations of some notes until the opposite extreme is reached. Listeners to this sequence will perceive the straightforward rhythmic interpretation of the first pattern and continue to maintain this interpretation through several of the intermediate steps. Then as the other extreme is neared, a jump is made to an interpretation matching the pattern at the opposite extreme. Rhythmic parsing is thus done *categorically*, with percepts assigned to one of a limited number of simply structured possibilities, where additional timing variations are perceived as expressive, not structural.

We have seen some basic tools for the manipulation of time in interactive systems, such as scheduling and time stamping. These techniques, however, are clearly on a level well below that of human temporal perception. The human experience of time can suggest important ways to organize and elaborate the programs' temporal facilities. Further, many efforts already extant in computer music provide tools for working with time that are far more powerful than the elementary techniques reviewed earlier.

Time Maps

The time map described in Jaffe 1985 provides a general method for coordinating temporal deformations among several voices of output. The idea is to be able to specify tempo fluctuations in such a way that voices are able to speed up or slow down independently of one another and to return to synchronization at any desired point. As an example, imagine that a composer would want slight ritardandi setting off the cadence of certain phrases: a time map would allow the notation of that phrase as regular (for example, a series of eighth notes) but would force the performance to include delays of slightly increasing duration between successive note onsets as we approach the cadence. A time map, then, is a function describing the deviation between the performed and notated lengths of the duration between two attacks. Such maps, or tempo curves, can be stored to affect the generation of temporal performance in real time. Similarly, tempo curves can be analyzed from real performances as a way to quantify the expressive timing added by virtuoso players.

As in the case of the example just outlined, these techniques have tended to be applied to score-driven models. As such, maps are applied most naturally in situations where there is a score or structural notation of the rhythmic content. To be able to use them in interactive systems with no score requires those systems to be able to assert goal points in their output or in some way to segment the material they are producing, such that a time map can meaningfully adjust the time offsets before performing the fragment. For example, indication of some output point as a phrase boundary can mark it as the goal of a slight decelerando, emphasizing that point's structural importance, even if the phrase has not been stored in advance. All that is required is that the system mark the fragment as a phrase and apply a map before performance.

This is not to suggest that finding goal points in unnotated output is trivial, but it indicates one motivation for attempting to identify them. Such gestures as phrase lengthening are important cues for the perceptual system and serve to accentuate structural articulations in performed music. Their more widespread application is critical to the continued development of interactive systems, particularly as those systems are used more commonly as equal partners in human instrumental ensembles. To use time maps well in performance-driven systems will require advances in two areas: the real-time specification of goal points in musical output, such as phrase or larger structural boundaries, and the flexible description of time deformations for fragments of any duration, together with their calculation in real time.

Several interactive programming environments provide timing facilities that could support these kinds of extensions. The CMU MIDI Toolkit, for example, allows the specification of sequences by several means: text editing, capturing a MIDI stream in real time, or converting standard MIDI files produced by some commercial sequencer or other source. Playback of these scores operates through a virtual time system, which can be varied with respect to real time. Affecting the clock rate of the virtual time system can produce variable playback speeds, allowing synchronization with external events (Dannenberg 1991). Such a facility could be used to apply stored time maps to designated portions of sequences in interactive performance. The problem of finding structural units across which to apply the maps remains; these must be identified by hand. But using a time map to vary the virtual time reference of the sequence playback, would allow the realization of performance-driven tempo variation on stored music fragments.

Time maps, or tempo curves, have deficiencies of their own which will require further study, however. The difficulty with such representations of expressive timing is that there is no general library of time maps that can be applied to any arbitrary piece of music and yield satisfactory results. In their article "Tempo Curves Considered Harmful," Peter Desain and Henkjan Honing (1991) systematically show how the map representation fails to retain the necessary expressivity through various transformations. As an example of their argument, consider the tempo control implemented in most commercial MIDI sequencers. The idea of a tempo control is that a user can shift the speed of a performance up or down, changing the overall tempo of a sequence without degrading the quality of the performance. Desain and Honing show that the use of simple arithmetic transformations to the time offsets between events will not yield a new performance that remains close to what a human player would do when modifying the tempo of a performance by a similar amount. A human player will apply different timing variations to the same piece when the tempo is increased by 50 percent, generally by using less variation, producing a "flatter" tempo map between the ideal and performed versions. Turning up the tempo control on a sequencer, however, will use the same map shrunk by 50 percent, making variations that were effective at the slower tempo sound clownish and inappropriate at the higher speed.

The compositional processes implemented in Cypher provide both directed and static means of temporal deformation. Directed temporal operations perform a linear transformation of the offset times separating events, either lengthening them (decelerando), or shortening them (accelerando). Static operations add smaller, nondirectional changes to the length of event offsets. These possibilities may, as is the case with all compositional methods, be applied on any level, in response to messages arriving from the listener. Level-1 applications will change offsets on a per-event basis (see the transformation modules *accelerator* and *decelerator* described in section 6.1). Level-2 applications will be invoked in response to regularity or phrase-boundary messages. Therefore, their action will be advanced with the frequency of the appropriate messages coming from level 2; temporal deformations attached to phrase boundaries will be advanced on a per-phrase basis, for example.

Dynamic Variation

Dynamic variation is another common conveyance of expressive performance. Changes in loudness are used to emphasize structural boundaries and to highlight directed motion toward some musical goal. Crescendo and decrescendo are clear examples of expressive dynamic variation, but they are far from the only ones.

As in the case of temporal deviations, slight, quickly changing perturbations of the dynamic level are a critical part of an expressive, or even just acceptable, musical performance. But dynamic variations cannot be applied randomly or by following only local musical constructs. The essence of expression is to use variation in pointing out structural boundaries, major articulations of the composition in progress.

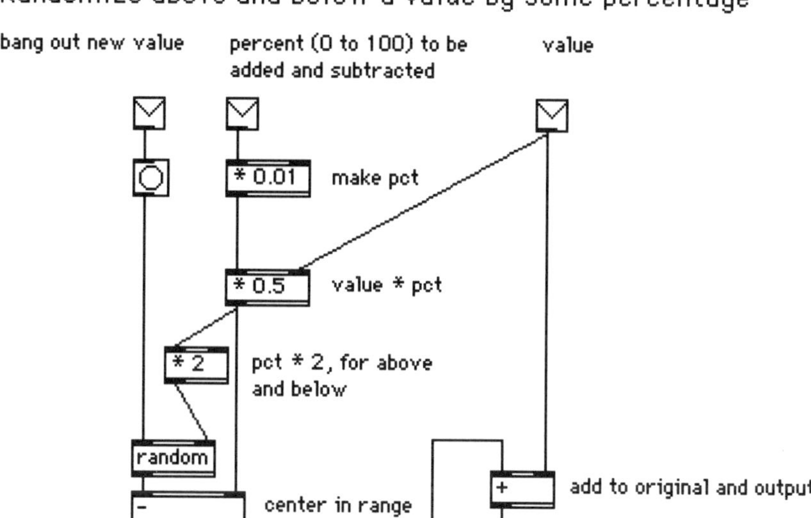

Figure 4.7

Unless some of that structure is present, either laid out by a human user, or found by the program itself, dynamic variation will add unpredictability to a computer performance, but will not enhance the performance of larger musical gestures, as a human performer normally would.

The Max subpatch in figure 4.7, written by Todd Winkler, shows a method for adding some random jitter to performance variables, within a specified percentage. Slight randomization of inter-onset intervals, or dynamic values, can eliminate some of the most egregiously "mechanical" effects of computer generated music. In fact, much of what is advertised as "human feel" in commercial synthesis systems is based on just such an idea. I have argued here that interactive systems need to move beyond strictly random variation in expressive performance, and I do not mean to suggest that Winkler proposes this patch as a solution to the problems of expression. Just such an approach can be quite effective, however, when used in conjunction with more structured variations—some fluctuation within an overall crescendo, for example, or perturbing the progression of an algorithmically generated accelerando.

Dynamic variation in Cypher can take three forms: crescendo, decrescendo, or a more quickly changing, unstable pattern of change in loudness. These possibilities subsume two kinds of directed motion (louder, softer) and one relatively static pattern of change. Further, these processes can operate simultaneously on different compositional levels. Imagine a series of decrescendi embedded in a larger, more global crescendo, or small, local dynamic changes within an overall decrescendo. The level structure of Cypher provides a framework for directing the application of dynamic variation to different structural planes of the compositional output. If a dynamic process is applied on level 1, for example, changes in loudness will occur on a per-event basis (see the *louder* and *quieter* transformation modules). Dynamic processes on the second level will be applied as a function of the listener message to which they are connected: a crescendo connected to the phrase boundary message, for example, will affect output on a per-phrase basis, with each successive phrase somewhat louder than the last.

Structural Anticipation

The performance of music is determined by the performers' understanding of the composition they are playing. Performance pedagogy on all levels emphasizes the skill of interpretation, transcending the mechanics of pure technique. Once a performer has a conception of the music to convey, all of the specifics of physical interaction with an instrument are executed in accordance with the expression of that conception (Clarke 1988). Further, different performance circumstances will engender different performance strategies, still with the goal of expressing the same underlying expression. External factors such as the size or resonance of a hall or faster tempi chosen by a conductor could cause the relationships between various parameters of the performance to change. These changes will, however, be made to optimize the conveyance of a performer's understanding of the composition's structure.

Many current interactive systems, including Cypher, are currently able to recognize some musical structures in a stream of events represented by MIDI. Recognition alone, however, is not enough. To perform expressively, a player (human or machine) must be looking ahead, anticipating the future motion of the musical discourse. A program performing expressively, therefore, must have knowledge of typical continuations in a style if it is to shape its performance in accordance with the anticipated contour of some musical structure.

Such anticipation can only come from familiarity with the norms of a musical style, providing another motivation for beginning to include a base of musical knowledge in computer music programs. Again, music theory and music cognition offer indications of how expectation works in the human experience of music. Phenomena such as tonal expectation have received significant attention including computer simulations, from music cognition. In chapter 7, we will review some of these efforts as we consider artificial intelligence applications in interactive systems.

The concluding point to be made here is that an understanding of structural functions shapes the composition, performance, and audition of music. Research in music cognition has been directed toward discovering the nature of that understanding and how it affects the performance of musical tasks. Music theory has long provided a rich collection of ideas on how musical structures are built and perceived. Interactive systems must come to grips with these problems, and they have already begun to do so. Without concepts of musical style sufficiently strong to anticipate probable continuations and points of articulation, computer programs will never be able to play music with the expression that is evident in human performances. Even the strategies humans employ in the structural cognition of music are only dimly understood. Interactive music systems need to advance in this area for the sake of their own performance levels; at the same time, interactive systems can provide a unique testing ground for theories advanced in other disciplines, such as applied theories of music and music cognition, by showing the function of theoretical constructs in real performance situations.

5 Machine Listening

One of the primary motivations for building an analysis section into an interactive music system is the opportunity it affords for generating new output whose relation to the musical context is readily apparent to a human listener. It is my belief that trying to follow the example of human cognition in building a machine listener will be fruitful not only because humans provide the best, indeed the only, model of successful music listeners but also because couching an interactive system in terms compatible with human listening categories will encourage the generation of music that, though procedurally generated, will resonate with the human cognitive processes for which it is ultimately intended.

The division of a computer music system into listening (or analytical) and composition components seems to be a natural one. Several efforts have explicitly described their structure using such terms, and others easily fall into them. Cypher is one system where a listener/composition axis is distinctly maintained. Another clear example is the T-MAX system built by Bruce Pennycook and his colleagues at McGill University (Pennycook and Lea 1991). The HARP (Hybrid Action Representation and Planning) system, built at the University of Genoa by Antonio Camurri and others, likewise has two subsystems: one for managing sounds and analyses and another handling scores and descriptions of pieces (Camurri et al. 1991). David Wessel's improvisation software is split into listening, composing, and performing assistants (Wessel 1991). Further, variants of the machine-listening task are evident in several applications for such things as the automatic transcription of audio recordings (Chafe, Mont-Reynaud, and Rush 1982) or tutoring systems for the piano (Dannenberg et al. 1990).

To say that building a listening capability into a computer program can enhance its musicality is not to imply that there is a generally agreed theory of what music listening is. Many competing versions of the cognitive process of listening exist, within and among fields specifically concerned with the question, such as music theory and music cognition. Building a machine listener demands making choices about the matter and means dealing with the consequences of those choices in live performance. This chapter will explore in considerable detail the listening engine of Cypher, expanding the discussion with references to other systems as these become relevant. Here as in the remainder of the text, it is crucial to note the way choices of representation and processing embody particular conceptions of the way music is experienced, thereby amplifying the power of a program to deal with musical situations in those terms and attenuating the same system's power to address other conceptions.

The transformations of musical information made by listening systems are not lossless. In other words, the abstractions made do not produce a representation that can be transformed back into the original signal, as, for example, a Fourier analysis can be changed back into a sound-pressure wave. The abstraction of MIDI already throws away a good deal of timbral information about the music it represents. The analytical transformations described here, similarly, cannot be used to reproduce the original stream of MIDI data. Information is lost; for that reason, it is critical to take care that the parameters of the representation preserve salient aspects of the musical flow.

We will be concerned for the most part with listening systems that assume the MIDI abstraction. A major part of human musical understanding arises from perceptions of timbre, and these are discarded when MIDI represents a musical flow. Some researchers have built listening capabilities into systems that begin on the signal level, trying to identify notes and articulations in a digital audio representation. Examples would include Barry Vercoe's recent work (Vercoe 1990), and the various forms of automatic transcription (Chafe, Mont-Renaud, and Rush 1982). Adding timbral information to machine-listening algorithms will certainly make them more sensitive to some of the most prominent aspects of music in human perception; although a reliance on personal computers and MIDI have made timbre hard to reach currently, chapter 8 will show how timbral representations could enrich already existing models.

5.1 Feature Classification

Cypher's listener, as we have seen, is organized hierarchically. Currently, two levels of analysis exist: the lowest level describes individual note or chord events, and the level above that describes the way these events change over time. To describe incoming events, the listener process on level 1 (a lower level, level 0, would be a timbral analysis) classifies each of them as occupying one point in a multidimensional featurespace. This is a conceptual space whose dimensions correspond to several perceptual categories; placement of an object in the space asserts that the object has the combination of qualities indicated by its relation to the various featural dimensions.

To illustrate the concept, consider a three-dimensional featurespace, bounded by the perceptual categories register, density, and dynamic. Points occupying such a featurespace are shown in figure 5.1. The position of the points in this example space are determined by assigning each event values for the three categories bounding the space; those values, taken as a vector, specify a unique location in the space for the event.

In figure 5.1, we see a cluster of points near the upper right back corner of the cube. These points represent sounding events that have been classified as high, loud, chords: the values assigned to each of these qualities is near the maximum endpoint of the scale. Similarly,

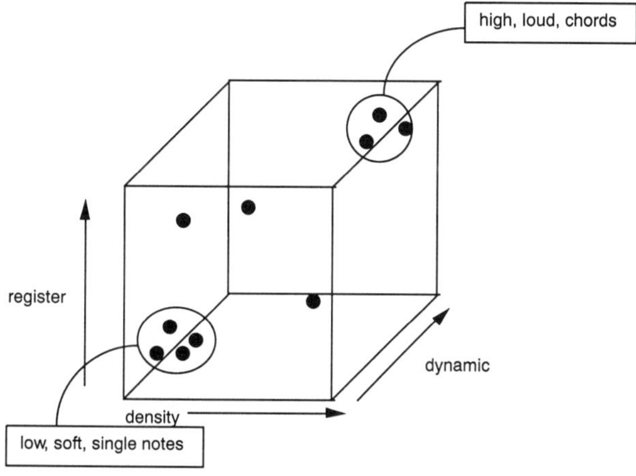

Figure 5.1

there is another cluster of points near the lower left front corner of the cube that, since the values assigned to all qualities are near the minimum endpoint, correspond to low, soft, single notes. We can see that events will be grouped more closely as their perceptual qualities are more closely related; points near each other in the space represent events with many perceptual qualities in common.

The featurespace actually used by the level-1 analysis has six dimensions: register, loudness, vertical density, attack speed, duration, and harmony. The values assigned to each feature are a function of the MIDI data associated with the input event and of the points in time at which the event begins and ends. For example, the *loudness* dimension is decided by simply comparing the event's MIDI velocity to a threshold: those velocities above the threshold are classified as loud and those below it as soft.

Classifying loudness into one of two categories is of course unnaturally restrictive: there are certainly many more musically meaningful dynamic gradations than two. The point of this research, however, is to work on the combination and communication of many analysis agents. Therefore, the individual analysis processes are kept skeletally simple. Scaling the loudness analysis up to much finer gradations would change nothing in the design of the system other than making it bigger. Because such a change is not central to the function of the program, it has been left out of the research version.

The featurespace classification combines the output of each feature agent into a single vector, which is the main message passed from the level-1 listener to the player. The contribution of any single feature can be easily masked out of the whole. In this way, the player is continually informed of the behavior of each feature individually, and in combination. Further, higher listening levels will use the featurespace abstraction to characterize the development of each feature's behavior over time.

Before continuing, it is worth clarifying some points of terminology. Cypher's basic architecture is derived from several ideas put forward in Marvin Minsky's book *The Society of Mind* (Minsky 1986). Two often-used terms from that work are *agent* and *agency*. Minsky describes the distinction between them as follows:

Agent Any part or process of the mind that by itself is simple enough to understand—even though the interactions among groups of such agents may produce phenomena that are much harder to understand.

Agency Any assembly of parts considered in terms of what it can accomplish as a unit, without regard to what each of its parts does by itself. (Minsky 1986, 326)

Thus, the feature agents described in the following sections, whose combined output specifies a point in the level-1 featurespace, are simple processes responsible for analyzing some aspect of a musical performance. As we shall see, agencies built from combinations of these simple processes are able to accomplish more complicated analytical tasks.

Note and Event

Before proceeding, let us examine some of the structures used by the program for representing music. The *Note* and *Event* structures are two of the most important ones.

```
typedef struct {
        unsigned char pitch, velocity;
        long duration;
        } Note;
```

A Note closely follows the MIDI standard's concept of a note: it records a pitch (using the MIDI pitch-numbering system, where middle C = 60) and a velocity, representing the strength with which the note was attacked. Cypher adds a *duration* to these parameters, where the duration is length of time in milliseconds between the MIDI Note On message initiating the note and the Note Off message that terminates it.

An *Event* structure holds at least one Note. Events are kept in doubly linked lists, which facilitate navigation forward and backward through temporally proximate events (the progressive perspective). The *prev* and *next* pointers point to the preceding and succeeding Events, respectively.

```
typedef struct ev {
        struct ev *prev, *next;
        long  time, offset;
        char  chordsize, external;
        Note  data[NOTEMAX];
        } Event;
```

The most important pieces of information added to the collection of Notes held in an Event are timestamps, which associate an Event with a point in time. There are two ways of identifying the onset time of a Event: the first records the absolute *time* of the Event relative to the beginning of program execution. The second method records the time *offset* of the Event relative to the Event preceding it. It is this second timestamp which is most often used; in fact, the absolute timestamp is used mainly to calculate the offset and the duration of Notes. The *chordsize* indicates how many Notes an Event contains and the *data* array holds the Notes themselves. The *external* field indicates simply whether the event arrived from the outside world or was generated by the program itself and is needed for some timing considerations.

Focus and Decay

Focus is a technique used to make feature judgments relative to the musical context actually heard. Rather than evaluating qualities against a constant scale, the measurement scale itself changes as new information arrives. When there is change within a very small range of values, the focus of the agent narrows to an area where change can be detected. When values are changing over a very wide field of possibilities, the focus pulls back to register change across a broader range of values.

Decay is the adjustment of the focal scale over time. The magnitude of the measurements made is relative to the range of change seen—the principle of focus. The scale against which measurements are made changes over time, as data that are not reinforced tend to recede from influencing the current context—the principle of decay. The first featural agent we will consider, the one classifying register, will provide a good example of these two techniques at work. The remaining agents make less initial use use of focus and decay; either their lack of precision or more vexing theoretical problems make them less amenable to such treatment. The relation of each agent to the concept, however, will be discussed as we proceed.

Register

The *register* agent classifies the pitch range within which an event is placed. At the most basic level, this classification distinguishes high from low in pitch space. Making realistic registral judgments requires more precision than a separation of high from low, however, and is further sensitive to the conditioning effects of context and timbre. Our considerations, limited by the representations of the MIDI standard, do not include timbre, and our precision is limited to two bits. Still, registral judgments in Cypher are made against a scale derived from the pitch information actually experienced by the program.

One way to classify register would be to divide a piano keyboard up into some number of equally sized divisions, compare incoming events against these divisions, and assign classifications according to which division contained them. The Max patch shown in figure 5.2 is an implementation of this idea. It is quite straightforward: Note On messages are checked to be within the expected limits of a MIDI keyboard. Then, in the *expr* object, 21 is subtracted from the pitch number, since 21 is the lowest pitch number on an 88-key keyboard. This makes the note numbers of incoming pitches range from zero to 87. Simply dividing the result by 22, then, yields 4 classifications, labeled from 0 to 3. This classification is seen in the number box at the bottom.

Although splitting up the 88 keys of the keyboard will work well for piano music and other ensemble textures that use most of the musical range, it makes little sense for other solo instruments or combinations of instruments using only a fraction of that span. Therefore, the register agent in Cypher keeps a scale of low to high based on the pitches actually analyzed up to any given moment (the principle of focus). As each new event arrives, it is compared to the scale stored for that event stream. If the event is lower or higher than either endpoint of the scale, the scale is adjusted outward to include the new event. For example,

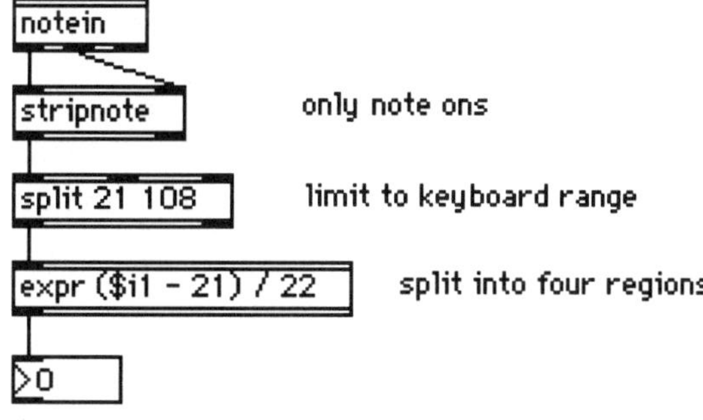

Figure 5.2

if the lowest point on the scale is MIDI pitch number 60 and a new event of 48 arrives, the low endpoint of the scale is changed to 48.

The precision of the classification reports is directly tied to the size of the scale against which the measurements are made. If the pitch scale for some stream is less than two octaves, the register agent will only distinguish between low and high. Once the span opens out to over two octaves, possible classifications expand to four: low, medium low, medium high, and high. Consequently, judgments made about pitches played in a small ambitus will have fewer gradations than judgments concerning pitches presented in a more varied context. In the case of chords, the overall register classification is decided by a "majority" rule: the register with the most pitches of the chord is declared the register of the event as a whole. If more than one register has the same number of pitches in a chord, that is, if there is a tie in register classification after application of the "majority" rule, the lowest classification among those tied will be chosen.

The adjustment of the endpoints of a pitch scale as new pitch information arrives is an example of focus in a feature agent. A necessary complement is the principle of decay, which also changes the endpoints over time, but in the opposite direction. These two operations together involve the register scale in a process of continual expansion and contraction. As we have seen, when new pitches arrive that exceed the bounds of the previously established range, the register scale grows by replacing one of the endpoints to match the new data. If an endpoint has not been reinforced for five seconds, that endpoint shrinks in toward the opposing endpoint by one halfstep (one MIDI pitch number). Thereafter, the endpoint will continue to shrink inward by one halfstep every half second. When a pitch arrives to reinforce or extend an endpoint, the scale again grows outward to meet it, and the decay timer is reset to five seconds. After a new duration of five seconds with no additional information near the extreme, the scale will again begin to shrink inward. The addition of focus and decay to the Max register agent shown in figure 5.2 would complicate matters but could easily be accomplished; Max's timing and statistical objects, such as *maximum*, *minimum*, and *timer*, would be appropriate tools.

Dynamic

The *dynamic* agent classifies the loudness of events. In this case, the nature of the feature demands careful consideration of the focus and decay principles. For MIDI data, there is already a highly significant scale of possible loudness values against which events can be compared: velocity information is encoded in seven bits, giving a range of values varying from 0 to 127. Unfortunately, the perceived loudness of two different synthesizer voices, even using the same velocity value, can vary widely. Real classification of perceived loudness would require signal processing of an acoustic signal, which Cypher deliberately avoids. The listener is forced instead to rely on the MIDI velocity measurement, which records the pressure with which a key was struck in the case of keyboards, and some approximation of force of attack when coming from a commercial pitch-to-MIDI converter following an acoustic source.

Accepting the MIDI velocity scale of 0 to 127, it was found that focus and decay had little effect on establishing any particularly more appropriate scale of values for measuring loudness. In fact, even with the MIDI scale there seems to be no way to establish good thresholds for distinguishing velocity levels. One keyboard played normally may readily give a MIDI velocity of 110, for example, whereas another must be hammered with all the strength at one's command to get the same reading. There is no clear way to compensate for this algorithmically – consistently low readings, for example, could come from an exceptionally delicate piece. Placing the loudness threshold in the middle of the values actually seen, then, would simply classify half of the events as loud when all of them are experienced as softly played.

For this reason, the dynamic agent is the only one that must be hand tuned for different instruments; an actual test with the physical instrument to be used must be performed to find out what MIDI velocity readings will be registered for various types of playing. With that information in hand, a threshold corresponding to the instrument can be established, distinguishing soft from loud playing. Once a threshold has been chosen, the agent simply compares the MIDI velocity of incoming events to it and reports a classification of loud or soft according to whether the event is above or below the threshold. Multiple-note events are classified as loud when more than half of the member notes are above the threshold and are classified as soft otherwise.

The Max patch of figure 5.3 is an implementation of the dynamic agent. The object

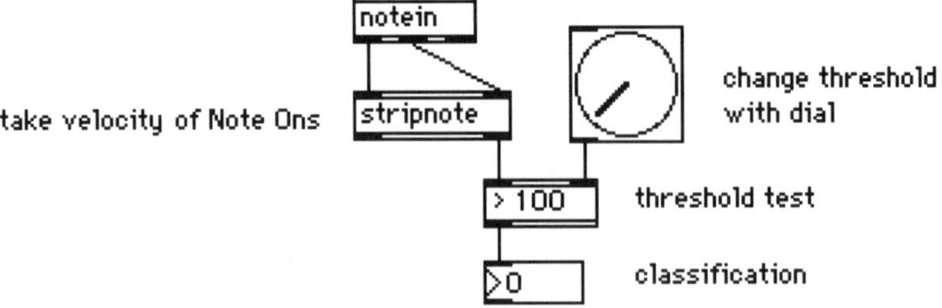

Figure 5.3

compares the velocity values of Note On messages against a threshold of 100. If the velocity is less than or equal to 100, the number box below will show a classification of zero; otherwise, the classification will be 1. The dial above the test can be used to set the threshold value.

Density

The *density* agent tracks vertical density. Vertical density refers to the number and spacing of events played simultaneously; this in contrast to horizontal density, the number and spacing of events played in succession. Horizontal density is treated by the *speed* agent. The techniques of focus and decay are laid aside when considering vertical density; this is because the perceptual difference between linear and chordal textures seems to remain constant regardless of the context. Similarly, though context does condition the perception of extension or clustering in chord voicings, the effect is still relatively weak. Because both of these aspects of vertical density (number of notes, spacing of notes) are represented with such low precision here, the coarser, more or less constant, perceptions are being modeled. Consequently, the thresholds used to decide classifications of density and spacing are constant as well.

The classification performed by this agent represents two related types of information: first, an event is judged to be either a single note or a chord. Second, if the event is a chord, the distance between extremes of the chord is considered, giving a classification of the chord's spacing. The first judgment, deciding if an event is a single note or a chord, is harder than it sounds. The main problem has to do with the way MIDI information is transmitted—serially, with notes from any simultaneity sent down the wire one at a time. Another problem is finding the boundary that separates fast trills from chords. At what point do the onsets of neighboring notes follow each other so quickly that they begin to be heard as a simultaneity? The answer to the second question, in Cypher, is 100 milliseconds. (Note that this constant was arrived at simply through experimentation with MIDI gear and does not represent any empirically justifiable mark.) Notes arriving within 100 milliseconds of the first note in an event are considered part of the same event. Establishing that threshold, however, leads directly to the first problem: Must we always wait 100 milliseconds to find out if any more notes will arrive?

It took a surprisingly long time to find a good solution to this problem. The final implementation works as follows: The computer running Cypher is attached to an interface that receives and sends MIDI messages. Incoming MIDI messages are parsed, timestamped, and buffered in a MIDI driver that responds to the interrupts generated when a new message arrives. Cypher reads the buffered events from the MIDI driver in its main loop. First, a single MIDI event is read from the driver, and its timestamp is recorded. This gives us the start time of the current event. A counter, which will be incremented each time a null event is read from the driver, is set to zero. (A *null event* is sent from the driver when an attempt is made to read it before a new MIDI event is complete in the buffer. Many null events can separate two MIDI events, even if the duration separating them is very small.)

Now, MIDI events are repeatedly read from the driver and added to the *Cypher* event under construction as long as the following two conditions are true: the duration from the start time to the time of the most recent MIDI event read is less than 110 milliseconds and the number of null MIDI events read is less than 50. These conditions are a consequence of the normal pattern of input accompanying a performed chord. Timestamps for the notes in the chord are close to one another but almost never simultaneous; however, a range of 110 milliseconds will almost always catch onsets that belong together. Second, even MIDI packets with the same timestamp will sometimes be separated by null events. This is why one cannot simply keep reading events until the first null event. Allowing 50 null events to be read before giving up on additional data seems to capture almost all chords as chords, without introducing delays to system response while the program is waiting for additional data to straggle in. There is still some confusion in vertical versus horizontal density: even with this method, fast trills will sometimes be read as groups of very compact chords. An additional rule could be added that would insert a chord boundary any time the same pitch was about to be added a second time to the same chord.

The Max patch shown in figure 5.4 accomplishes a similar operation. The

thresh 100

object will collect all incoming integers arriving within 100 milliseconds of each other. Then, using the objects *iter* and *counter*, the number of pitches in the list is counted. If this is greater than one, the event is classified as a chord (labeled 1), and otherwise as a single note (labeled 0).

There are two differences between this and the Cypher scheme: The Max patch of figure 5.4 will always wait 100 milliseconds before reporting the pitches recorded; because of the additional "null event" counter, Cypher is usually able to produce all the notes of a chord without waiting the full duration. Second, Cypher goes beyond the chord/note distinction of the Max patch: if it has been established that the density of an event is greater than one, the agent classifies the spacing of the chord. To do this, the extreme notes are identified, then the distance between extremes is measured. Chords falling within an octave are *octave1*; chords covering between one and two octaves are *octave2*; and chords spanning more than two octaves are *wide*.

Attack Speed

The *speed* agent classifies the temporal offset between the event being analyzed and the event previous to it in time. The offset is the duration in centiseconds between the attack of the previous event and the attack

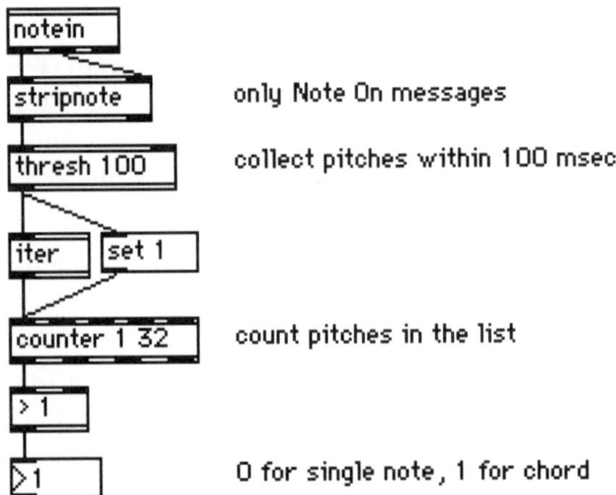

Figure 5.4

of the analyzed event: this duration is sometimes referred to as the inter-onset interval (IOI). Measuring the inter-onset interval indicates the horizontal density of events; a low IOI separates events closely spaced in time.

The speed agent currently uses an absolute scale to classify the IOI into one of four categories: events with an IOI longer than 2100 milliseconds are classified as slow; those between 2100 and 1000 milliseconds are classified as medium slow; those between 1000 and 300 milliseconds are medium fast; and those shorter than 300 milliseconds are fast. Note that the ranges decrease in size as the speed increases: the range of offsets for medium slow events is 1100 milliseconds, down to a range for medium fast events that covers 700 milliseconds.

The Max patch in figure 5.5 is a version of the speed agent. With each arriving note, a bang goes to both inlets of a *timer* object. This yields the time in milliseconds between each Note On message. Then a series of *split* objects classify the inter-onset interval. The object

```
split 100 300
```

will pass durations between 100 and 300 msec out the left outlet, and anything else out the right outlet. Two more splits help classify the IOI into one of four categories, as in Cypher. The main difference between

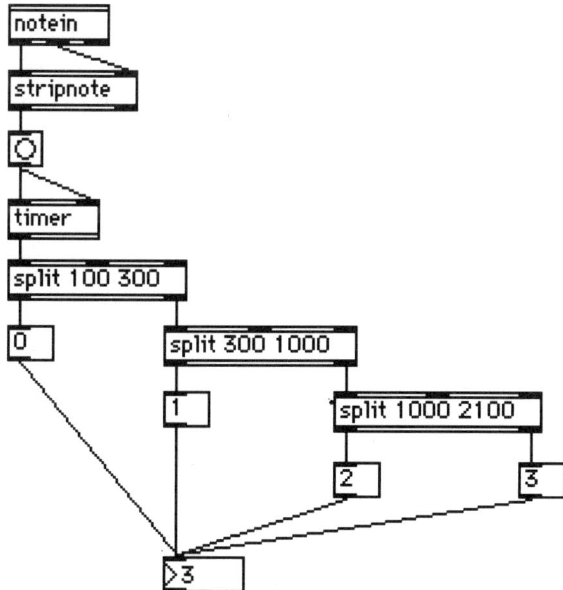

Figure 5.5

this patch and Cypher is that the latter is also performing the chord-gathering algorithm described in the previous section. Therefore, rather than measuring all arriving Note On messages, as are produced by the *notein* object in figure 5.5, the speed agent measures the IOI between Cypher events, which could be either individual notes or chords.

In Cypher, the threshold at which horizontal density becomes vertical density is 100 milliseconds: all raw MIDI events arriving within 100 milliseconds of the onset of a Cypher event are grouped together in that Cypher event as a chord. In other words, Cypher events constructed from MIDI data arriving from the outside world will never have an IOI less than 100 milliseconds (Cypher events being wholly generated in the composition section, however, might be spaced more closely). The 100-millisecond threshold means that the range for fast offsets is limited to 200 milliseconds (the difference between 300 milliseconds, the upper bound, and 100 milliseconds, the limit below which no offsets will be recorded).

The speed feature clearly could benefit from a focus scale. A sliding series of thresholds able to reflect relative speed variations according to context would give a more lifelike representation of the experience of attack speed. Indeed, with adjustments by focus and decay, speed might be represented with somewhat less precision than would be needed without them, since the reduced classification set will always be referring to meaningful gradations. In other words, rather than having a large set of possible speeds, many of which remain unused in some context, a smaller set, adjusting itself to the data arriving, could give a more accurate picture of what is actually happening.

Duration

The *duration* agent classifies the length of Cypher events. A duration is the span of time between the onset, or Note On message, at the beginning of an event and the Note Off message terminating it. Unlike the agents reviewed so far, the duration agent adds a classification to the featurespace characterizing the event *previous* to the one whose attack has just been recorded. This is because the level-1 featurespace analysis is done as quickly as possible after the initial attack of an event. A good part of the perceptual information accompanying a musical event is generated at the onset, particularly if that event has been represented in MIDI. If it is MIDI, and continuous controller information is ignored, *all* of the relevant information is present at the onset—except for the event's duration.

There are two ways to respond to this problem: either analysis can be delayed until an event has finished, or the current event can be analyzed for everything but duration. The second solution has been chosen, since durations tend to remain relatively constant from event to event, and because the responsiveness of the system improves markedly if the current event is the one analyzed and complemented by the composition section.

At present, an absolute scale is used to classify duration. Events whose duration exceeds 300 milliseconds are classified as long, and the rest as short. The duration classification should be given more precision and made available as a value relative to the current beat duration. Much as combining chord and key classifications yields the function of the chord in the key, combining durations and beat periods would yield an expression of an incoming duration in terms of whole and fractional parts of beats. Having durations available in such terms (one quarter note, dotted eighth note, etc.) could produce sequences amenable to treatment by the pattern processes described in chapter 6.

The implementation of focus on duration is problematic: a combination of sliding and fixed scales seems to be the correct way to proceed. For example, a grace note (a note of very short duration preceding some primary pitch) always has about the same length and is always experienced as very short, no matter how long the surrounding durations are. So grace notes should always be classified as (very) short—the classification should not change as the primary pitches become shorter or longer. More typical note durations are sensitive to context, however: an eighth note surrounded by thirty-second notes will sound longer than an eighth note of the same duration surrounded by whole notes. Perhaps relatively extreme durations should receive constant classifications, and those in the usual duration range should be subject to a more context-sensitive focal scale.

The Max patch in figure 5.6 is a schematized version of a duration agent. The *select* object separates Note On messages from Note Offs. When a Note On arrives, the left inlet of the *timer* receives a bang. For a Note Off, the right inlet is banged, yielding the time in milliseconds between the two. This duration is then compared against a threshold of 300 milliseconds, and a classification of long (1) or short (0) results.

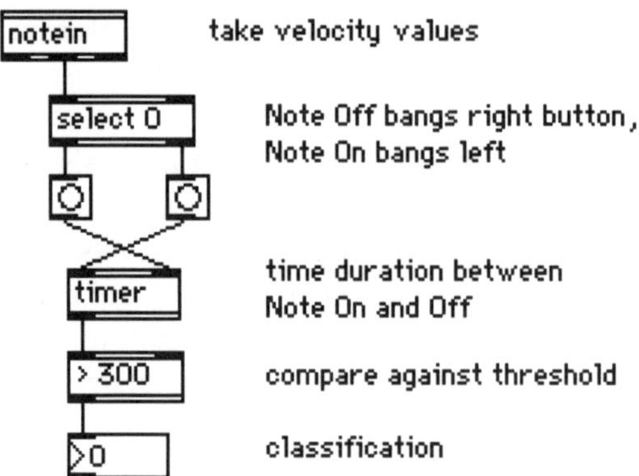

Figure 5.6

Note that this patch is too reduced to be very useful in its present form: here it measures durations between any Note On and any Note Off regardless of whether those messages correspond to the same pitch.

5.2 Harmonic Analysis

The characteristic trait of categorical perception (the human propensity for separating some percepts into different distinct classes) is that the perceiver will tend to classify a stimulus as belonging to one category and then switch to another category as the stimulus is continually varied along some dimension that defines class membership. In other words, the perceiver will usually classify the stimulus as being one thing or the other and rarely as an object with some qualities of both. In the following two sections, I describe listening tasks resembling categorical perception: The first, harmonic analysis, maintains a theory of the current root and mode of the chordal area through which the music is passing, and, on a higher level, of the key to which those chords are related. The second task, beat tracking, performs the categorical analysis illustrated in the previous example: separating structural beat durations from the expressive and otherwise irregular spacings of event offsets.

Chord Identification

The goal of chord identification is to determine, in real time, the central pitch of a local harmonic area. The harmonic sense implemented here models a rather simple version of Western tonality. The choice of this particular orientation was made for two reasons: first, a pragmatic desire to test the function of categoric harmonic perception on easily understood tonal examples, and second, because a rudimentary understanding of tonality seems a reasonable capacity to give a program that attempts to deal with a wide variety of musical styles. To be sure, the tonal sense discussed here will be inadequate to describe many harmonic systems—a listener of many twentieth-century examples, in particular, should be programmed with a more wide-ranging vocabulary. The chord and key identification techniques described achieve a good measure of success within the target style, however, and mark out a path for adding supplemental harmonic competencies.

With the aforementioned motivations, a series of tests were performed to determine a reliable method for finding the root and mode, in a simple tonic sense, of musical passages played in real time on a MIDI keyboard. The first method closely followed the model described in Scarborough et al. 1989. In this approach, connectionist principles are applied to the problem of analyzing harmonies. A neural network with twelve input nodes is used, where each input node corresponds to one of the twelve pitch classes in the tempered scale, regardless of octave. As each incoming MIDI note arrives, positive increments are added to theories associated with six chords of which the note could be a member, and negative increments are added to all other theories.

In figure 5.7, we see an arriving "c" MIDI note shown as the leftmost input node at the bottom of the figure. Positive activation is seen spreading out from that node to the six simple triads (shown as output nodes at the top of the figure) of which the note could be a member: C major, C minor, F major, F minor, A♭ major, and A minor. The negative increments, sent on to all the other output nodes, are not drawn.

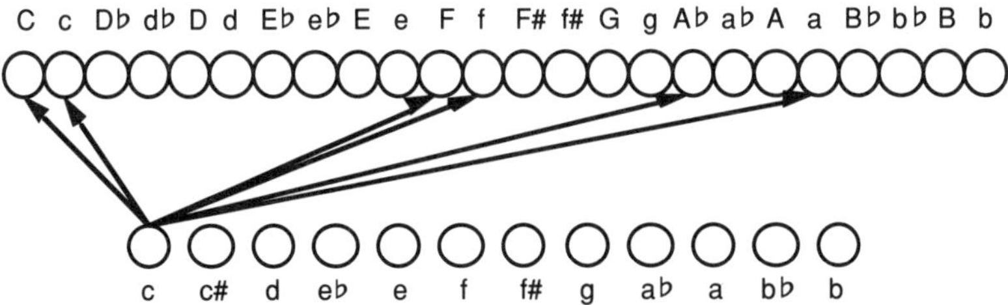

Figure 5.7

The chord theories correspond to major and minor triads built on each of the twelve scale degrees. This is done not to restrict the harmonic discourse to major and minor triads but to direct the analyzer to find a likely root and mode (major or minor) for any arbitrary chord. Therefore, the network will report a root of F not only for F major or minor triads but for any chord that is more like F than anything else. Further, the output will be conditioned by the context, since a large amount of activation built up in some node will tend to keep that node dominant if subsequent input is ambiguous. The increments sent to each output node were developed by hand, through trial and error and a rudimentary consideration of traditional music theory. It would change nothing in the overall structure of the program to train a "real" neural net through back propagation and use the learned weights.

At any point in time, the root and mode of the current chord are taken to be those corresponding to the theory with the largest score. This method is a plausible first approximation of a tonic harmony analyzer; the unadorned version attains accuracy rates of better than 70 percent on Bach chorale examples. Successive refinements to this analysis method, however, were made not by concentrating on the weights associated with particular nodes but rather by consulting a continually growing network of related features in an effort to make the job of the chord analyzer simpler. Similarly, another network topology, including a layer of hidden nodes, might produce better results from the connectionist analysis (see section 7.5 for an overview of neural network design). The improvements gained from connection to an agency of additional analysis processes, however, would presumably still hold.

Connecting Additional Agents

Translating performed musical gestures to a MIDI stream causes simultaneous events (chords) to be serialized and sent down the wire one note after another. The effect of this serialization on connectionist analysis can be seen from the two trials shown in figures 5.9 and 5.10. The data analyzed is taken from the first phrase of the chorale *Ach Gott, vom Himmel sieh' darein* by J. S. Bach (figure 5.8).

The graphs of data shown for each trial should be read as follows: the row of pitch names at the top shows the 24 possible chord theories, where an uppercase letter indicates the major mode and lowercase indicates minor. So, the first two entries correspond to C major and C minor. The leftmost column shows incoming notes; these are considered without octave references and so are shown by pitch name only.

Reading across each row from the incoming pitch name, the tally associated with each chord theory is shown. Those theories with the highest value are followed by the sign "]"—for example, a value of 5] for a given theory means that that theory's tally equals 5 and that 5 is the highest tally of all theories in that row (though there may be others with the same score). Finally, the rightmost column shows the *confidence* of the analyzer in the winning theory (or theories). Confidence is simply a measure of the strength of the winning theory relative to all the scores in that row, as in

certain = (high_theory/total_points_in_row)*100.

Therefore, the more a winning theory captures the points available at any one time, the higher its confidence rating will be.

Figure 5.8

	C	c	C#	c#	D	d	Eb	eb	E	e	F	f	F#	f#	G	g	Ab	ab	A	a	Bb	bb	B	b	
e	1			1					5]	5]									3	3					27
e	2			2					10]	10]									6	6					27
g#			3	5					11]			1					5	5							36
b									14]	3					1			6					5	5	41

• played bottom to top

Figure 5.9

	C	c	C#	c#	D	d	Eb	eb	E	e	F	f	F#	f#	G	g	Ab	ab	A	a	Bb	bb	B	b	
b									3	3					1			1					5]	5]	27
g#			3	3					4			1					5	6]					2	2	23
e	1			4					9]	5									3	3					36
e	2			5					14]	10									6	6					32

• played top to bottom

Figure 5.10

In the first trial, the E major chord at the beginning of the chorale was arpeggiated with the notes played from bottom to top (to force an evaluation in that order); in the second trial, the same chord was arpeggiated from top to bottom. The absolute value for a theory of E major, after all four notes have passed, is the same in both trials (14). The certainty rating is slightly different (41 in the first trial, 32 in the second). The intermediate results, however, are strikingly different. The second trial begins with a theory of B (major or minor), and passes through G sharp minor before settling on E major. The first trial produces E major (or, at the outset, minor) throughout.

The same phenomenon will be observed for any chord when the order of evaluation is changed. Each successive pitch serves to direct a search further through the space of chord theories; different orderings of pitches necessarily result in different search paths. We are able to skirt the problem of internal path deviations arising from evaluation order differences by consulting the density agent. When that communication is added, the listener knows which notes are part of a chord and which have been played separately. Therefore, a simple refinement of the chord agent allows it to reserve classification until all the notes of a chord have been processed. The internal path through the chord theories is rendered irrelevant, since it is never seen by the rest of the system. Only the final theory, which remains reasonably stable (though certainty ratings are seen to change from one ordering to another) is broadcast.

Next, a communication path is established to the register agent. In Western tonal music, significant harmonic information tends to be presented in relatively lower registral placements. The bass voice of a four-part texture is more likely to be consonant with the prevailing harmony than the soprano: higher voices often include pitches dissonant to the harmony as passing tones or in ornamentation. Therefore, the chord identification agency was modified to give greater weight to information coming from the lowest register than to messages from higher registral areas.

We can see this illustrated in the data of figure 5.11: the pitches that have been found in the lowest register are marked by an asterisk in the far right column. The effect of these pitches on the chord theories can be seen from their greater weight; the bass "e" from the first chord, for instance, gives twice as much emphasis to the E major theory (10 points) than does the "e" higher up (5 points).

	C	c	C#	c#	D	d	Eb	eb	E	e	F	f	F#	f#	G	g	Ab	ab	A	a	Bb	bb	B	b		
g#			3	3					1			1					5]	5]							27	
e	1			4					6]	5									3	3					27	
b									9]	8					1			1					5	5	31	
e	2			2					19]	18									6	6					35	*
___																										
a					6	6			9	8	2			2					16]	16]					24	*
e	1			1					14	13									19]	19]					28	
c	6	5							1		3	3					1		4	20]					46	

• bass emphasis

Figure 5.11

Finally, the beat agency is consulted. The heuristic here is that pitch information on the beat is more likely to be consonant with the dominant harmonic area than pitches off the beat. The beat agency conducts an initial pass over the data before the chord agency is called; so the chord process is able to obtain good information from the beat tracker about the current event. Weights associated with events on the beat are given 1.1 times the emphasis of events off the beat.

The chord identifier is able to return two kinds of information in response to query messages: the first is the current theory number. The theory number conveys both the root and mode of the chord, since twenty-four separate theories are maintained. Major and minor mode versions of the same root are paired, such that C major is theory 0, C minor is theory 1, and so on. Because of this ordering, querying processes can find the mode of the chord by taking the theory number modulo 2 (even theories are major, odd ones are minor) or can find the root of the chord by dividing the theory number by two. The second piece of information returned is the confidence rating of the analyzer in the theory. This can be used by other agents to discard theories with low confidence levels.

Key Identification

In Western tonal harmony, there is a clear hierarchical relationship between the concepts of chord and key. Chords are local harmonic areas dominated by the root of a collection of pitches in a small temporal area. On a higher level, chords are related to keys—harmonic complexes whose central pitch affects the perception of tonal relations through longer spans. The level-2 harmonic analysis (hereafter referred to as key identification) has, like the chord agency, a connectionist core. The input nodes of the chord net are activated by the pitch classes of all Cypher events present in the listener's input stream. The key identification network has twenty-four input nodes, which are activated by the chord classifications from the harmonic analysis agency one level down. Each arriving chord classification, one per event, will activate an input node, which in turn spreads activation among the twenty-four output nodes interpreted as corresponding to the minor and major modes built on each of the twelve scale degrees.

The key theories that are most positively influenced by an incoming major chord are those for which the chord could be the tonic, dominant, or subdominant. Other increments vary by the mode and scale degree of the chord and the mode of the prevailing key theory (since chords on some scale degrees will be minor in the major key and major in the minor key). In figure 5.12 we see twelve input nodes represented, for major mode chord reports from the twelve scale degrees. The complete network has twenty-four input nodes. In the figure, positive activation is spreading from the input to key theories for which the chord is tonic, subdominant, or dominant. Negative activation, which is simultaneously spreading from the same input node to all other key theories, is not shown.

The weights used were determined by trial and error rather than by a machine-learning technique such as the back-propagation algorithm. Again, these weights could easily be replaced by a new set developed with a learning rule. In developing them by hand, we noticed that finding good negative increments for key weights, as for chord weights, is in a sense more important than establishing positive ones. In this scheme, only four theories receive positive increments from a chord input. The other twenty theories receive negative or null increments. Well-chosen negative weights are important because they break down an established theory and make room for a new one to emerge. Particularly when keys are being tracked, one theory will tend to

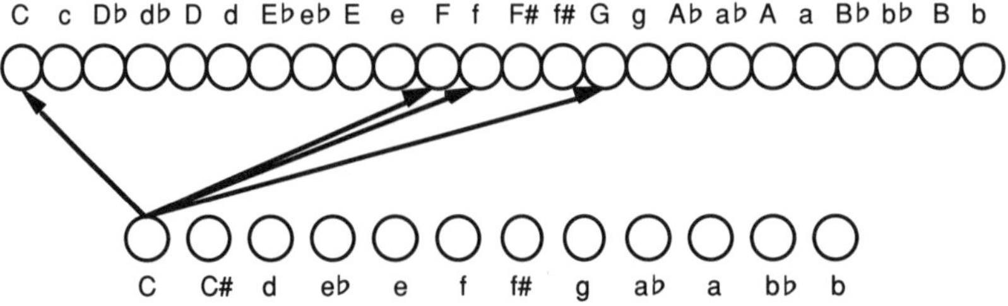

Figure 5.12

remain strongest for a long period, but must be supplanted by another rather quickly. Negative weights, coupled with an upper bound on theory strength, keep any theory from becoming so dominant that the analysis will become sluggish at finding changes of key.

Key Agency Connections

The connectionist part of the key identification process is again at the core of a larger agency, in which other featural and higher-level agents are linked together with the key net to form a complete, more accurate reading of the current harmonic context. The first agent added to the key net is the one tracking vertical density. Information is sent from the chord agency to the key agency with every input event. It is of interest to the key analyzer, however, to know the vertical density associated with arriving chord reports. Many Western musical styles will present nonharmonic pitches in passing tones, ornaments, or other kinds of linear embellishments to a more chordal texture. This heuristic is represented in the key agent by giving greater weight to harmonic information presented in simultaneities. Linear pitch material will still contribute to the analysis but will accumulate more slowly than chordal input. This connection to an analysis of vertical density enables us to know what kind of behavior to expect given the three possible textural types: (1) all chords: harmonic analyses carry the same weight, since there is no difference in vertical density, (2) completely linear: key analyses change more slowly than in denser textures, (3) combinations of linear and chordal material: denser material will advance harmonic analyses more quickly than do the (typically) more nonharmonic linear voices.

Information flows from the chord identification to the key analyzer; an improvement to the chord identification algorithm was made by including a feedback path from the key to the chords. This is because the chord finder often produces ties between two rival chord theories. One typical case is confusion between major and minor theories based on the same root. This situation can not be disambiguated until a third comes along. Ties between other theories frequently arise, however, particularly when the analysis is in transition from one dominant theory to another. In these instances, the current key analysis is consulted. A table of probabilities for each chord in each key is consulted, and the most likely chord for the current key is chosen for the output of the chord identification process.

The chord agency includes the neural net chord analysis core, informed by the register, density, and key analysis agents. Each of these agents performs its own specialized task and communicates the results of this analysis to other agencies that profit from a broader context. The chord agency itself could benefit from an expanded repertoire of contributing agents: duration and dynamic could also help indicate relative importance among incoming events, such that the pitches associated with louder or longer events receive greater weight in the chord identification process.

In figure 5.13, we see the connections between the network core of the chord agency and other contributing agents. Dynamic and duration are connected by dotted lines to indicate their potential, but not actual, contribution. Beat tracking has a two-way connection to the chord net. The two-way link indicates that the agencies are consulting each other. Chords and keys are similarly connected in both directions. Finally, the density and register agents are shown sending information to the chord and/or key analyses.

Bruce Pennycook's team at McGill University has built similar agency-style networks of expertise to perform real-time listening tasks. Their *tracker* object, built into a specialized Max environment, is able to track the beat period, metric placement, and chord progression of a jazz trio consisting of piano, bass, and drums (Pennycook 1992). The beat-tracking agent estimates a beat period from the drum lead-in to

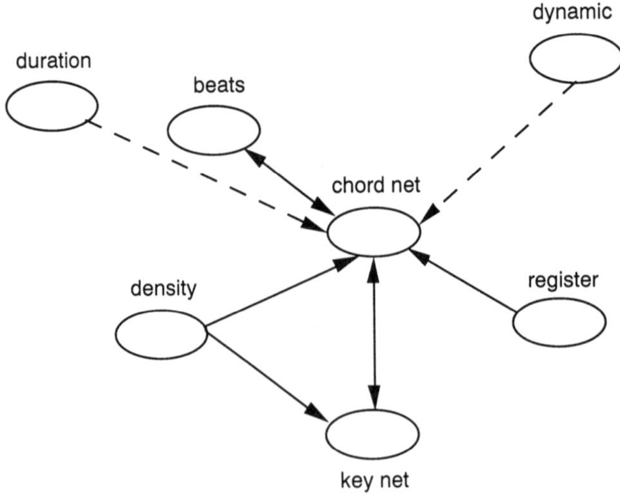

Figure 5.13

a performance. In an algorithm similar to the one discussed in the following section, the durations of various subdivisions of the basic period are calculated and compared against actually arriving inter-onset intervals. The current beat period is then adjusted as the real durations deviate from the estimated attack arrivals. Further, this system can distinguish beats in a measure because of regularities in the lead-in. Using that knowledge, harmonic information coming from the bass instrument on the downbeat is given a privileged status in the calculation of the current chord. Here again we see an interplay between harmonic and rhythmic tracking, where heuristic knowledge of rhythmic activity serves to strengthen harmonic estimates.

5.3 Beat Tracking

Beat tracking is the process of finding a duration to represent the perceived interval of a beat, described as that level of temporal periodicity in music to which a listener would tap a foot, or a conductor move a baton (Chung 1989).

Grosvenor Cooper and Leonard Meyer distinguish between three levels of rhythmic activity: the first level is a pulse, a regularly recurring succession of undifferentiated events. The second level is meter, which differentiates among regularly recurring events, and the third is rhythm, in which particular patterns of strong and weak beats arise (Cooper and Meyer 1960). We can use these distinctions to discuss the beat-tracking capabilities built into interactive music systems. Several of them, including Cypher, attempt to identify only the lowest level of rhythmic activity—the program's task is to find the interval of a basic pulse in the music without grouping these pulses into a sense of meter.

In all of the applications we will consider here, there is no representation of expected input available to the program. In other words, no pattern matching can be done between live input and a stored score. Score followers, reviewed elsewhere, effectively perform beat tracking by matching in this way. Here the problem is to find a beat pulse in completely novel input. Further, we are interested in finding the beat in real time. A number of systems scan musical representations in several passes to find a beat (Chafe, Mont-Reynaud, and Rush 1982). Although we will look at how these techniques could be adapted to real time systems, such programs will not be our primary focus.

Beat Tracking in Cypher

Cypher accomplishes beat tracking with an agency built around a connectionist core tuned to find beat periodicities in MIDI data. The beat agency is quite similar to the agencies for chord and key identification in this respect and in fact consults many of the same agents that contribute to the other tasks. The beat agency sends to the chord, key, and phrase agencies the progress of its analysis and in turn consults the feature agents and the chord agency to assist in determining a plausible beat interpretation of the incoming MIDI stream.

The connectionist core of the beat agency maintains a large number of theories, which represent possible beat periods. Theories are maintained for all possibilities between two extremes judged to be the limit of a normal beat duration. The limits in this case were taken from the indications on a musical metronome, which has historically been found sufficient for typical beat durations. These limits are 40 beats per minute on the slow end, and 208 beats per minute on the fast end. Metronomic beat periods then fall in the range of 288 to 1500 milliseconds. In the multiple theory algorithm, separate theories are maintained for all possible centisecond offsets within this range; in other words, offsets from 28 to 150 centiseconds (a total of 123 possibilities) are regarded as possible beat periods.

There are two parts to a beat theory: the theory's points and an expected arrival time. There are also two ways for a theory to accrue points: First, each incoming event spawns a list of candidate beat interpretations. The members of this list are all awarded some number of points. Second, the arrival time of incoming events are checked against the predictions of all nonzero theories. Theories whose prediction coincides with the real event are given additional points. Figure 5.14 illustrates this principle: the top row of arrows represents actual

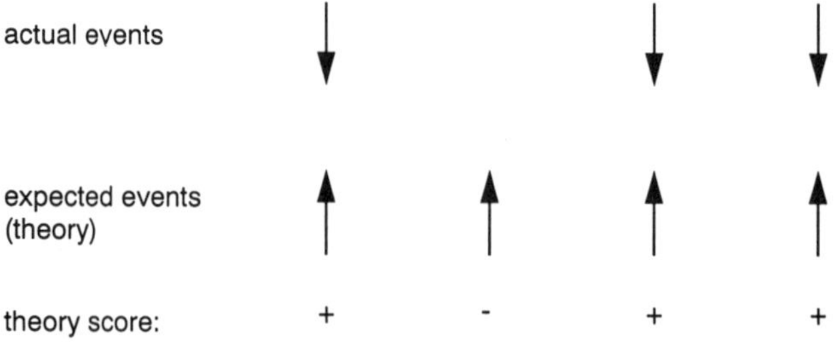

Figure 5.14

incoming MIDI events. The lower row of arrows represents the event arrivals predicted by a beat theory. When the arrows of actual events line up with the predicted arrivals, the corresponding theory is positively incremented. When no actual arrow aligns with a beat prediction, the theory loses strength.

The algorithm works as follows: When an event arrives for analysis on level 1, it is passed to the beat-tracking agency. The first thing the tracker does is to examine the expected event arrival times of all theories. If the real arrival coincides with an expected arrival for any nonzero theory (within a small margin to allow for performance deviations), points are added to that theory's score. If the real arrival comes before an expected arrival, the real offset is subtracted from the expected offset, so that on the next event the agent will still be looking for a "hit" at the same absolute time. If the real offset arrives later than an expected offset, points are subtracted from that theory's score. The heuristic here is that syncopations are unlikely; that is, true beat pulses will usually have events aligned with them.

The beat tracker can return two different values in response to queries: (1) the absolute time of the next expected beat, and (2) the current beat period. The first response allows other processes to schedule events to coincide with the expected next beat. The second value can be used to schedule events at regular intervals corresponding to the calculated beat period.

Generating Candidate Interpretations

The first part of the beat-tracking algorithm uses the syncopation heuristic; theories whose estimated time of arrival coincides with a real event are rewarded, and those theories with ETAs *before* the incoming event (that is, the incoming event is syncopated with respect to the theory) are penalized.

The second step in the algorithm looks for the five most likely beat interpretations of the incoming event offset. Two candidates are found from the offset itself and from the offset of the previous event. Then a set of factors is used to generate the rest: the members of the set are each multiplied in turn with the offset of the incoming event to produce a possible beat duration. If the resulting duration is inside the acceptable range (on the metronome scale), it is added to the list of candidates. If the factored offset is off the metronome (outside the approved range), it is rejected, and the next factor on the list is tried. This process continues until five candidate interpretations are found.

Initially, two candidates are generated independently of the factors set. The first interpretation evaluated is always the offset associated with the incoming event; if that offset by itself is within the accepted range, it is given first place on the list. The second interpretation evaluated is the result of adding together the current and previous event offsets. The idea here is that the true beat duration will often not be directly present in the input, for example in the case of a regularly recurring quarter/eighth duration pattern (such as might arise in 6/8 time). In such a situation, the true beat duration is a dotted quarter; that duration, however, will be rarely present in the input. It would arise from the factorization process, as we shall see in a moment. It is quite effective to consider the simple possibility of adding adjacent offsets, however, since (as in the example) these will often yield the appropriate duration. For the second candidate, then, the current and previous offsets are summed and added to the list if the result is on the metronome.

All other candidates are generated from the set of factors. This set assumes the usual Western rhythmic subdivisions of two or three, or multiples of two or three, to a beat. The factors interpret the incoming offset as if it represents half the beat duration, or twice the beat duration, or 1/3 the beat duration, or 1.5 times the beat duration, etc. The set of factors follows:

```
static float factors[FACTORS] =
{ 2.00, 0.50, 3.00, 1.50, 0.66, 4.00, 6.00, 1.33, 0.33, 0.75 };
```

The trace in figure 5.15 was generated in real time from an analysis of a live performance. The rhythm played was the following, where 8 stands for a played eighth note, and 4 a quarter note, in moderate tempo: 88 88 88 88 4 4 4. There is one fewer row in the activation trace

	0	1	2	3	4	R	E
38	38[6]	53[5]	114[1]	84[1]	150[0]	345	380a
39	38[12]	80[6]	115[2]	53[2]	150[0]	382a	420b
37	37[18]	113[7]	78[7]	54[3]	148[1]	422b	459c
39	38[24]	77[12]	115[8]	148[2]	150[0]	459c	496d
38	38[30]	77[13]	114[9]	53[5]	150[0]	496d	534e
37	37[36]	76[18]	112[14]	148[1]	150[0]	532e	569f
35	36[42]	74[19]	108[15]	144[2]	52[1]	568f	604g
38	37[48]	73[24]	111[16]	144[3]	150[0]	605g	642
77	37[41]	75[30]	107[13]	150[0]	149[0]	683	720
78	76[40]	38[34]	112[14]	150[0]	149[0]	760	836

Figure 5.15

than in the rhythm, because two notes must pass to give an initial inter-onset interval.

This and subsequent beat theory activation traces are to be read as follows: the first column indicates the offset in centiseconds of the event being analyzed, measured from the attack of the previous event. Then, the trace has five columns marked from 0 to 4. In these columns are recorded the five beat theories with the highest scores. For each theory, there are two values shown. The first is the projected beat duration for the theory; the second (following the duration in brackets) is the points currently associated with that theory. So, an entry of 38[6] would indicate a beat duration theory of 38 centiseconds, which currently has a score of six.

In the example (figure 5.15), we see the eighth-note duration hovering around 37 centiseconds, with a typical performance spread covering a total of about 4 centiseconds. The quarter notes also show relatively constant values, more or less twice that of the eighth notes. The eighth-note tempo is initially accepted as the beat offset, because it is "on the metronome." When the quarter notes arrive, however, the quarter note duration quickly takes over as the beat duration. This process is seen clearly at the input of 77, the second quarter note (at the end of the first quarter-note duration). Because this duration arrives later than the expectation for the eighth-note pulse, the eighth-note theory loses seven points (drops from a score of 48 down to 41). The input falls directly on the expected quarter-note arrival time, however, and this theory gains six points. When the final quarter note comes (at the end of the second quarter-note duration), the same thing happens, and the quarter-note beat duration takes over first place.

The most interesting entries on the activation trace are those at the far right of the figure, the columns marked "R" and "E." These mark the "real" and "expected" event arrival times. The "real" time is the clock time recorded when the incoming event was analyzed, and the "expected" time is the arrival time calculated for the next event after the analysis. Therefore, the expected time in any row should match a real time in some later row, if the tracker is working correctly. In the figure, I have marked the correspondences between expected and real arrival times. Lowercase letters are placed beside correctly predicted event times, with the same letter next to the prediction and the actual event. We see a quite acceptable alignment of expected and real event arrivals, up to the moment when the performance changes from eighth notes to quarter notes. The events predicted to arrive at times 642 and

720 never do arrive: the real events are syncopated with respect to them. By the end of the example, the quarter-note pulse has taken over, and the next expected arrival is anticipated at one quarter-note duration later.

Accommodating Performance Deviations

Even in this most simple example, which should present no performance difficulties whatever, we see the inevitable onset deviations that mark human playing. Such deviations will be even more pronounced with more difficult music, or when a performer is consciously adding expressive transformations to the offset times. The beat and meter analysis described in Chafe, Mont-Reynaud, and Rush 1982 corrects for these deviations by finding a threshold that will allow them to determine notes of equal duration. That is, if the deviation between two notes is within the threshold, they will be treated as having the same

Figure 5.16

value. Once a workable threshold has been found, adjacent note values can be classified in terms of greater than, less than, or equal. Rhythmic, or agogic, accentuation results from short-long pairs, and these accents are used as landmarks, together with harmonic accents, to decide the meter of a musical section.

Cypher attempts to accommodate expressive variations as follows: before points are awarded, the beat-tracking algorithm searches the immediate vicinity of a candidate theory for other nonzero theories. Nonzero neighbors are taken to be a representation of the same beat, but with a performance deviation from the candidate. If such a neighbor is found, the tracker asserts that the composite theory is midway between the neighbor and the candidate and adds together the points from the neighbor and those due to the candidate. Then the neighbor and candidate theories are zeroed out, leaving one theory in that vicinity—the average duration calculated from previous and current inputs.

We can clearly see this "zeroing in" behavior in the next trace (figure 5.17), taken from a live performance of the opening of the Bach chorale example shown in figure 5.16. The tracker maintains the quarter-note pulse as the leading theory throughout. Because of the performance

	0	1	2	3	4	R	E
74	74[6]	148[1]	111[1]	94[1]	150[0]	382	453a
70	72[17]	146[6]	150[0]	149[0]	148[0]	449a	521b
71	71[28]	143[7]	106[1]	150[0]	149[0]	520b	591c
67	69[34]	140[12]	150[0]	149[0]	148[0]	589c	657
35	69[35]	140[13]	35[6]	102[1]	52[1]	624	658d
34	69[40]	138[14]	34[12]	102[2]	150[0]	658d	727
34	68[41]	34[18]	137[15]	102[7]	51[1]	695	729e
35	68[46]	34[24]	138[20]	103[8]	150[0]	730e	798
35	69[52]	34[30]	139[21]	104[9]	52[1]	765	799f
36	70[57]	35[36]	141[22]	106[14]	150[0]	803f	872g
73	71[68]	35[29]	143[27]	107[15]	150[0]	876g	947h
70	70[74]	143[28]	35[22]	106[8]	150[0]	947h	1016i
37	72[80]	145[29]	36[28]	106[9]	55[1]	984	1019
32	70[85]	136[34]	34[34]	101[10]	150[0]	1017i	1086j
38	70[91]	36[40]	136[31]	107[15]	53[5]	1056	1087
33	70[96]	34[46]	134[32]	103[16]	150[0]	1089j	1158
35	69[102]	34[52]	137[33]	104[17]	52[1]	1124	1157k
32	68[107]	33[58]	132[26]	100[22]	150[0]	1157k	1224
36	68[108]	34[64]	138[27]	104[23]	54[1]	1193	1225
18	70[109]	35[65]	138[24]	106[24]	54[6]	1210	1226
21	70[110]	37[70]	138[21]	106[21]	19[12]	1232	1302
34	69[111]	35[76]	104[26]	137[22]	56[12]	1267	1301l
35	69[116]	35[82]	104[27]	138[15]	54[13]	1301l	1370
36	70[117]	35[88]	106[28]	141[16]	54[6]	1337	1371m
38	72[122]	36[94]	110[33]	141[13]	52[11]	1377m	1449

Figure 5.17

deviations, however, the period of the beat duration moves slightly throughout the trace, starting at 74 centiseconds and moving as low as 68 with an average value around 70. Again, I have marked correspondences between expected and actual arrival times with lowercase letters—identical letters show successful predictions of event arrivals.

The tracker does a respectable job on this example: 13 out of 14 quarter notes are correctly predicted, 12 of them within 4 centiseconds. It is interesting to note where the predictions break down: the sixteenth notes at the end of measure 4 are performed a little slowly, which leads to an incorrectly predicted downbeat of measure 5. By the second beat of measure 5, however, the prediction again matches reality.

The Bach example is of limited rhythmic complexity but demonstrates the kinds of rhythmic behavior the tracker can handle well. This method is more erratic with rhythmically complex input; passages with fast figuration around a slow underlying beat particularly tend to confuse it (such examples are an exaggerated form of the sixteenth-note mistake in this example). Probably such mistakes could be improved with better weights, more sophisticated candidate selection, and added constraints indicating typical rhythmic progressions. The point of this study, however, was not to develop the perfect beat tracker but rather to include beat tracking in a network of many competencies, all able to help each other achieve better performance on their specialty. The chord agency and dynamic agent are two entities whose reports affect the calculation of beat periods. In chapter 7, I will explore in more detail the relationships the beat tracker joins into with other agents.

Meter Detection

The digital audio editing system developed by Chafe, Mont-Reynaud, and Rush (1982) determines the second level of Cooper and Meyer's hierarchy of rhythmic behavior: a meter of strong and weak beat relationships across the basic pulse. Their program does not function in real time, but it is interesting for its approach to the derivation of meter from an undifferentiated representation. For the purposes of this discussion, we can treat the basic material as MIDI data: the representation they actually used came from a lower level of audio analysis, yielding pitch and timing information much like MIDI.

First-pass processes find accents, either melodic or rhythmic, in the succession of events. Then these accentual anchors guide the generation of bridging structures, spanning several events between anchors. When a regularly recurring bridge interval has been found, it is applied forward and backward through the remainder of the example to find attacks that may coincide with a continuation of the bridge in either direction. "With the method used, the system looks ahead from simple bridges to see if it can extend to a note an equal bridge-width apart. Any remaining unconnected zones are examined in reverse on a second pass. The method of targeting ahead (or behind) for a particular time interval enables the system to ignore intervening syncopated accents and frees it to latch on to any note placed within a prescribed distance of the target" (Chafe, Mont-Reynaud, and Rush 1982, 544).

Good bridge intervals are then clustered together, and these clusters are examined for lengths in simple relations with each other, preferably in a ratio of 1:2:4 or some similar integer sequence. Durations within a bridge are brought into line with similarly simple subdivisions of the span. Some possible note value interpretations are accepted following stylistic heuristics, such as considering double-dotted values less likely for fast tempi than slow ones. Finally a meter is chosen from stylistically acceptable candidates. Again simple integer ratios are preferred, in duple or triple meters. The derived meter is then used to produce a barred notation of the performed music. This system was shown to work well for examples on the order of Mozart piano sonatas but would break down for more rhythmically complex inputs, particularly those with many syncopations.

Longuet-Higgins and Lee

In their article "The Rhythmic Interpretation of Monophonic Music," H. C. Longuet-Higgins and C. S. Lee (1984) develop a partial theory of how listeners are able to arrive at a rhythmic interpretation of a stimulus presented as a succession of durations only—that is, no further cues from dynamics, harmonic activity, rubato, text, etc. are available. They present their considerations with respect to notated music examples, rather than live performances: "The expressive qualities of live performance vary so widely that we have felt it essential to restrict the discussion in some way, and we have done this by concentrating on those directions about a performance that a composer customarily indicates in a musical score" (Longuet-Higgins and Lee 1984, 151).

The authors consider traditional Western meters as hierarchical structures in which successive levels represent duple or triple subdivisions of the level above. A 4/4 meter would, in this system, be represented by the list [2 2 2 . . .], which indicates that each level in the hierarchy forms a duple subdivision of the level above. Similarly, a 3/4 meter is represented as [3 2] (three beats in a bar, with duple subdivisions), and 6/8 as [2 3] (two beats per bar, with triple subdivisions). They present a set of context-free generative rules, which produce possible rhythms within a given meter. Then "the relationship between the rhythm and the meter may be simply stated: The former is one of the structures that is generated by the grammar associated with the latter" (Longuet-Higgins and Lee 1984, 155).

Even with such a generative description of rhythm, many situations arise that could be equally well described by more than one structure. Such situations give rise to rhythmic ambiguity in music. Still, ambiguities are usually assigned a particular interpretation by most listeners, and the forces behind these assignations occupy Longuet-Higgins and Lee. They begin by looking at syncopation, a phenomenon whereby a "strong" event is displaced relative to an underlying meter. "We may suspect that this is a general characteristic of 'natural' interpretations: that when a sequence of notes can be interpreted as the realization of an unsyncopated passage, then the listener will interpret the sequence in this way" (Longuet-Higgins and Lee 1984, 157). Accordingly, the authors define regular passages to be those with the following characteristics:

1. Every bar, except possibly the first, begins with a sounded note. (This ensures that there are no syncopations across bar lines.)
2. All the bars are generated by the same standard meter.
3. There are no syncopations within any of the bars. (Longuet-Higgins and Lee 1984, 158)

If a passage is regular, the authors assert, the metric structure can be derived from the durations of the sounding notes. A set of rules is introduced along with a procedure for applying them. Basically, the shortest metrical unit is identified with a first pass through the passage. Then longer durations are found and compared in length with the shortest. Multiples of the short duration that produce the longer ones then are used to calculate the meter.

The method advanced by Longuet-Higgins and Lee is not immediately appropriate for use in an interactive system: for one thing, their algorithm relies on several passes through the data, a technique generally unavailable to real-time programs interested in responding as quickly as possible. We can notice two features of their work, however, that could be adapted to interactive implementation and that in fact are already found in beat-tracking methods: first, a reliance on the heuristic that syncopations are unlikely, the same operative principle behind Cypher's beat tracker; and second, a preference to find larger durations from multiples of small ones. There are basically two ways to relate the durations of a musical passage: the small ones can be regarded as subdivisions of the large ones (division), or the large ones found to be multiples of the small (multiplication). In the some of the beat-tracking methods reviewed in this text, we find George Lewis advocating a multiplication scheme, as Longuet-Higgins and Lee have done, with other researchers favoring the division approach, as in the Mont-Reynaud beat tracker.

The work of Longuet-Higgins and Lee is significant for the development of interactive meter detectors because it can be regarded as an incremental improvement of the beat-tracking methods already developed. If a program is able to find the beat duration accurately, the syncopation and multiplication rules they propose offer a promising avenue for extending an analysis to the metric level.

5.4 High-Level Description

In chapter 4 we reviewed some of the considerations involved in separating musical structure into different hierarchical levels. Here we will look at some of the analytic methods that have been developed for describing behavior on higher levels of such music hierarchies. There are a number of problems specific to the description of higher-level behavior, among them grouping, classification, and direction detection. Of these, the first is the most fundamental and has received the most attention. David Wessel's improvisation engine uses principles derived from Lerdahl and Jackendoff's grouping rules to find phrase boundaries in live MIDI performances. The HARP system of Camurri et al. deals with "music actions," defined to be musical "chunks" or phrases. The CompAss project described by Andreas Mahling of the Institut für Informatik in Stuttgart provides phrase structure editors.

In Cypher, the listening processes on level 2 describe the behavior of several events. They examine the featurespace reports from level 1 and look for two main types of structure in the behavior of the features over time. First, one agent tries to group events together into phrases. Another agent looks at all events within a phrase and decides whether each of the level-1 features is behaving regularly or irregularly within it. A third agent, as yet unimplemented but part of the same conception, would look for direction in the motion of lower-level features.

These three tasks (grouping, observations of regularity and direction) correspond to a general view of music in which change (or the lack of it) and goal-directed motion form the fundamental axes around which musical experience revolves. Such a view is espoused, for example, in Wallace Berry's book *Structural Functions in Music*: "By recurrent reference to interrelations among element-systems, reciprocal and analogical correspondences are indicated in which the actions of individual elements are seen to project expressive shapes of progressive, recessive, static, or erratic tendencies. Progressive and recessive (intensifying and resolving) processes are seen as basic to musical effect and experience" (Berry 1976, 2).

Not all music exhibits such directionality, and therefore does not comfortably bear description using such terms; however some music, particularly much Western music, is about directionality and change. Cypher is biased toward looking for goal-directed musical behavior; however, the listener will still have something meaningful to say about music that is not primarily goal directed. In that case, useful analysis will be shoved down, as it were, to level 1. Classifications of individual features and local musical contexts will take precedence over longer-term descriptions of motion and grouping.

Phrase Finding

Locating meaningful phrase groupings in a representation of music is one of the most important problems in interactive music and one of the most difficult. "I do not expect much more to come of a search for a compact set of rules for musical phrases. (The point is not so much what we mean by *rule*, as how large a body of knowledge is involved)" (Minsky 1989, 645). Minsky seems here to be pointing to the musical commonsense nature of phrase grouping, and commonsense reasoning is notoriously difficult to capture, particularly through a small, generalized set of rules. The CYC project is a current attempt to approach common sense, through an elaborate, cross-connected network of knowledge taken from newspaper accounts, encyclopedias, textbooks, and the like (Lenat and Guha 1991). Perhaps a vast network

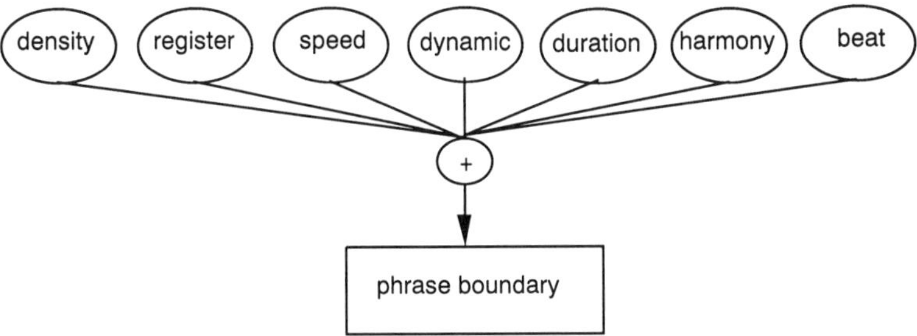

Figure 5.18

of similarly constructed musical knowledge would help us identify phrases; in any event, some systems already look for phrase boundaries, and we can try to evaluate their approaches and levels of success.

In Cypher, phrases are musical sequences, commonly from around two to ten seconds in duration, that cohere due to related harmonic, rhythmic, and textural behaviors. The level-2 listener detects boundaries between phrases by looking for discontinuities in the output of the level-1 feature agents. Each agent is given a different weight in affecting the determination of a phrase boundary; discontinuities in timing, for instance, contribute more heavily than differences in dynamic. The phrase boundary agent collects information from all of the perceptual features, plus the chord, key, and beat agencies. When a discontinuity is noticed in the output of a feature agent, the weight for that feature is summed with whatever other discontinuities are present for the same event. When the sum of these weights surpasses a threshold, the phrase agent signals a group boundary. Note that this signal will correspond to the initial event of a new phrase; the discontinuities are not noticed until after the change.

The remaining feature dimension, harmony, is treated somewhat differently. The weight of the harmonic analysis is decided by the function of the current chord (local harmonic area) in relation to the current key. In other words, a chord analysis of F major will not be considered in isolation but as a functional harmony in some key. If the current key were also F major, for instance, the chord would have a tonic function (or function number zero, in the Cypher numbering scheme). Following the conventions of Western tonal harmony, tonic and dominant functions are given more weight as potential phrase boundaries than are chords built on other scale degrees. The table shown in figure 5.19 lists the phrase boundary weights given to the various chord functions.

The phrase boundary analysis relies heavily on the progressive perspective; neighboring events in time are compared, and split into different groups according to their similarity or dissimilarity. Another manifestation of this reliance is an extension of the functional harmony contribution: adjacent events' functions are checked to see if they manifest a dominant/tonic relationship. That is, if the harmonic event for the last event has a function a perfect fifth above that of the current event, the evidence for a phrase boundary is strengthened. Another contribution comes from the beat tracker: events on the beat are given more weight as potential phrase boundaries than events not landing on a predicted beat point.

Further, the phrase boundary calculation implements a version of the techniques of focus and decay. Initially the phrase boundary threshold is set to a constant. When a new phrase boundary is found, the number of events in the new phrase is checked: if there are under two events in a phrase, the threshold is incremented—phrase boundaries are being found too quickly. On the other side, there is an maximum limit to the number of events in a phrase. If the event count

Function	I	i	bII	bii	II	ii	bIII	biii
Weight	4	4	1	1	2	2	1	2
Function	III	iii	IV	iv	#IV	#iv	V	v
Weight	2	0	3	3	1	1	5	5
Function	bVI	bvi	VI	vi	bVII	bvii	VII	vii
Weight	1	2	2	0	1	2	2	2

Figure 5.19

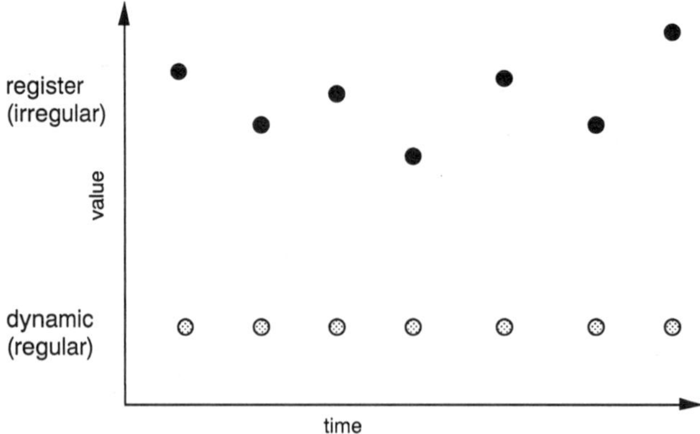

Figure 5.20

passes this limit, a phrase boundary is declared and the threshold is set lower—phrase boundaries are not being found quickly enough. In this case, the heuristic for moving the threshold up seems to work well. The decay part of the rule seems too arbitrary, however; there should be a more musical way to decide that phrases are too long than by counting events.

Regularity

The second higher-level analysis task carried out by Cypher is to describe regular and irregular behaviors by the features tracked on level 1. Within each phrase, the regularity detectors look to see whether the classifications for each feature are changing often or remaining relatively static. Features whose classifications do not change much are deemed regular, while those with more dynamic behaviors are called irregular.

In figure 5.20, we see the feature classifications for several Cypher events played out over time. The black dots represent the register classifications for each event, and the grey dots, the dynamic values. In this case, dynamic behavior would be termed regular by the level-2 listener, and registral behavior would be flagged as irregular.

The phrase boundary agency uses discontinuities between feature classifications for adjacent events as evidence of phrase boundaries. The *regularity* report on level 2 is closely allied to the group detection phase: the classification of regularity and irregularity is done over the history of a group. That is, once a group boundary has been found, regularity/irregularity tracking begins anew. The first event of any phrase, therefore, will always be regular for all features, since it is the only event in the phrase. Once two and more events are present in the current phrase, regularity judgments will again characterize a significant population of events. Then, for each feature, the number of discontinuities among events within the current phrase is calculated each time a new event arrives. If there are more discontinuities than identities, the feature is said to be behaving irregularly. If feature transitions are identical more often than they are different, the feature is behaving regularly.

5.5 Computer-Generated Analysis

The following sections document a real-time musical analysis of a performance of the Bach chorale shown in figure 5.16. This chorale was chosen because it presents a challenging tonal language, stretching the capabilities of the harmonic analysis. The rhythmic level of the piece, on the other hand, is less challenging but still presents some variety. Simpler, more easily handled examples could have been presented instead, but in the following exposition the ways in which the process falters are as instructive as the successes. All of the charts were generated by Cypher as the chorale was being played; as such, they represent the quality of the information about the piece that would be available to the rest of the program during performance.

Bach Chorale

We will first consider the output of the key agency. Incoming chord agency reports are shown in the leftmost column of figure 5.21. The activation associated with each key theory is shown in the 24 following columns. The highest activation for a key theory in any row is followed by a "]" symbol. So in the very first row the chord agency reported an E major chord, spawning a key theory of E major. Each measure in the original score has been marked in the trace with a dash in the chord column. Accordingly, there is a dash after the first E major report, since that measure contains only the pickup chord. The dashes are a convenience for comparing the trace to the score.

Notice the first key change, in measure 7. The tonic moves from A minor to E minor, which has taken over by the middle of measure 7. The move back to A minor is more circuitous; the agency notes the ambiguity at the onset of measure 8, with the F major chord, and abandons E minor for C major. The E major to A minor transition between the second and third beats, however, is enough to reestablish A minor. Another instability occurs at the beginning of measure 9, when a first inversion A minor chord is misread as C major. These reports, and the D minor report in measure 8, would be ignored, since key changes that are not confirmed by at least two successive reports are discarded. The tonal ambiguity of the end of the piece is instructive: the accumulation of accidentals in the final two measures leads to uncertain chord reports, contributing to a wandering key analysis as the piece closes. Here it is possible for the key agency to make different analyses on different performances. Sometimes the piece comes out in A minor and sometimes in E major: the instability of the chord reports, caused by ambiguous chords such as the penultimate D# diminished seventh, means that the key tracker will be less stable as well. The key

	C	c	C#	c#	D	d	E♭	e♭	E	e	F	f	F#	f#	G	g	A♭	a♭	A	a	B♭	b♭	B	b
E									4]										2	2			1	
- m2																								
a											1				1	1				7]				
b															2				1	8]				5
a											1				3	1				13]				
b															4				1	14]				5
a											1				5	1				19]				
- m3																								
E									4										2	21]			1	
b									3						1				3	22]				4
a											1				2	1				27]				
D					4										4	3			1	27]				
E					4				4										3	29]			1	
b					4				3						1				4	30]				5
- m4																								
a					3						1				2	1				35]				
d	1	1				4					1				1	1				35]	1			
E						3			4										2	37]			1	
E						3			6										3	38]			1	
F	1										4									31]	2	2		
G	2	1									4				2					29]				
e	3				1	1				5					2					29]				
c		5															1			29]	1	1		
d	1	6				4														29]	2			
- m5																								
E						3			4										2	31]			1	
A					1	4			4										4	30]				
E					1	4			6										5	31]				
E					1	4			8										6	32]				
a						4			1		1				1	1			1	37]				
D					4	1									3	3			2	37]				
- m6																								
D					8										5	5			3	37]				
f#					9				1	1				5					3	30]				
e	1				10	1				6									2	30]				
B					4				2	8			1						2	29]			4	
A					5	1			2	8									4	28]			1	
e	1				6	2				13									3	28]				
F#			1		1					12			4							21]			2	2
- m7																								
e	1				2	1				17										21]				2
G	3	2			3	1				13					4					16]				
G	4	3			3	1				11					6					14]				
G	5	4			3	1				9					8					12]				
B									2	11			1		3					11]			4	
e	1				1	1				16]					3					11				
e	2				2	2				20]					3					11				
- m8																								
F	3									13]	4									4	2	2		
d	4	1				5]				4	4									4	3			
C	8]										6	2			1						3			
d	9]	1				4					6										4			
E	4]					3			4		1								2	2			1	
a	4					3					2				1	1				7]				
b															2				1	8]				5
- m9																								
C	4										2	2			3					4]				
C	6]										3	3			3					2				
E	1								4]										2	4			1	
a	1										1				1	1				9]				
a	1										2				2	2				14]				
- m10																								
E									4										2	16]			1	
a											1				1	1				21]				
C	2										2	1			1	1				19]				
d	3	1				5					2					1				19]	1			
e	4				1	6				4										19]				
g	3					6	1			4	1	1				5				10]				
C#			2			4				1			1	1		2				7]				
- m11																								
D					4	1									2	4			1	7]				
E					4				4										3	9]			1	
f#					5]				5	1				5					3	2				
E					5				9]										5	4			1	

Figure 5.21

analysis is particularly useful in going through the phrase boundary analysis, shown in figure 5.22.

The phrase boundary trace should be read as follows: the first five columns report the weights added by featural discontinuities between events. When one of these columns has a nonzero value, the corresponding feature has changed classifications between the event on that row and the preceding event. Then in the column marked *chord*, the weight added for chord function is reported. The function reported for each event is also noted. Next, key changes show up as an additional four points. Events on the beat are awarded an additional two points, shown in the next column. The next to last column is the total of the activation from all the previous ones, and the number in the far right column is the current phrase boundary threshold. Therefore, if the value in the second to last column for any row is greater than the last number (the threshold), a phrase boundary was reported for that event. I have added asterisks to the trace to mark the identified phrase boundaries.

In the phrase detection for the Bach example, notice that the phrase threshold is initially too low. There are double hits and spurious boundaries, such as the first two events of measure two. The phrase agency notices this as well, and we see the threshold moving up with each double hit. By the time the threshold gets to about 9, better boundaries are being found. The beginning of the phrase on the last beat of measure 5, for example, is found correctly. The following phrase beginning, at the end of measure 7, is also correctly identified. Here we see the double-hit problem arise again, however. Evidence for phrase boundaries in this scheme seems to accumulate and dissipate too slowly, leading to identifications of phrase group boundaries on neighboring events. The final phrase boundary in the example, at the end of measure 9, shows exactly the same behavior: the correct boundary is identified, but the following event is chosen as well. This problem can be easily corrected in the program simply by ignoring double hits. The main cause of the problem is the speed change weight. After the fermatas, the program finds the change in duration between events and contributes to the boundary identification. Since the speed change at a fermata is so pronounced, however, successive events tend to report changes in classification, leading to the double hits.

Den	Reg	Speed	Dyn	Dura	Chord		Key	Beat	Total		
1	1	0	0	0	3	I	0	0	5	7	
- m2											
0	0	4	0	0	3	i	0	2	9	7	*
1	1	0	0	0	1	ii	4	2	9	8	*
0	1	0	0	0	3	i	0	2	6	8	
1	1	0	0	0	1	ii	0	2	5	8	
1	0	0	1	0	3	i	0	0	5	8	
- m3											
1	0	0	1	0	5	V	0	2	9	8	*
1	1	0	0	0	1	ii	0	0	3	8	
1	1	0	0	0	3	i	0	2	7	8	
1	0	0	1	0	2	IV	0	0	4	8	
1	0	0	0	0	5	V	0	2	8	8	
1	1	4	1	0	1	ii	0	0	8	8	
- m4											
1	0	4	0	0	3	i	0	2	10	8	*
1	1	4	0	0	2	iv	0	0	8	8	
1	1	4	0	0	5	V	0	0	11	8	*
1	1	0	0	0	5	V	0	0	7	9	
1	1	0	0	0	0	bVI	0	0	2	9	
1	1	0	0	0	0	bVII	0	2	4	9	
1	1	0	0	0	5	v	0	0	7	9	
0	0	0	0	0	1	biii	0	2	3	9	
1	1	4	0	0	2	iv	0	0	8	9	
- m5											
1	1	0	0	0	5	V	0	2	9	9	
1	1	4	1	0	6	I	0	2	15	9	*
0	1	0	1	0	5	V	0	2	9	9	
0	1	0	1	0	5	V	0	2	9	9	
1	1	0	0	0	6	i	0	0	8	9	
0	1	4	1	2	2	IV	0	0	10	9	*
- m6											
0	0	4	0	2	2	IV	0	0	8	9	
0	0	0	1	0	0	vi	0	2	3	9	
0	1	0	1	0	5	v	0	2	9	9	
1	0	0	0	0	1	II	0	0	2	9	
1	1	0	1	0	3	I	0	2	8	9	
1	0	0	1	0	5	v	0	2	9	9	
0	0	0	0	0	1	VI	0	2	3	9	
- m7											
1	1	0	0	0	5	v	0	2	9	9	
0	1	0	0	0	0	bVII	0	2	3	9	
1	1	0	0	0	0	bVII	0	2	4	9	
0	1	0	0	0	0	bVII	0	2	3	9	
1	1	0	1	0	1	II	0	2	6	9	
0	1	4	0	2	3	i	0	0	10	9	*
1	0	4	1	0	3	i	4	0	13	9	*
- m8											
1	1	0	0	2	0	bII	0	0	4	10	
1	1	0	0	0	3	i	0	2	7	10	
1	1	0	0	0	3	I	0	2	7	10	
1	1	0	1	0	1	ii	4	2	10	10	
1	1	0	1	0	1	III	0	2	6	10	
1	1	0	0	0	3	i	0	0	5	10	
1	0	0	0	0	1	ii	4	0	6	10	
- m9											
0	0	0	0	0	0	bIII	0	0	0	10	
1	0	0	0	0	0	bIII	0	2	3	10	
1	1	0	0	0	3	I	0	2	7	10	
0	1	0	0	0	3	i	0	0	4	10	
1	1	4	0	2	3	i	4	0	15	10	*
- m10											
1	0	4	0	2	5	V	0	2	14	10	*
0	0	0	0	0	6	i	0	2	8	11	
1	0	0	1	0	0	bIII	0	0	2	11	
1	0	0	1	0	2	iv	0	2	6	11	
1	1	0	1	0	5	v	0	0	8	11	
1	0	0	0	0	1	bvii	0	2	4	11	
1	0	0	1	0	4	III	0	0	6	11	
- m11											
1	0	0	0	0	2	IV	0	2	5	11	
0	0	0	1	0	5	V	0	0	6	11	
0	1	0	0	0	0	iii	0	2	3	11	
0	1	0	0	0	3	I	0	2	6	11	

Figure 5.22

6 Machine Composition

As a simple but understandable figure of the imagination, we each have in our minds a committee of "experts" which are the criteria we will consult when making decisions. These criteria are of various kinds: some are inherited, some are needs, but there are also appointed criteria, and there is a time in which they can and will be in this appointed position. If, however, you find repeatedly that this committee doesn't come to a conclusion you actually approve of, you fire it. But then you have to find other criteria. Composition is a wonderful method for discovering not-yet-appointed criteria.
—Herbert Brün

Chapter 3 reviewed an array of existing interactive music programs, describing them integrally and in terms of their relation to the dimensions of the evaluation framework developed earlier. Here we will similarly abstract principles of existing programs away from their original vehicle of implementation, looking at formalisms for composing music with a computer. Strictly speaking, it is inaccurate to say that these programs are concerned with modeling human compositional techniques: usually, they are used to work out some procedure with greater speed, more accuracy, and less "cheating" than their human creators would be able to muster. In particular, composers use compositional algorithms to develop high-level methods, procedures that operate on a control plane governing the long-term evolution of notes and durations without forcing the composer to consider each event individually.

I consider composition methods as belonging to three broad classes: (1) *sequencing*, or the use of prerecorded musical fragments, (2) *algorithmic generation* from some small collections of pitch or rhythmic elements, and (3) *transformation*—simple, modular changes to already complete musical material.

• A *sequence* is a list of stored MIDI events, which can range in duration from gestures of a few seconds, to entire compositions many minutes long. Sequencing is by now quite familiar because of the collection of commercial editors available for recording and manipulating sequences. Most of the familiar systems, however, are not designed for real-time interactive use in live performance. Rather, the operative bias is in favor of preparing complete compositions to be played back from beginning to end, perhaps with some timing variations to synchronize with video or other machines. Our particular interest here will be in how such sequences can be varied and conditionally integrated with live musical contexts.

• The second class of composition methods comprises *generative algorithms,* which produce material from some stored collections of data (such as pitch or duration sets), often using constrained random operations to spin out a distinctive gestural type from the seed elements. Such routines can often be invoked with a number of performance parameters, to set such things as the duration within which to continue generation, a pitch range to be observed, the speed of presentation, etc.

• The *transformation* of material is accomplished by taking the input to an interactive system and systematically varying it along some parameter. A simple example would be to take all arriving Note On messages and add two to the pitch number before playing them back out. The effect of such a transformation would be, naturally, to transpose all incoming material up a whole step. Several transformation systems allow the combination of many simple changes, resulting in more complex, compound relations between input and output.

6.1 Transformation

Richard Teitelbaum developed an intricate form of transformation in his *Patch Control Language,* written with Mark Bernard (Teitelbaum 1984), and in the more recent Max implementation of the same idea. Transformation in Teitelbaum's system arises from combinations of a number of simple operations, such as delay, transposition, or looping. The generation of output with these modules is controlled by the composer during performance, as he calls up stored patches and applies them to some incoming MIDI stream. The mode of performance is predominantly improvisation, and the decisions of the composer concerning the choice of patches, which of several inputs to send through them, and the sounds to use in articulating the result shape the structure of the whole.

The Max patch shown in figure 6.1 is an adaptation of the *inverter* module from the version of Teitelbaum's software implemented by Christopher Dobrian. The leftmost inlet turns the inverter on or off; pitch and velocity numbers are sent to the next two inlets across the top. If the inverter is on, 120 is subtracted from incoming MIDI pitch numbers. The absolute value of that result is taken as the new pitch number. Therefore, the point of symmetry is middle C (MIDI note 60): the absolute value of (60 – 120) is 60 again. Any pitch other than middle C will be flipped around to form the same interval with middle C as the original, but in the opposite direction—the C an octave above middle C will come out an octave below, and so forth. Compare this with the *mirror* module shown in section 3.5. The inversion algorithm used by Jean-Claude Risset has much the same effect but can change the point of symmetry. These inverters are perfect examples of the idea

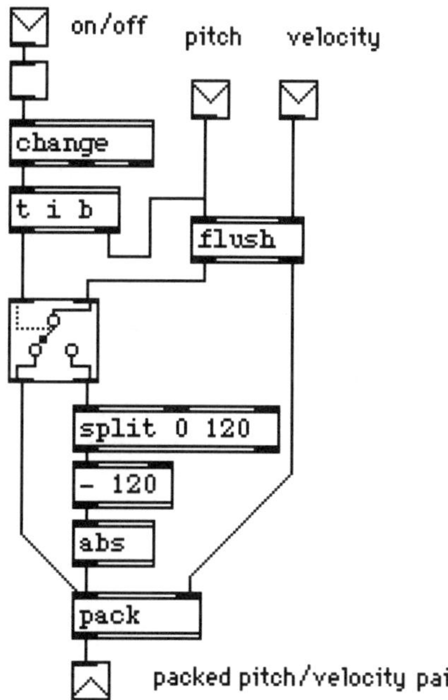

Figure 6.1

of transformation: input from some source is modified in a consistent, simple way and sent back out again or on through further transformations.

Transformation seems to be a method quite well suited to works involving improvisation; Teitelbaum's usage is an example. Daniel Weymouth similarly makes prominent use of transformations in his composition *This Time, This* for Zeta violin and a Max patch written by the composer. The violin score is a combination of notated music and indications for improvisation; the improvisations sometimes follow constraints. For example, the pitch may be notated and the rhythmic presentation left free; conversely, pitches are sometimes improvised to notated rhythms. The computer part is an intriguing blend of transformation and generation. Material from the violin performance is often used as a seed for rather elaborate responses: at the center of the work, a harmonic complex used repeatedly throughout is compressed into a series of chords, which are triggered by single pitches coming from the violin. At other times, the work takes advantage of the fact that the controller can send information from each separate string on individual MIDI channels: toward the end of the piece, the upper strings spawn soft, high chords, while the lower ones provoke bursts of sound that break up into reverberation. An excerpt from *This Time, This* can be heard on the companion CD-ROM.

Transformation in Cypher is accomplished through the chaining of many small, straightforward modules. The action of these modules is cumulative: if more than one is used on some material, they are applied serially, with the output of one operation being passed to the input of the next. Although the action of any module taken singly is simple and easy to follow, longer chains of transfomations can build up material that is quite complex, though deterministically derived from its inputs. In figure 6.2, a source chord is first sent through the arpeggiation module, which separates the pitches, and then through the looper, which repeats the material given it.

Level-1 Filters

The transformation objects implemented in Cypher all accept the same three arguments: (1) a *message*, which selects one of two possible methods in the object, (2) an *event block*, a list of up to 32 events to be transformed, and (3) an *argument*, whose function changes according to the message. The two messages accepted by transformation objects

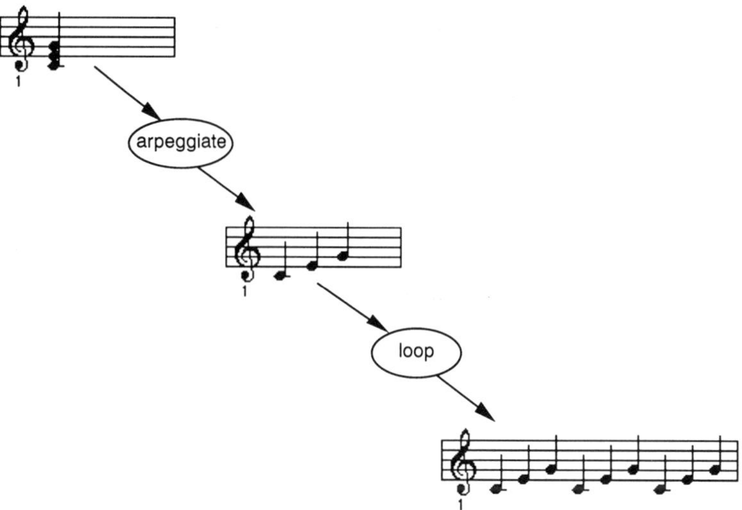

Figure 6.2

are xform and mutate. The xform message selects the method that applies a transformation algorithm to an *argument* number of events in the *event block*. The mutate message will use the *argument* to change the value of some parameter controlling the behavior of the transformation algorithm. In this case, the *event block* is left untouched. When called with the xform message, all transformation objects return a value that represents the number of events in the block to be output after the transformation is applied.

Often, several transformations will be applied to the same event block. In this case, the transformations will be executed serially, with the output of one transformation sent through to the input of the next. In this situation, it makes a difference in which order the transformations are applied. For example, the objects *arpeggiate* and *grace* will produce two different effects, depending on which of the two is applied first. If applied as *grace* → *arpeggiate*, a quick grace note pattern will lead up to an arpeggiation of some input chord. In the *arpeggiate* → *grace* order, the arpeggiation would be done first, and then all notes in the arpeggio would have a separate grace note figure added to them. Because of this difference, each transformation filter has associated with it a priority. Before applying a series of filters, the composition section will order the filters to be used by their priority index. Then, the filters will be executed serially, with the highest priority transformation performed first, the result of this sent on to the next-highest priority transformation, and so on. The user can change the priority of any filter through a simple manipulation of the interface. The association of priorities to filters is remembered from execution to execution as part of the program's long-term memory. Further, priority orderings can be changed in performance as different reaction types demand different application sequences.

Descriptions of the level-1 transformation objects follow. The descriptions will be in terms of how the object changes the event block arriving as input, and what kinds of changes to the transformation behavior can be effected by incoming mutate messages.

Accelerator

The *accelerator* shortens the durations between events. Cypher events have associated with them a value called an *offset*, which is the duration separating it from the previous event. Shortening this value causes an event to be scheduled for execution sooner than would be the case were the offset left unaltered; this quickening of execution time results in the events being performed at an accelerated rate. The state variable controlling the behavior of the accelerator is called *downshift*. In the normal case, *downshift* is just the number of milliseconds subtracted from every event offset in the block. A mutate message can be used to change the value of *downshift*. Increasing it will cause events to be scheduled more quickly; decreasing the downshift value will slow down event scheduling.

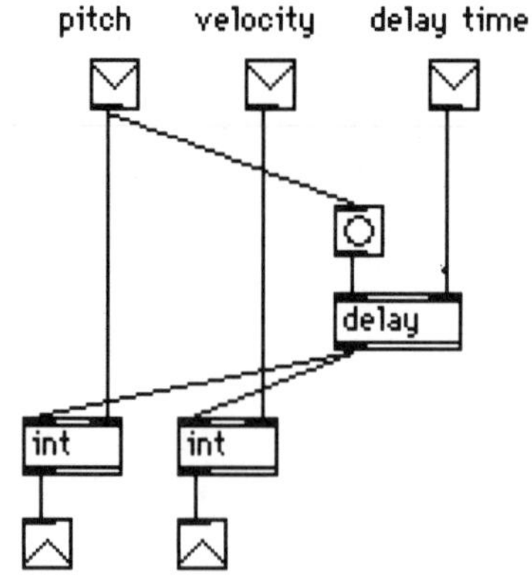

Figure 6.3

The acceleration algorithm is applied to all events in the input block except the first. The first event in every block has something of a special status: normally, the first event will be performed with no delay. This is because we generally want the response to be as fast as possible. And in fact, a transformed event with no delay will be virtually simultaneous with the original input. To achieve the greatest responsiveness, the first event in a block is given an offset of zero, before all transformations. Accordingly, the accelerator has no effect on the first event (unless some other transformation has already replaced its offset with a positive value).

The Max subpatch in figure 6.3 could form the kernel of several kinds of time transformation, acceleration being one of them. The patcher shown has three inlets and two outlets. The inlets take MIDI pitch and velocity values and a delay time in milliseconds. The same pitch and velocity values sent to the object will be output after the specified delay has elapsed. To realize a Cypher-like accelerator, this fragment could be applied to stored events each comprising a pitch, velocity, and delay time. To make the events played faster, simply decreasing the stored delay time before sending the events through the delay patcher would suffice.

Accenter

The *accenter* puts dynamic accents on some of the events in the event block. There are two state variables associated with it: a *count*, which keeps track of how many events have been processed; and the variable *strong*, which indicates how many events are to pass before an accent is generated. The effect of the module is to place a dynamic accent once every *strong* events. A mutate message can be used to change the value of *strong*. Using mutate, higher-level processes can change the accentuation pattern. An accent is described in terms of the MIDI velocity scale, in which 127 is the loudest onset amplitude. The *accenter* sets the velocity of strong events at 127 and of other events (to highlight the accentuation) at a significantly lower value.

The Max patch in figure 6.4 performs the *accenter* algorithm. MIDI Note messages with a velocity of zero (Note Off) are passed through unchanged. The *select* object connected to the *notein* velocity outlet sends nonzero velocities (associated with Note On messages) to the *counter*. With each incoming velocity, the counter is incremented by one. When the counter resets to zero (because it has reached the maximum), the *select* object beneath it will bang a message box, setting the velocity to 127. For every other value coming from the counter the velocity is set to 70. The number of notes which must pass before an accent is played can be changed with the dial.

Arpeggiator

The *arpeggiation* method unpacks chord events into collections of single-note events, where each of the new events contains one note from the original chord. The algorithm is straightforward: for each note in the input event, a new event is generated, with the pitch and velocity taken over from the original chord note. The state variable available for mutation is *speed*, which determines the temporal offset separating the events of the arpeggio. Arpeggiated events will be scheduled to play at intervals of *speed* milliseconds; therefore, increasing the speed variable will slow down the succession of arpeggiated notes, and decreasing the speed variable will quicken them.

The rudiments of a Max arpeggiator are shown in figure 6.5. The pitches of the chord are stored in a table, and the *counter* object steps through them. There is an inlet to the subpatch, which expects the total number of notes in the chord. After each note is played, a bang is sent to the *delay* object, which will pass it on to the *counter* after some number of milliseconds has elapsed; this duration is set with the dial connected to *delay*'s right inlet. When the bang is passed on, the next note will sound, and so on. Note that this fragment is a perpetual arpeggiation machine: once begun, it loops through the chord indefinitely. Adding

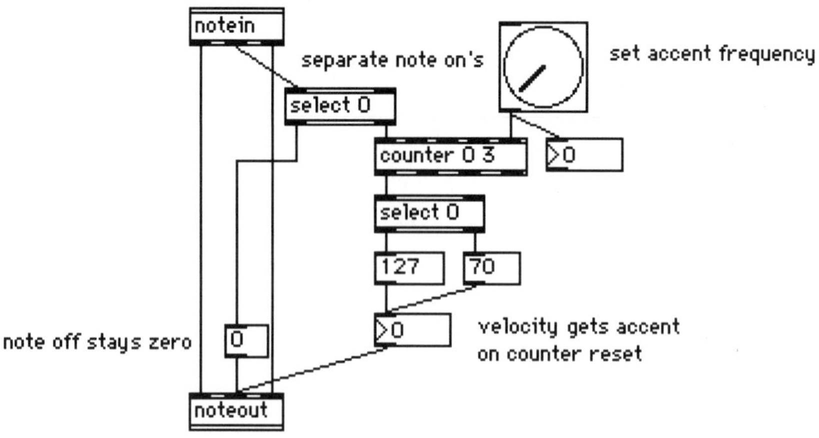

Figure 6.4

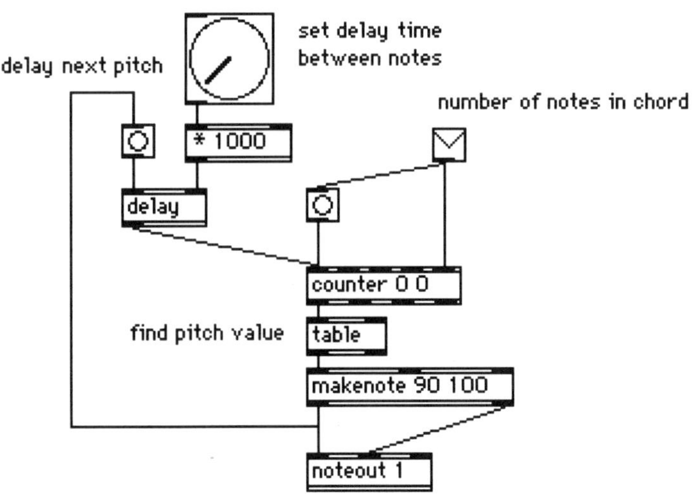

Figure 6.5

a termination path once the *counter* hits the maximum would make it equivalent to the Cypher arpeggiator.

Backward

The *backward* module takes all the events in the incoming block and reverses their order, so that the event which would have been played last will instead be output first, and so on. There is no mutation message provided for *backward*. In Max, a similar effect could easily be achieved by simply changing the direction inlet of a *counter* object reading through a *table*.

Basser

Basser plays the root of the leading chord identification theory, providing a simple bass line against the music being analyzed. The state variable *sensitivity* is available for mutation in this routine. Sensitivity refers to the confidence rating returned from the chord identification agent for the current theory. Each time *basser* is called, it queries the chord identifier twice: once to get the current root and again to read the confidence level. If the confidence level is higher than the value of *sensitivity*, a bass note will be played; otherwise the module remains silent.

Root notes are played within the second full octave on a piano keyboard, that is, within the MIDI pitch range 36 to 47. Further, new bass notes will be played no faster than one every 25 centiseconds; it is usually hard on synthesized bass sounds, and somewhat disconcerting, to hear a bass line with attacks several times a second. *Basser* does not funnel its output through the event block mechanism, but schedules its own performance. This is because there is no transformation of the input being performed; a new voice is being generated in addition to the original events.

Chorder

The *chorder* module will make a four-note chord from every event in the input block. There is an array of three intervals, which will be used to limit the pitches in the chord. For every event in the block, the first pitch in the event is taken as a starting point, and the other three pitches are generated as intervals within the bounds given by the interval array. For example, the first additional pitch is chosen at random within 7 half-steps of the original note. The second must be within 15 half-steps, and the last within 23. If any pitches exceed the upper limit of the keyboard range, they are changed to the highest pitch on the keyboard. Using this algorithm, all chords generated by the *chorder* will be smaller than two octaves in total span, and contain four pitches more

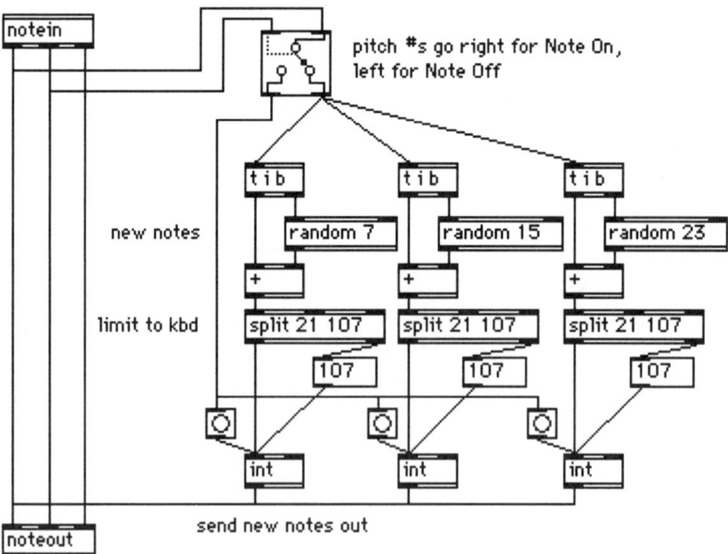

Figure 6.6

or less evenly distributed throughout that range. There is no mutation message available for this module.

The Max patch in figure 6.6 is an implementation of the *chorder* algorithm. The velocity of incoming note messages controls the direction of the graphic switch at the top of the patch. Note On messages spawn new notes through additions to constrained random numbers. These additional pitch numbers are saved in the *int* objects at the bottom, after first being limited to the keyboard range, and sent on to *noteout*. When Note Off messages arrive, their zero velocity sends the pitch number out the left outlet of the graphic switch. Then they bang out the saved pitch numbers, turning off the same chord that was turned on initially.

Decelerator

The *decelerator* lengthens the duration between events. Increasing an event offset causes it to be scheduled for execution later than would be the case were the offset left unaltered; this slowing of execution time results in the events being performed at a decelerated rate. The state variable affecting the behavior of the decelerator is the *upshift*—the number of centiseconds added to every event offset in the block. A mutate message can be used to set the upshift to a new value. Increasing the upshift will cause events to be scheduled more slowly; decreasing the downshift value will speed up event scheduling.

For every event in the input, *upshift* is added to the offset if that lengthening results in a value less than 400 centiseconds. If the new offset exceeds that threshold—in other words, if the resulting offset would cause the event to be delayed by more than 4 seconds—200 centiseconds are subtracted from the offset instead. This will cause the event to be scheduled two seconds earlier, in effect an acceleration; however, this quickening also means that subsequent decelerations will again cause a slowing within the 4-second margin. The overall behavior will be a gradual slowing, to the 4-second limit, one quick acceleration, and another gradual decelerando. The Max subpatch of figure 6.3, shown in connection with the acceleration module, could similarly form the basis of a decelerator. The only difference between the two would lie in the calculations used to determine the delay sent to the subpatch's rightmost inlet.

Flattener

The *flattener* is one of the few modules that will undo variation found in the input block. This module flattens out the rhythmic presentation of the input events, setting all offsets to 250 milliseconds and all durations to 200 milliseconds. The result is a performance that is significantly more machinelike than most inputs, since all attacks will be exactly evenly separated one from another. There is no mutation variable associated with this transformation. Again, the simple Max subpatch of figure 6.3 could achieve the same effect if it were sent a constant delay time with every pitch/velocity pair.

Glisser

The *glisser* adds short glissandi to the beginning of each event in the input block. There is one state variable available for mutation, which controls the maximum length of the generated glissandi. The first step of the transformation method calculates a glissando length as follows: `howmany = ((rand()%length)+1);`. The random number generator is called, and its output used modulo the *length* variable, to limit the upper bound. One is added to the result to ensure that all executions will add at least one new event to each incoming event. Therefore, mutating the *length* variable will change the maximum number of notes allowed in a glissando.

Glissandi are generated from below the input note and run up to it in half-step increments. The interval between the input event and the first note of the glissando, therefore, depends on the calculated length. If, for instance, a glissando length of five is needed, the first pitch will be a perfect fourth below the input event, to allow five half steps of ornamentation going up to the original pitch. These new pitches are generated with a constant speed (70 milliseconds apart) and velocity (rather loud—MIDI value 110).

Figure 6.7 is a Max glissando patch. When a new note arrives, it provokes a new random number within the range set by the dial and opens the gate used to control the *delay* object later. The random number is subtracted from the pitch to set the value of a *counter*; the pitch itself sets the counter's maximum value. Then, the *counter* will play through the pitches of the glissando; after each one is produced, a bang message is delayed 70 milliseconds before making the next note. When the gliss has reached the original pitch number, the gate flips to

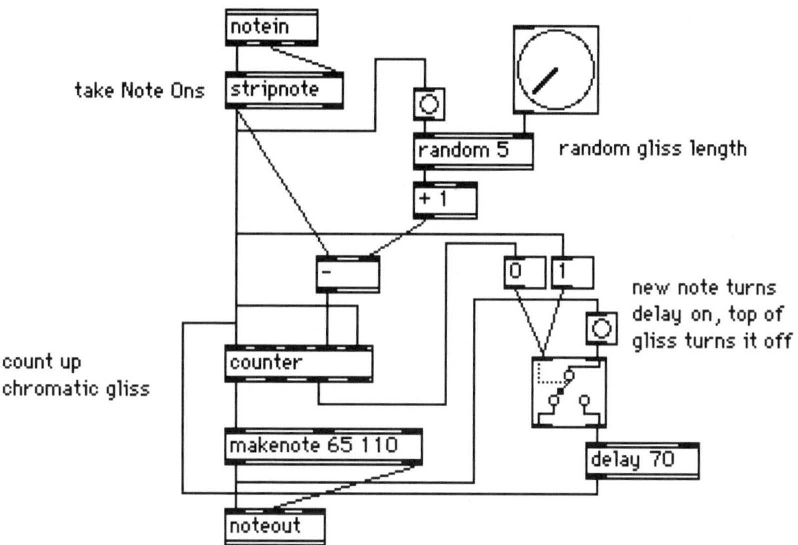

Figure 6.7

the left outlet, and no more bangs will reach *delay*, thus stopping the process.

Gracer

The *gracer* appends a series of quick notes leading up to each event in the input block. Every event that comes in will have three new notes added before it. All of these new notes will be at offsets of 100 milliseconds, resulting in a fast, grace-note-like ornamentation of the original event. The added pitches are chosen at random from a range set by the *space* variable. Grace notes will usually be chosen to appear below the original pitch; random numbers are generated within the *space* range and then subtracted from the event pitch. If this results in a note below MIDI number 40, the modification is instead added to the original pitch, producing a grace-note figure that leads down to the original event. The *space* variable can be modified with a mutate message, changing the pitch range within which grace notes will be selected.

The Max patch in figure 6.8 performs a transformation like the *gracer*. For every pitch played, three new notes will be produced at random within 15 semitones below the original (this range can be changed with the dial). Offsets of 100 millisecond separate each pitch. After the three grace notes, the original pitch is played out, and the process stops until another note is performed. The only difference between figure 6.8 and the Cypher version is that no notice is taken here of the tessitura; grace notes will come from below no matter how low the original pitch is in the range.

Harmonizer

The *harmonizer* modifies the pitch content of the incoming event block to be consonant with the harmonic activity currently in the input. The basic idea of the algorithm is the following: After ascertaining the current chord and key, pitches in the event block are nudged into a scale consonant with those analyses. The contour of the pitches is maintained as closely as possible; pitches dissonant with the chord and/or key are moved up or down one or two half steps to a consonant pitch. For example, an F sharp found in an event block associated with the tonic chord in C major would be nudged up to a G natural, changing a highly dissonant pitch to a consonant member of the tonic triad.

The specifics of how to modify incoming pitches are maintained in the *nudge* array, which has three dimensions corresponding to mode, function, and original pitch. The first dimension, *mode*, has two possible values, which represent major and minor versions of the current

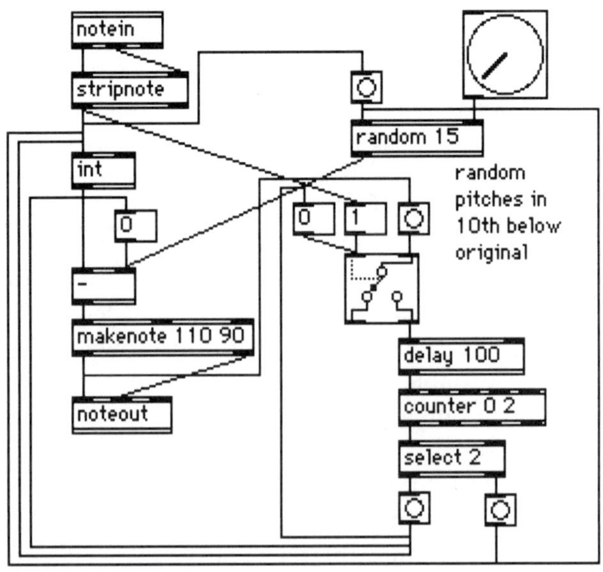

Figure 6.8

key. This allows an immediate selection between two kinds of modification, one for each mode. The second dimension goes into the mode-specific transformations and finds the list associated with the *function* of the current chord. Function is used in the music-theoretic sense here: a C major triad in the key of C major, for example, has a tonic (or, in the program's numbering scheme, zero) function. There are 24 possible functions, corresponding to the major and minor versions of triads built on the twelve scale degrees. The final dimension of the *nudge* array comes from the pitch number of the incoming note, which is considered regardless of octave, meaning that the value of this dimension can be one of twelve possibilities.

With these three dimensions, the harmonizer is equipped to transform any incoming pitch class, played against any chord function in either the major or minor modes of the key. There are no mutation possibilities associated with this module, but there should be: according to the style of music being performed, the *nudge* array itself should be replaced. Some styles place stricter constraints on allowable dissonances, and the way these are resolved, than others. If the program were able to recognize styles and had at hand a repertoire of *nudge* arrays corresponding to them, it could swap in the appropriate harmonic behavior for each known style.

Inverter

The *inverter* takes the events in the input block and moves them to pitches that are equidistant from some point of symmetry, on the opposite side of that point from where they started. In other words, all input events are inverted around the point of symmetry. For example, if the symmetry point were middle C, all pitches above middle C would be transformed to others the same distance below middle C as the original pitches were above it. High becomes low, and the higher the original pitch, the lower the transformed pitch. The point of symmetry can be altered with a mutate command: the default setting is 64, which is the MIDI pitch number for the E above middle C, the exact center of an 88-key piano keyboard. A mutation can change this point to any other MIDI pitch number. Pitches that, after transformation, would exceed the MIDI pitch boundaries are pinned at either the highest or lowest possible pitch, whichever is closer to the calculated value. We have already seen two Max versions of the same idea: the *mirror* subpatch from Jean-Claude Risset's *Duet* in section 3.5, and the *inverter* from Richard Teitelbaum's software shown in figure 6.1.

Looper

The *loop* module will repeat the events in the input block, taken as a whole. In other words, all of the events in the block will be performed once, then all will be performed again, and so on, until the desired number of loops is reached (in contrast to a looping scheme in which each individual event would be repeated some number of times before continuing on to the next). The number of loops performed depends in part on the *limit* variable. There are always a minimum of two loops performed, including the original events. So the least action taken by this module would be to repeat the original events once. Additional repeats are generated at random, up to the value of *limit*. For example, if *limit* were equal to four, the module would perform randomly from one to five repeats. The *limit* can be reset with a mutate message.

The Max patch of figure 6.9 is the essence of a looper. Banging on the button at the top of the patch will cause it to loop through the first four elements in the table three times. The carry count outlet of the *counter* object tells how many times the counter has gone from its minimum to maximum values. Once the carry count has reached 3, in this patch, the switch sending bangs through the delay back up to the counter is set to the off position. In this example, all the patch does is flash the bang button under the table object twelve times. One can easily imagine how this could be extended to provide a Cypher-style looper: if the table were filled with MIDI pitch numbers, routing the

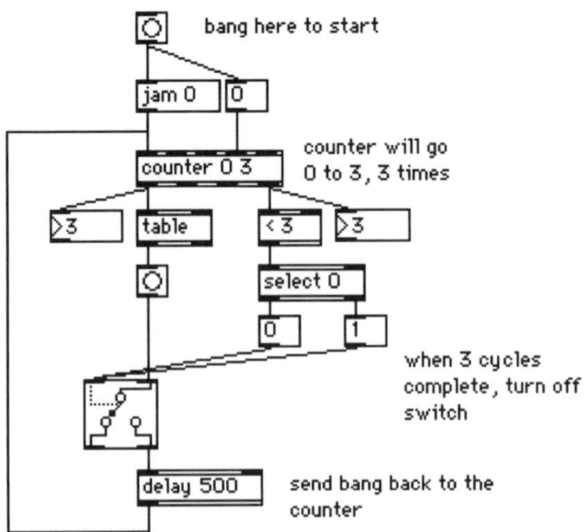

Figure 6.9

table outlet to a makenote/noteout pair, for example, would loop through the pitches in the table.

Louder

The *louder* module adds crescendi to the events in the input block. This is another case in which the transformation would not be heard on blocks of only one event. The solution here is to add a second event to singleton blocks. The amount of velocity change is arrived at quasi-randomly; that is, the following calculation is used: change = (rand()%limit)+1;. This varies the velocity modification randomly up to a maximum set by the variable *limit*, with a minimum value of 1.

Each event in the block will receive an increasing augmentation of its velocity. The first event has *change* added to it. Before each succeeding event, *change* is increased, then added into the next event velocity. If ever the new velocity exceeds the MIDI maximum (127), the value of *change* itself is used. Then the algorithm proceeds as before. The effect is a crescendo, more or less gradual (depending on the value of *limit*), up to the MIDI limit, followed by a sudden drop in loudness, followed by another gradual crescendo. A mutate message can be used to change the value of *limit*, effectively varying the speed of loudness change.

Obbligato

This module adds an obbligato line high in the pitch range to accompany harmonically whatever activity is happening below it. The algorithm for doing this is very simple: the chord agency is queried for the root of the current harmonic area. The root is played out in the octave starting two octaves above middle C. The other wrinkle on this behavior is that the module only plays out an obbligato note for every fourth event in the incoming event block. This ensures that the obbligato line will move more slowly than the other material. The frequency, in events, of obbligato output can be changed by sending the module a mutate message with a new setting.

Ornamenter

Ornamenter adds small, rapid figures encircling each event in the input block. Two new events are added for each one coming in. The new events will circle the original pitch, with one new event above it and one below. The distances above and below the original pitch are chosen at random, within a boundary controlled by the *width* variable. The calculation is change = ((rand()%width)+1). *Width* keeps the output of the random number generation within a boundary; one is added to make sure that all new pitches will differ from the original by at least one half step. The new events have a constant offset (100 milliseconds) and velocity (110 MIDI). The width variable can be changed with a mutate message.

The Max patch in figure 6.10 implements an ornamenter. When a new note arrives, it causes random numbers within the range set by the dial to be sent to the *plus* and *minus* objects on the left side of the patch. First, the random number is subtracted from the original and played out. After a delay of 100 milliseconds, the same random number is added to the original and played. Finally, 100 milliseconds later, the original pitch itself is performed, and the process stops.

Phraser

The *phraser* module temporally separates groups of events in the input block. Adding a significant pause between two successive events plays on one of the strongest grouping cues and tends to induce a phrase boundary at the break. The state variable *phrase_length* determines how many events will pass before a pause is inserted. When *phrase_length* events have gone by, the offset of the following event will be length-

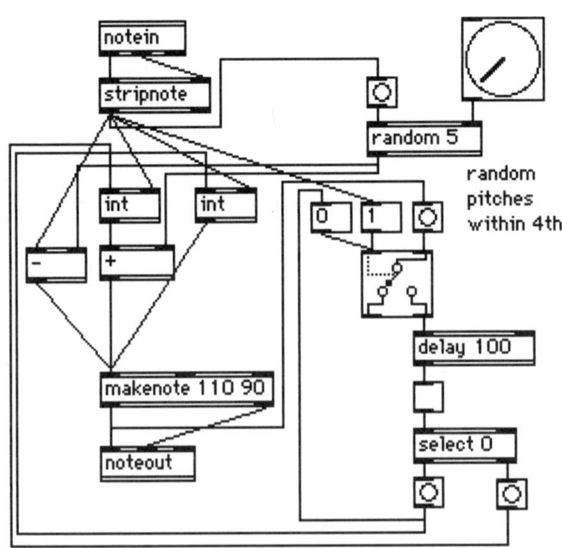

Figure 6.10

ened at random by a duration somewhere in the range of 400 to 1670 milliseconds. The value of *phrase_length* can be changed with a mutate message.

Quieter

Quieter adds decrescendi to the events in the input block. Again, the effect would not be heard on blocks of only one event, so a second event is added to singleton blocks. The amount of velocity change is arrived at quasi-randomly; that is, the following calculation is used: change = (rand()%limit)+1;. This varies the velocity modification randomly, with a maximum somewhere below the value of *limit* and a minimum of 1. The value of *change* is subtracted from the velocity of the first event in the block (which have become two if the original input was a single event). For each succeeding event, first the value of *change* is augmented, and then the event's velocity is diminished by that value. If the newly calculated velocity goes below 10, *change* is subtracted from 127 (the maximum MIDI velocity), and the result is used as the new event velocity. The effect will be a gradual decrescendo (the speed of which is determined by *limit*), an abrupt jump to a loud velocity, and another gradual descent. The value of *limit* can be changed with a mutate message, varying the speed of loudness change.

Sawer

This module adds four pitches to each input event, in a kind of sawtooth pattern. It is similar to the *ornamenter* in that it also adds new material above and below the original pitch. In this case, two pitches will be added above and two below, in alternation. The amount by which these new notes will deviate from the input is determined by the state variable *width*. The value of *width* can be changed with a mutate message.

Figure 6.11 is a sawer patch produced with some modifications to the ornamenter shown in figure 6.10. Here, there is a *counter* object after the delay. A *modulo* operation follows the counter, such that even counts will cause a pitch above the original to be generated, and odd counts, a pitch below the original. This sawer will generate the incoming pitch first, then four new pitches, two above and two below, in alternation. The interval between the original and modified pitches will change with each note, because the *random* object is prodded for a new value each time.

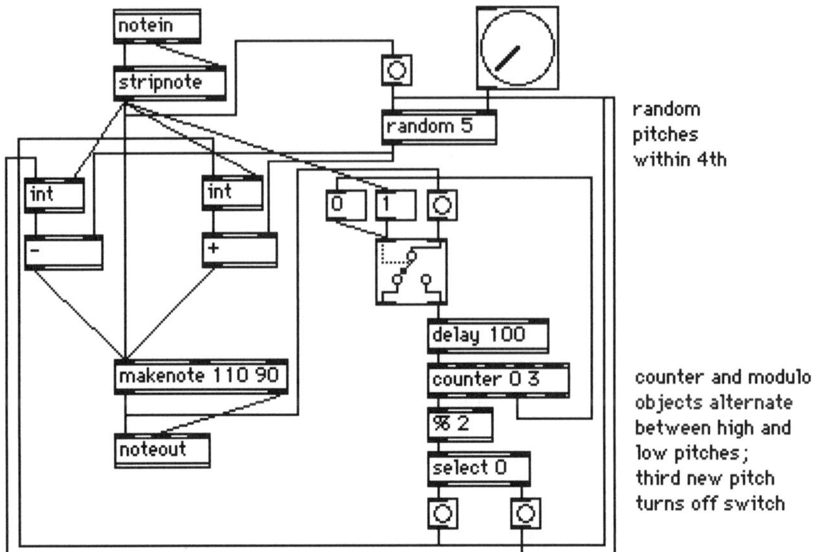

Figure 6.11

Solo

The *solo* module is the first step in the development of a fourth kind of algorithmic style, lying between the transformative and purely generative techniques. Because its operation is not a transformation in the same sense as the other processes described in this section, I will reserve discussion of *solo* for section 6.4.

Stretcher

The *stretcher* affects the duration of events in the input block, stretching them out beyond their original length. The state variable *mod* controls the range of variation that will be introduced. The calculation of the new duration for each event in the block is coded thus: duration = (rand()%mod)+500. First, a random number is generated; this is limited to the maximum specified by *mod*. The result of the modulo operation is added to 500, giving a minimum lengthening of 500 milliseconds. The maximum lengthening is determined by *mod*, and the value of *mod* can be changed with a mutate message. A similar effect could easily be implemented in Max; a calculation such as the one outlined above would be needed to produce duration values fed into a *makenote* object, for example.

Swinger

Swinger modifies the offset times of events in the input block. The state variable *swing* is multiplied with the offset of every other event; a value of *swing* equaling two will produce the familiar 2:1 swing feel in originally equally spaced events. If the input events are not equally spaced to begin with, the swing modification will have more complex results. The value of *swing* can be changed with a mutate message.

Thinner

The *thinner* reduces the density of events in the input block. Most of the transformations, if they change the number of events presented at the input, change it by adding new events. Consequently, the density of events emanating from the composition section can reach quite significant levels. *Thinner* is one tool for reducing the amount of material coming from the player. The state variable *thin* controls how the reduction is done. A count is associated with the module, which is incremented with each note of every event. When *thin* divides evenly into the count, the corresponding Note is deleted, and the offset of the Event that contains the Note is increased by one second. For example, if *thin* were 3, and an incoming event held six Notes, two of the Notes would be deleted and the offset of the Event would be increased by two seconds. The density of incoming material will be reduced, then, in two ways: some chords will hold fewer notes, and pauses of one or more seconds will be added between some events. The value of *thin* can be changed with a mutate message.

TightenUp

To do the *tightenUp*, events in the input block are aligned with the beat boundary. On entering the module, the beat agency is queried for the current beat period. Next, the offset times of all events in the input block are added together. If the combined offsets are equal to the beat period, then the final event of the block will sound on a beat boundary. This is the desired effect of the module: if the offsets are already in such an alignment, the method returns with no further action. If the combined offsets have a duration less than the beat period, the last offset is extended by the difference between the two—again placing the final event in the block on the beat. If the combined offsets' duration is longer than the beat period, the difference is divided by the number of events in the input block, and the result is subtracted from every event offset. In other words, all events are quickened by a constant value to make the final event again fall on the beat. There is no mutate message associated with this module, and the transformation does not add any events to the ones already present on input.

Transposer

Transposer changes the pitch level of all the events in the input block by some constant amount. The distance by which the pitches will be moved is calculated as follows: interval = (base%limit), *base* is a random number, *limit* will keep the value of this random number within some bound, and *interval* is set to the result. Then, for each event in the block, *interval* is added to the current pitch. If the resulting pitch exceeds the upper limit of the pitch range, interval is instead subtracted from the original event pitch. So, transpositions will generally be upward, though near the top of the pitch space they will move the other way. The value of *limit* can be changed with a mutate message. A good Max transposer from Richard Teitelbaum's software is shown in figure 3.19.

Tremolizer

The *tremolo* module adds three new events to each event in the input block. The new events have a constant offset of 100 milliseconds. They surround the original pitches, with two new events above the original and one below, or two below and one above; in either case, the higher and lower new events alternate. The distance new pitches will be removed from the original is determined by the following calculation: first a random number is generated. This is limited to a maximum of 12, then added to 2. The addition ensures that all new pitches will differ from the original by at least one whole step. The maximum deviation between original and new pitches is an octave plus one whole step. There is no mutate message associated with this module.

A few small changes allow us to change the sawer patch from figure 6.11 into a version of the tremolizer, shown in figure 6.12. Here, the intervals of the new pitches are the same in both directions, because the random object is not asked for a new value between attacks. Further, a simple change to the counter ensures that three new pitches will be generated for each incoming event, not four. This demonstrates, first, that Max patches can easily be modified to achieve a range of similar behaviors from one basic algorithm. Second, if the changes being made here were subject to modification during performance (adding a dial to set the upper bound of the *counter* object, for example),

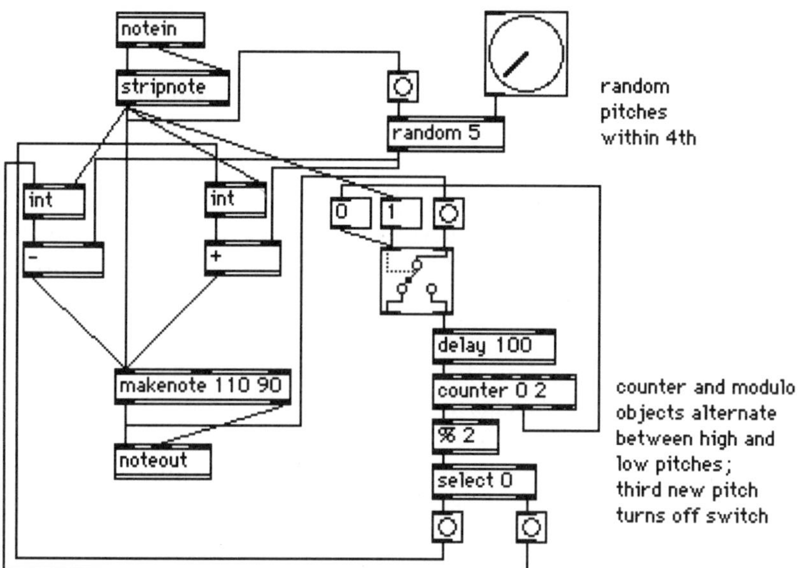

Figure 6.12

this same range of behaviors could be generated onstage in response to varying musical circumstances.

Triller

Triller adds four new events to each event in the input block. These will be performed as a trill above or below the original pitch. The new events have a constant offset of 100 milliseconds. The placement above or below the source pitch is determined randomly, but trills that would come out below MIDI pitch 30 are always played above the source, and trills that would come out above MIDI pitch 100 are always played below. The trills will be the source pitch alternating with a trill pitch either a half step or a whole step above or below it. The entire figure will begin and end on the source pitch, alternating with two trill notes. The choice between half- or whole-step trills is made randomly. There is no mutate message associated with this module. Again, a simple modification of the basic Max patch shown in figures 6.10, 6.11, and 6.12 could produce the same effect: if the tremolo patch from figure 6.11 were initialized to produce random numbers not larger than 2, a version of the Cypher triller would result. The only difference is that the Max version would not be sensitive to register and that the Max patch begins on the source note, but does not end on it.

6.2 Generation Techniques

A small but critical distinction separates transformation methods from generation techniques. As we have seen, transformation methods perform some operation on representations emanating from an external source. In the case of generation techniques, the output of a compositional formalism is derived solely from the operation of the formalism itself, possibly aided by stored tables of material. A way to distinguish between generation techniques and transformation, then, is to note that transformation methods require live input and generation techniques do not. This distinction is a fine one, and tends to blur easily, as do many of the classification metrics we have been discussing. Still, it seems to capture a noticeable difference in the way composers approach algorithmic methods: either the machine is changing something it hears or is generating its own material from stored data and procedures.

In Cypher, generation methods are used to produce clearly distinguishable textures and accept messages to influence their behavior during any particular performance. For example, the *tremolo* algorithm produces a rapidly changing pitch field that sweeps up the keyboard range, folding around to the bottom of the range when it has reached the top. The overall duration of the process is established with the set message. Within that duration, the algorithm calls itself many times, using continue messages. The temporal offsets between these self-invocations are determined by a calculation that alternately lengthens and shortens the duration between calls. Each invocation of the routine includes a seed pitch, and a fixed set of three intervals determines the notes generated around this seed. Every seed will produce ten new pitches, arrived at by continually cycling through the array of intervals. Three and one-third repetitions of the interval array are heard for each invocation of the routine. The seed pitch itself, then, is shifted upward with each new call of the routine until it reaches the top of the range, at which point it is folded back around to the bottom. The entire process continues until the duration specified in the set message has elapsed. All of the generation methods produce short fragments when selected from the *alg* menu; they will use the *Bank* and *Timbre* sounds currently selected.

Clarence Barlow has a highly developed algorithmic music generation method, which he has implemented in a real-time program called AUTOBUSK (Barlow 1990). Following the ideas laid out in his article

"Two Essays on Theory" (Barlow 1987), and brought to compositional fruition in the remarkable *Colgluotobüsisletmesi* for solo piano (1978), AUTOBUSK uses concepts of stability, clarity, consonance, and dissonance to affect the microtonal and rhythmic behavior of musical textures. It is a generation method that uses seed material supplied by the user to spin out music according to its algorithmic principles. Each instance of the program can realize three voices in real time. "AUTOBUSK can be run autonomously or—using more than one computer—in series or in parallel: a serial connection causes MIDI output to be interpreted as input control by the next computer along in the line, whereas a connection in parallel permits synchronized sets of six, nine or higher multiples of three voices" (Barlow 1990, 166).

Pat-Proc

An example of an interactive generation method is the Pat-Proc program written by Phil Winsor of the Center for Experimental Music and Intermedia at the University of North Texas (Winsor 1991). Pat-Proc is divided into two parts: the first part generates pitch material for manipulation by the second part, which performs various operations, prominently including looping techniques. The program first realized generation methods derived from minimalism and later expanded these to cover a wider stylistic range. The two hallmarks of generative methods are quite easily seen from the way the program is divided: stored material is manipulated by procedures generating recognizable musical textures. The procedures are governed by control variables whose manipulation allows the composer to affect the generation of any particular output.

In fact, the division of Pat-Proc into two tasks, material definition and melody writing, allows two levels of generation method. In the first task, a number of procedures are available for generating the pitch material, which will be elaborated further during melody writing. To define the basic pitch material, a user may define the pitch set by hand, use a constrained sieve to generate pitches, or define a basic interval set, which will be spun out into scales by the program. The melody-writing section of the program generates linear voices from the basic scales, using a collection of methods. Pitches can be chosen from the scale serially, following a random distribution, or through an interval sieve. Further, the user can specify percentages of rests to be included or of the number of notes to receive ornamentation. Several voices can be generated in parallel, and rhythmic procedures can be applied to control their polyphonic presentation.

Pat-Proc is not used in live performance, but a great many of its features could easily be adapted to such usage. As it exists, Pat-Proc performs all the necessary calculations for each voice in the resultant texture and then produces output in one of a variety of formats—an alphanumeric note list, MIDI sequence, or conventional music notation. The characteristics of the algorithm, however, are what interest us here: Pat-Proc, as it is conceptualized and used, exemplifies an algorithmic generation method. In a two-stage process, some stored basic material is defined and then elaborated compositionally by a number of procedures whose function can be affected by a user through a collection of control variables.

Markov Chains

Markov chains formed the basis of several compositions by Lejaren Hiller and his colleagues from the early 1960s, and have since been implemented in a number of interactive systems. Markov chains are series of linked states. Each state moves to a successor state, in what is called a *transition* (Ames 1989). The state at the beginning of a transition is the *source*; the state at the end is the transition's *destination*. In a Markov chain, each successive destination of one transition becomes the source of the next. The behavior of the chain is captured by a table of transition probabilities, which gives the likelihood of any particular destination being reached from some source.

In Experiment 4 of Hiller and Isaacson's *Illiac Suite* (1957), the transition table was weighted to produce melodies favoring harmonic (consonant destinations) and proximate (small-interval destination) continuations (Ames 1989, 176). Markov chains can be made to index transition tables that rely on more than one source event. The number of previous states used to determine the next destination state is called the *order* of the chain. Chains that use only the source state to determine a transition are called *first order*; chains that use the two most recent states to find the transition to the next are *second order*, and so on.

In interactive systems, either explicitly Markov-like transition tables or closely related probability schemes have been used as generative algorithmic techniques. A realization of Markov techniques in Max, developed by Miller Puckette, has been used at IRCAM in compositions by Philippe Manoury, including *Jupiter* and *La partition du ciel et de l'enfer*. Saxophonist and interactive system designer Steve Coleman has written a drummer program, which uses probabilities to decide on the placement of percussion sounds on any sixteenth pulse of a phrase, in a variety of styles. These probabilities are conditioned by immediately preceding choices, in first-order Markovian fashion. Similarly, George Lewis uses probabilites to select from tables of stored melodic and rhythmic material, and these probabilities are again modified by the successions actually played out.

Max Generation Objects

We have reviewed extensively the use of Max to transform musical material; several composers have used the language to implement more strictly generative processes as well. Jeff Pressing described a general method for algorithmic composition in his article "Nonlinear Maps as Generators of Musical Design" (Pressing 1988). On the companion CD-ROM, the Max patch *quaternmusic* implements a realization of these ideas. The user controls the behavior of the generator by manipulating four variables: "The behaviour of the central equation, a four-dimensional quaternion logistic map, depends critically on the value of the parameter *a*. The four components of *a*, that is, a_1, a_2, a_3, and a_4, are the parameters manipulated by the musician. Depending on the value of *a*, the equation can produce fixed points, limit cycles, intermittency, chaos, divergences to infinity, and other types of behaviour" (Pressing 1991, 1).

The Max object MAXGen was developed at the Université de Montréal by composer Jean Piché and his team. MAXGen allows the specification and execution of arbitrarily complex control functions, which can be applied to synthesis or compositional parameters in real time. Envelopes, tendency masks, and step functions can be drawn in a graphic editor within Max or "played" into the object through MIDI. Once defined, functions can be stretched, compressed, copied, or merged.

Figure 6.13 shows an editing window from MAXGen. The tool icons arrayed in the upper left-hand corner represent various drawing and selection operations. Other controls change the representation on the screen and initiate processing of selections from the editing window, including stretching and the other operations listed previously. The notion of a tendency mask is extensively supported in MAXGen: in the work of several composers, including most notably G. M. Koenig and

Barry Truax, tendency masks are used to vary the range of a random number generator over time. As the limits of the mask are adjusted, they set the upper and lower bounds for the generation of random numbers. The resulting values are then used to control pitch, durations, or synthesis parameters.

Gary Lee Nelson has developed a number of pieces based on explorations of fractals in music that are implemented in Max. Aspects of Benoit Mandelbrot's fractal theory that have attracted composers, among them Nelson, J. C. Risset, Michael McNabb, and Charles Wuorinen, include the property of self-similarity, in which forms are repeated on several scales simultaneously, and "strange attractors," numbers in a fractal system that tend to exert a particular pull on the field around them. The application of these ideas to musical form has come in several guises; some researchers have taken fractal principles to the level of sound synthesis, where the forms of the pressure waves resemble the form of entire phrases and compositions (Yadegari 1991).

In *Fractal Mountains*, Gary Lee Nelson uses fractal graphs, whose method of generation ensures self-similarity on several levels. A collection of three graphs governs pitch, rhythm, duration, and density values in a microtonal, algorithmically generated environment. One graph controls pitch and rhythm by mapping the vertexes onto frequency (the y axis), and attack point (the x axis). Similarly, another graph affects the duration of notes through a function determining the number of sounds that should be heard simultaneously, affecting the overall density. The third graph maps onto dynamics, through MIDI velocity values. The entire system is made interactive by a technique that generates the graphs in real time from notes played on a MIDI

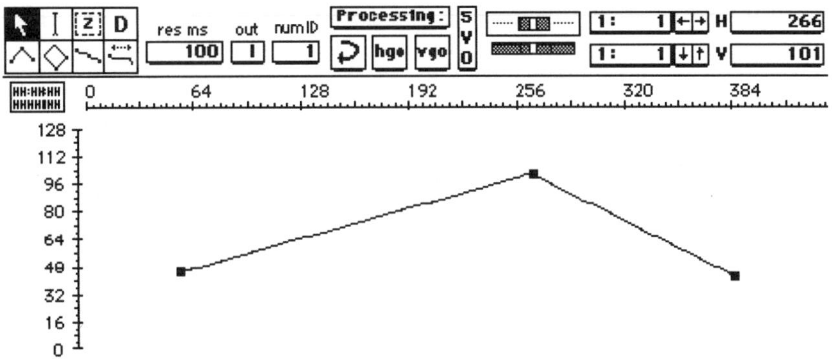

Figure 6.13

wind controller. The pitch and velocity values from incoming wind controller events are used to place points on the graphs, which generate "fractal mountains," and proceed to spawn new musical continuations based on the principles previously described.

6.3 Sequencing and Patterns

The most widespread applications yet developed for computer music are the class of programs collectively known as *sequencers*. A sequencer provides recording and editing capabilities for streams of MIDI data. More recently, tracks of audio information can be coordinated with the MIDI tracks as well. Several interactive systems have developed ways to incorporate sequences in performance, modifying aspects of the playback in response to live input. The Max programming language, for example, has a number of facilities for recording and using sequences.

Because of the normal use of commercial applications, sequences are usually thought of as successions of Note On and Note Off messages, with some occasional continuous controls and program changes thrown in. Stored strings of MIDI data not including Note messages can be used quite effectively in interactive performance, however: Roger Dannenberg's composition *Ritual of the Science Makers* employs sequences in just this way (Dannenberg 1991). Rather than recording Note commands, sequences in *Ritual* record parametric changes. For example, values fed to digital signal processing algorithms are changed over time by a sequence of control information initiated at the appropriate moment in the performance. Another section of the work transforms pitches arriving from the ensemble of flute, violin, and cello into chords: these transformations, then, are varied through the section by a sequence of transposition values.

Sequences can be specified in several ways: one of the most common is to use a commercial application to capture and order MIDI data, then dump the results into an interactive environment through the use of the Standard MIDI File Format. Another way is simply to capture a stream of MIDI in real time during performance, as we will see Max's *seq* object do presently. A third way relies on some form of text editing to specify events and their arrangement in time. This way in particular allows function calls and manipulation of program variables to be interspersed with Note and controller information. The text-based score language of the CMU MIDI Toolkit, called Adagio, supports the integration of function calls with more traditional score information. The *qlist* concept used at IRCAM in Max is another expression of the same idea.

Sequencing in Max

The basic sequencing object in Max is called, appropriately enough, *seq*. The *seq* object records a stream of MIDI messages coming from the *midiin* object and can play these back out in a variety of ways to the *midiout* object, as shown in figure 6.14. There are three message boxes attached to the inlet of *seq*, which will instruct it to perform these functions: hitting the `record` message will start *seq* recording the MIDI stream coming from *midiin*. `Start` makes *seq* start playing back whatever messages it has recorded, from beginning to end, and `stop` will halt either recording or playback.

The more extensive patch built around the *seq* object shown in figure 6.15 was developed for part of Dinu Ghezzo's composition *Kajaani Nights*, premiered by the New York University Contemporary Players in November of 1991. The patch includes three sequencers, with separate record, start, and stop messages, as well as controls for independently varying the speed and transpostion level of playback.

The record, delay, start, and stop message boxes are all connected to the left inlet of their respective sequencers; the connections are "hidden on lock" here to make the mechanism more easily visible. In the performance, an operator recorded material from an opening chorale, using the "3way Record" button at the top. Once the chorale was loaded into the sequencers, the separate controls for each were used to layer the material with various transpositions and speed changes.

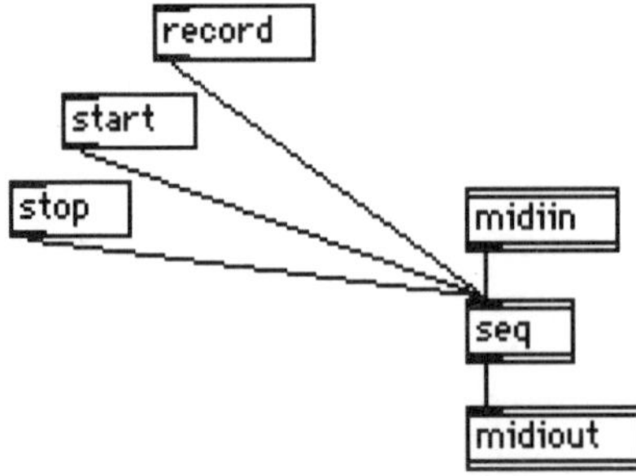

Figure 6.14

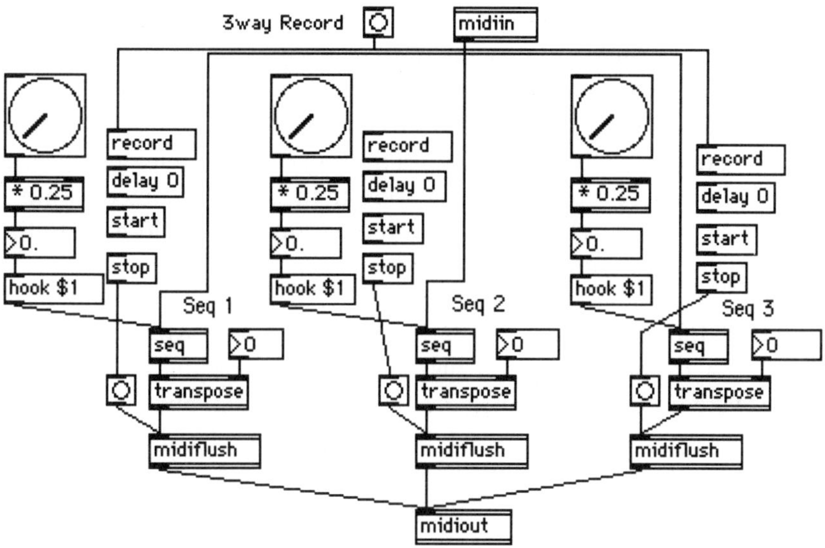

Figure 6.15

MIDI-LIVE

The composer and performer Bruce Pennycook led the development of the MIDI-LIVE interactive computer music environment, an important component of which is the ability to record and play back sequences in performance. MIDI-LIVE grew through the realization of a series of five compositions, all part of the *PRAESCIO* series written by Pennycook. The name "praescio" came from a vision of interacting "prescient" partners, human and computer, each of whom would "'know' a portion of the musical material for the work but only during the moment of realization—the performance—would the completely formed piece unfold" (Pennycook 1991, 16).

Sequences for MIDI-LIVE were described with *mscore*, a version of Leland Smith's *score* program. The sequences could be assigned to tracks accessible by MIDI-LIVE, and each piece specified conditions under which the tracks would be triggered by performer actions. MIDI note numbers, program change buttons, and foot switches were among the devices used to affect the state of MIDI-LIVE. A simple production system controlled the coupling between performer actions and machine responses. The production system consisted of <if-then> pairs, where the <if> conditions of the rules consisted of logical expressions on the state of performance devices (the foot switches, program change buttons, etc.), and the <then> actions were sets of program responses. For example, a simple rule in the production system might indicate that when a foot switch is depressed, the computer will record MIDI data coming from a keyboard, and when the foot switch is released, recording will cease. Production rules were themselves arranged in numbered sequences, where each rule in the sequence would have to fire before the next would become active.

The sequencing facilities offered in MIDI-LIVE enable some basic kinds of interaction between performers and prerecorded MIDI material. First, the performer controls the timing of recording and playback. The system does not implement tempo following, but the initiation time of any sequence is chosen by the performer. Further, controlled improvisation sections give the player access to a palette of sequences, which can be called up and played in any order. MIDI-LIVE allows extensive use of continuous control information to incorporate such devices as MIDI mixers in real-time performance. Finally, many simple transformations have been built in that can be used to vary the playback of any sequence track: output channel assignment, looping, transposition, tempo and velocity scaling, and harmonization are among them.

Sequencing in Cypher

Sequencing is little used in Cypher, primarily because the emphasis has been on the algorithmic techniques of generating an appropriate response in real time, rather than calling up a prerecorded response under certain conditions. The capability of using sequences in this way, however, is supported by the software, and the idea of launching fragments from a small library of possibilities when associated structures are encountered in the input is part of the orientation of the enterprise. The main implementational concern is that processing of the sequences should not degrade the performance of other listening and compositional tasks.

Sequencing was better supported in an earlier version of the program: the current implementation, however, is not far from providing the same facilities. The basic idea is this: A process that commences performance of a sequence file can be attached to any listener message. Such a process becomes a composition method like any other. Once initiated, a pointer to the sequence file is kept in a list of open sequences. Then, in the main Cypher loop, the sequence scheduling routine schedule_next_second() will be called.

Schedule_next_second() looks at the list of open sequences each time it is called. For each pointer in the list, one second's worth of sequenced material is read from the file and sent to the scheduler. All sequencer files follow the standard MIDI file format; events in such files are timestamped with their offset from the previous event (as is done in Cypher). Therefore, schedule_next_second() can send file events to the scheduler, adding up successive offsets until one second's worth of events have been read.

When one file has the required duration of events scheduled, the routine goes to the next pointer in the list until all sequences have been processed. The idea behind this handling of sequences is that Cypher makes a complete pass through its main loop at least once a second. If all open sequences have one second's worth of events scheduled each time through, they are guaranteed to continue playing until the following execution of schedule_next_second(). The program will never get stuck scheduling all of a long sequence while other processing waits, however, because files are never read all at once (unless they are quite short to begin with). Because scheduling of sequence files is interleaved with all other processing, Cypher can handle the performance of several sequences simultaneously, without a noticeable degradation in its ability to respond to other live input. Similarly, the listener can be pointed at a sequence file, and respond to the music in it through the usual listener/player mechanism, even while it is playing back the original sequence itself.

6.4 Cypher's Composition Hierarchy

We have seen the structure of Cypher's listener hierarchy. Level-1 analyses of individual sounding events are passed up to level 2, which groups them and describes their behavior over time. On the composition side of the program, a similarly hierarchical function can be found. Methods on the first level operate, generally speaking, on individual sound events. Second-level methods are concerned with the direction and regularity of groups of events. This distinction between levels is blurred, perhaps even more so than is the case on the listener side. Level-1 methods often deal with local transitions between groups of two or three notes; level-2 methods could well end up affecting only a single event.

Level 2

Level-2 composition processes are invoked by messages arriving from the level-2 listener and affect the behavior of the composition section over phrase-length spans of time. The messages sent out from the listener have to do with grouping and regularity. The processes on the composition side are clustered around those types of messages and effect various kinds of change to the musical flow. One common strategy on level 2 is to make and break connections between features and transformations on level 1. This is a good way to achieve the complement to some kind of behavior observed by the listener. Reports of regularity for some feature, for example, could be met by processes generating change in the same domain. Another strategy is to mutate the level-1 transformation modules; control variables relevant to the transformation method can be changed according to the nature of the input being reported by the listener and the current state of the variable. For example, the accelerando module can be made to accelerate its input more or less than it already does as a function of the speed feature found by the listener and the accelerando rate currently active.

Level 2 is also the appropriate place to perform processes of expressive variation, which extend across groups of sounding events. Variation in timing or loudness can be used to accentuate structural boundaries between events as they are produced. The ideas of second-level composition are closely allied with the concerns of level-2 analysis: the regularity, or types of change, of collections of events; the grouping together of such collections; and the direction of regular change are attributes to be generated in the music emanating from processes on the second level of the composition section.

Descriptions of implemented level 2 composition processes follow:

VaryDensity
This process is used to establish and break level-1 connections between the density features and certain transformations. It will be invoked by whichever level-2 listener message is connected to it; then the process examines the featurespace classification to determine if the current input is a chord or single note. If it is a chord, a level-1 connection will

be drawn between the chord feature and the arpeggiation transformation. If the input is a single note, a level-1 connection will be drawn between the line feature and the chord transformation. In other words, the density of the input to the listener will be reversed in the Cypher composer's output.

UndoDensity
This method disconnects all level-1 methods from the vertical density features, so that no transformations will be invoked from the *line* or *chord* classifications. This method can be used, for example, to cancel the effect of *VaryDensity*. Regular behavior of some feature could be used to call *VaryDensity*, establishing density-activated transformations on level 1. Irregular behavior of the same feature might be tied to *UndoDensity*, causing all level-1 density-activated transformations to cease.

Phrase
Primarily used as a way to mark phrase boundaries. When invoked, the routine sends out a loud MIDI event and adds a significant delay to the offset of an event block about to be played, emphasizing a potential phrase boundary. The method is designed to be called by the *Phrase* method on level 2; that is, whenever the phrase agency detects a phrase boundary, a message identifying the boundary will be sent out. If *Phrase* is hooked up to that message, it will announce the arrival of the boundary with an audible bang.

JigglePitch
This method sends out a single event, containing one pitch placed randomly anywhere in the keyboard range, every seventh time it is invoked. All other invocations will have no effect. *JigglePitch* is most often used for "jiggling" composition methods that may be stuck in a repetitive pitch pattern or area and so can be profitably connected to level-2 listener messages denoting regularity.

MakeBass
MakeBass establishes a connection on level 1 between the *all* message and the *basser* transformation module. Connecting a player process to the *all* message means that the player process will be called for every input event, no matter what its features. The *basser* module queries the chord agency for the root of the current harmonic area, then plays out

a single event, containing the root pitch, in the octave two below middle C.

BreakBass
The *all* message on level 1 is disconnected from the *basser* transformation module. *BreakBass* acts as the complement to *MakeBass*, undoing the effect of that module. For this reason, the *basser* module is only disconnected from *all*; any other level-1 features linked to *basser* will remain in force.

BeatPlay
This method looks at the period of the current beat theory and schedules bass notes to be played on the beat. If input is arriving, the beat period will be constantly adjusted to match the most recent theory. If no more external information is arriving, bass notes will be continued, using the period from the most recently calculated beat theory.

BeatStop
The complement to *BeatPlay*, this method will stop any currently scheduled beat task from continuing. Again, these methods are paired and are often hooked to opposite poles of irregular/regular messages for some feature. For example, a report of regular speed could trigger the beat player, and a subsequent report of irregular speed could be attached to *BeatStop*, causing all beat activity from the player to stop.

AccMutate
This is the first of a series of mutator processes, which take advantage of mutation facilities built into the transformation modules. *AccelMess* sends a mutate message to the *accelerator* level-1 module to vary the rate of acceleration performed. The new values sent will follow the form of a ramp: they will increase linearly to a maximum of around 450 (which will be the number of milliseconds subtracted from event offsets by the *accelerator*), jump back down to 100, and increase slowly from there again.

SawMutate
SawMutate is another mutation process, this time sending messages to the level-1 *sawer* module. *Sawer* will change the width of sawtoothlike ornamentations in response to mutate messages. *SawMutate* changes this width randomly, up to a maximum of two octaves.

Introspection

One easily detected, but nonetheless crucial, condition for the program to notice is when the music coming from the outside world has stopped. Among the possible causes of such a condition are that the piece is over, players are stopping a rehearsal to discuss the performance, the building is on fire, or that it is time for the computer to take a solo. Cypher is an enthusiastic soloist: it always takes the absence of other input as a signal that it should play more.

Since the most common generation method for the composition section involves transforming received input, the absence of any input would seem a crippling limitation. When performing alone, Cypher's composer continues generation by transformation through the simple expedient of transforming its own output. This method of soloistic generation I call composition by *introspection*. Music is generated from a controlled feedback loop: the player produces some output, which is analyzed and characterized by a listener. The listener sends messages to the player about what it has heard (in other words, what the player just produced), and the player is instructed, through the connections between listener messages and composition methods, to transform its own previous output in some way. The feedback path from the player to the listener is indicated with a heavy black line in figure 6.16.

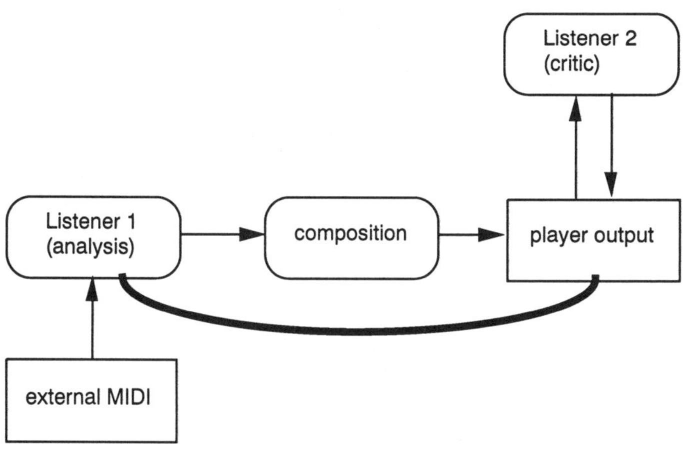

Figure 6.16

Introspection is a way for the user to control the connection of listener messages to composition methods. This facility provides another type of interaction with the program, allowing a human director, or a script of connection sets, to regulate the performance of Cypher during computer solos. Applying the transformations to their own output turns out to be an interesting way to observe their effect. Feeding back on themselves, many transformations lead to registral, temporal, or dynamic extremes, where they will remain until something disrupts the state. Using the connection mechanism to reorder the modules called by different configurations of the featurespace provides just such a disruption. Another approach is to mutate the low-level transformations when level-2 analysis finds features behaving regularly. Pinned behaviors are flagged as regular, and a subsequent mutation of the transformations, ordered by the level-2 player, sends output off in another direction.

The Critic

Any number of distinct player streams can be assigned their own Cypher listener. A listener is called with a new event and a pointer to some stream's analysis history. A player stream can emanate from any MIDI source, such as that coming from a human performer, from another computer program, or from Cypher's own player. Cypher's current architecture maintains two listeners, each with its own history. One listener is tuned to MIDI input arriving from the outside world; the other is constantly monitoring the output of the composition section.

We have just reviewed in some detail the process of analyzing a MIDI source, sending messages to the composition section, and producing novel musical material in response. The second listener shown in figure 6.16 represents a compositional "critic," another level of observation and compositional change, designed to monitor the output of the Cypher player and apply modifications to the material generated by the composition methods before they are actually sent to the sound-making devices.

Interactive music systems typically have no way of evaluating their output—the composer/user of such systems steers the program in one direction or another without any way of measuring success other than by ear. One reason the problem has been so neglected is that it is treacherous; evaluating musical output can look like an arbitrary attempt to codify taste. I choose to look at it another way: developing a computer program with a capacity for aesthetic decision making, though it is certainly arbitrary, is interesting in its own right and is valuable for the quality of information that becomes available to the human developer in further evolving the program.

The information provided by the "critic" listener forms the foundation of a rule set governing the featural attributes, grouping, and regularity in the output. The critic functions as a production system: a set of rules controls which changes will be made to a block of musical material exhibiting certain combinations of attributes. Tracing the analysis produced by the critic listener and the changes introduced by the production system, an informed evaluation can be made both of the music being produced by the composition section and of the effectiveness and stylistic traits of the critic.

When a MIDI event has been analyzed by the listener, it is copied into a scratch event block for processing by the composition section. According to the connections established between listener agents and composition methods, events in the block will be modified, or new events will be added. It is possible, particularly during introspection or in communication with another computer program, that events will arrive more quickly than they can be processed. Even more common is the case that the program will generate more data than the sound synthesis gear can produce. For this reason, the program will sample input that is too dense to be treated successfully.

An important function of the critic is to find "interesting" material in the output of the player for further manipulation by the composition methods. When performing introspectively, Cypher often must sample material generated by the player. When tracking a human performer, the program is almost always able to keep up with the rate of events arriving for evaluation and response. When the program begins to perform through introspection, analyzing and transforming its own output, however, data can easily begin to arrive with so much density that sending out transformations of it all would swamp both the synthesis gear and the comprehension of the listener. (The same observation holds for any input with a high enough density of events; introspective composition is the most common case, but others, such as input arriving from another computer program, are handled in the same way.) Therefore, the critic needs to select events from the wealth of material emanating from the player, which are then analyzed and used to germinate a fresh round of compositional processing.

To select interesting events for further processing, the critic uses the phrase boundary messages coming from the "critic" listener. A listener will identify phrase boundaries in a musical stream by monitoring discontinuities across feature classifications between two events. When discontinuities have arisen in enough features, the phrase agency reports a boundary. The critic listener performs this operation on material coming from the player. Events that the listener identifies as beginning a new phrase are considered "interesting" by the critic and are sent back to the "analysis" listener for another round of evaluation and response.

It may well happen that no phrase boundary is noticed in a block of material. In that case, the critic will select the event with the most differences from its predecessor. Essentially the same criterion is being used: events with many discontinuities relative to the previous event will be marked as interesting. If several events have the same level of difference from their predecessor, the earliest such event will be used.

Already in such a simple application of the critic, we can see that the rules associated with it form, in effect, an aesthetic bias for the program. Declaring events whose feature classifications differ markedly from their predecessor to be "interesting" is no more or less than an aesthetic choice; there is no inherent reason to find any musical event more interesting than any other. Aesthetic biases can be codified in terms of preferred actions to be taken in response to material exhibiting certain kinds of regularity, or feature classifications, or harmonic behavior—in short, preferences can be established for all of the situations reported out of the listener.

Aesthetic Productions

The rule set associated with the critic forms just such a collection of aesthetic preferences, applied to the incipient output of the player. The rules are expressed in the form of a production system: a set of condition-action pairs, where the condition parts are expressed in terms of logical operations on listener messages and the action parts consist of transformations to be applied to the musical material. The productions are applied just before the material is sent to the synthesizers. When events are first scheduled, there is no way of knowing how much additional material will be scheduled to be played at the same time. For that reason, whenever the composition section schedules some new output, it is first sent to a routine called Gather(), which will consolidate events destined for the same point in time. Further, Gather() will arrange for the consolidated material to be sent through the critic one clock tick before the time comes for it to be played.

Here is a simple example: the critic will prefer to reduce the vertical density of material being presented at a high speed (high horizontal density). Such a rule can be expressed as

```
if (FastVal(featurespace) > 2) Thinner(...).
```

The critic first computes the featurespace and regularity words for the event. A set of routines such as FastVal() is available to examine the classifications being returned for any of the level-1 or level-2 features and regularities. In this case, FastVal() will return the value returned by the level-1 analysis for the current event. If this value is greater than 2, the speed of this event has reached the highest possible rate. In that case, the material will be reduced through application of the transformation module *thinner*.

The aesthetic productions held in the critic are now static; that is, Cypher has a particular style that it will enforce on the music it plays. In a full implementation, the critic's rule set should be swapped in and out as a function of the style of music being played to the system. Rather than having a simple set of rules applying to the output of the program generally, specific stylistic rule sets could be invoked for known genres arriving from the outside world.

An extension to the static critic implements this idea: a further set of production rules can be invoked from the interface, or through a command in a score-orientation script. When the additional rules are used, several changes are made to the responses stored in the connections manager according to the characteristics of the music being put out by the composition section. This is another way to approach the manipulation of the player: rather than editing the program's output directly, the way the output will be generated in the first place is changed. Possible manipulations programmed into the action part of these productions include making and breaking level-1 connections, changing the sound banks and timbres used, and reducing the length of time the program will wait before beginning to perform introspectively.

Combination Techniques and the Solo Method

In the preceding review of composition methods, I have roughly divided the algorithms presented into three classes: processes of transformation, of generation, or of sequencing. Another possibility, however, is to construct compositional strategies that combine aspects of all three classes; human improvisation certainly arises from a combination of these. The methods employed most by humans and Cypher are nearly inverted, in that the technique which is most difficult for humans (immediately adopting and transforming the material of others) is what Cypher does best and most often. Human improvisers rely much more heavily on remembered sequences, which can be called up and adapted to different performance situations, and on the manipulation of sets of basic elements (scales, rhythmic patterns). In this section, I will first describe an implemented composition method that incorporates elements of all three algorithmic styles. Then I will review techniques and motivations for building composite players out of several compositional agents.

The *solo* method is available as a level-1 module; however, the algorithm it implements is not a transformation of material presented at the input, as are the other level-1 modules. The only relations *solo*'s output bear to the events in the input block are that it is harmonically related, and its horizontal density in time will tend to increase and decrease along with the density of the input material. In that respect, *solo*'s behavior is related to the transformative class of algorithms we have already extensively considered; it is not, however, strictly a transformation, since the input events themselves remain unchanged. Their only effect is to guide the generation of the module, through their harmonic content and horizontal density.

Solo is a hybrid of the transformative and generative styles: we have already seen the sense in which it is transformative. In fact, that part of the algorithm might more properly be termed simply responsive, since it looks at the input, but does not change it. The output of the module is a monophonic melody; the part of the algorithm that produces pitches generates them from an array of interval preferences, matched against reports coming from the chord agency. This part of *solo*'s operation is more generative, the second algorithmic style included in the module's hybrid form.

Each time it is called, *solo* adds between zero and four new events to each event in the input block. The offset between events will be chosen at random between 20 and 50 centiseconds. An array of intervals helps determine the pitches of the new events, through the following calculation:

```
next = (WhichChord(DUMP, 0)/2)+72+melody[rand()%5];.
```

First, the root of the current harmonic area is determined by querying the chord agency. The answer returned is divided by 2, to discount the mode of the harmony. Then, the root is added to 72, to place the activity of the *solo* module at least two octaves above middle C. Finally, one of the intervals from the melody array is chosen at random and added to the other elements. If the pitch calculated for any event is the same as the pitch of the event before, it is shifted down one half step.

The offsets for all the new events are added together and recorded. If the *solo* module is called again before all of the events from the most recent invocation have been performed, the module returns without producing any new events. It is this part of the algorithm that tends to match the horizontal density of *solo* to the density of the activity around it. Output from the module will never overlap itself; all of the events from one invocation are guaranteed to finish before the next group begins. If the input events are quite sparse, some time will pass before a new event spurs fresh output from *solo*. For inputs beyond a certain density level, however, *solo*'s output will be more or less continuous; a new event triggering more response will present itself quite quickly after any given group has finished playing.

7 Interactive Architectures and Artificial Intelligence

Techniques from artificial intelligence (AI) have been used in musical applications for many years. Each successive wave of AI technology, in fact, seems to find its way into several music programs. Here we will examine some of those efforts, including the influence of AI on the development of Cypher. This will not, however, be an exhaustive review of the many projects combining music and artificial intelligence. Rather, I will concentrate on branches that have already had an influence on the construction of interactive systems or that seem to hold particular promise for such an impact in the short term.

Artificial intelligence has often been attacked for concentrating on the "rational" processes of mind and for being unable to address the more subjective, emotional aspects of thought (Dreyfus 1979). A parallel notion holds that music engages precisely those parts of the mind that can least accurately be modeled formally, again usually termed emotional, irrational, or aesthetic (Clifton 1975). Taken together, these observations would seem to indicate a limited range of application for artificial intelligence techniques in music. A partial reply can be found in Marvin Minsky's essay "Music, Mind, and Meaning": "Our culture has a universal myth in which we see emotion as more complex and obscure than intellect. Indeed, emotion might be 'deeper' in some sense of prior evolution, but this need not make it harder to understand; in fact, I think today we actually know much more about emotion than about reason" (Minsky 1989, 639).

If such fundamental limitations to the operative power of artificial intelligence exist, they should be rapidly exposed in programs attempting to function musically. As we proceed through an examination of several extant systems, we will notice in some cases an unsuspected power of traditional formal techniques, and in others, new hybrid models that combine logical operations with non-rule-based components. To be sure, widespread limitations and compromises surrounding the musical intelligence of these efforts will be noticed as well. As attempts to implement musicianship in computer programs continue, interactive music systems may well serve to demonstrate empirically the power of formalized thought for the representation and generation of music; for some time to come, the failures may be as instructive as the successes in this regard. Further, the compartmentalization of cognition into "rational" and "emotional" components could become blurred as well, if those "emotional" thoughts prove to be at all amenable to treatment by techniques generally regarded as purely "rational." In fact, some practitioners regard the confrontation with a computer performer as a stimulus to exploration of the irrational:

> My approach to the art of musical improvisation is concerned with developing the musically expressive resources of one's unconscious mind. During an improvisation, which can begin without any preconceived score or plan, the unconscious mind of a performer generates an initial act or gesture, expressed sonically through the vocal or instrumental medium. As it evolves, the improvisation develops as a kind of dialogue between the freely associative unconscious mind and its sonic manifestations, mediated by the physical actions of the performer.
>
> Musical improvisation within the medium of live electronics can have the effect of further objectifying and detaching the perceived, sounding image; the image becomes detached both from its unconscious source and from the physical actions employed in its production. The "electronic double" takes on a life of its own—physically displaced in space, often amplified larger than life, perhaps costumed in new modulations, distortions and syntheses. (Teitelbaum 1991)

7.1 Cypher Societies

I will begin with a review of the borrowings from artificial intelligence found in Cypher. The most pervasive influence should be mentioned first: the theory of intelligence and cognition put forward by Marvin Minsky in his book *The Society of Mind* (Minsky 1986). The central idea of Minsky's theory is that the performance of complex tasks, which require sophisticated forms of intelligence, is accomplished through the coordinated action and cross-connected communication of many small, relatively unintelligent, self-contained agents.

Similarly, the basic architecture of Cypher, on both the listening and playing sides, combines the action of many small, relatively simple agents. Agencies devoted to higher-level, more sophisticated tasks are built up from collections of low-level agents handling smaller parts of the problem and communicating the progress of their work to the other agents involved. We have seen in the discussion of the listener, for example, that the process of chord identification is accomplished by an agency of interconnected feature classifiers and harmony experts.

This chapter will discuss in depth the design of an agency-based program architecture, describing the methods of communication and coordination that go into building high-level processes from smaller agents and the way a particular view of musical comprehension and composition is captured by such a design. First we will review in some detail the basic construction of the program and the representations used for various tasks. Gradually, a picture showing the cooperation of many agents will emerge, enabling us to look at the shared responsibility for various tasks spread through the program.

Feature Agents

When a Cypher event is sent to a listener, first of all a collection of low-level feature classification agents is trained on it. These agents can be considered independent of one another, at least at this stage.

Cypher events are built from incoming MIDI data, and can represent either single notes or chords. In figure 7.1, we see three feature agents analyzing a new Cypher event. (In this and all subsequent illustrations, the arrows indicate the direction of information flow. In figure 7.1, information from the Cypher event is going up into the feature agents.) The three features shown (density, register, and dynamic) are all calculated at attack time. Only one of them is context dependent and therefore requires access to memory: the scale against which the register classification is made has been established by the analyses of preceding events.

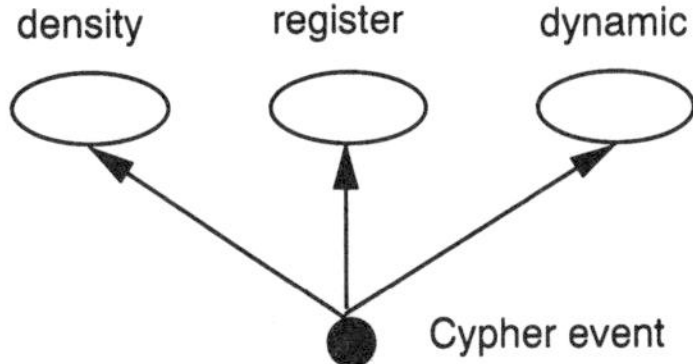

Figure 7.1

In the expanded figure 7.2, the context of previous events has been added. The register agent, then, classifies the new event within the context established. The duration agent, moreover, depends directly on earlier events to perform its analysis task. In another expansion of the original processing diagram (figure 7.3), we see the addition of two more feature agents: one measuring the speed of attacks and the other tracking duration.

The speed agent classifies the temporal distance between two events and therefore relies on one event before the current one to make its calculation. Accordingly, the very first speed classification will be meaningless, since it only measures the length of time between the beginning of program execution and the performance of the first note. An even greater reliance on previous information is shown by the duration agent: because featural classification is done at attack time, it is impossible to analyze the eventual length of the new event. For that reason, the duration classification for the *previous* event is included in the current report.

Rather than being a limitation, this procedure seems to reflect the way music is actually heard; the program will react to the duration of

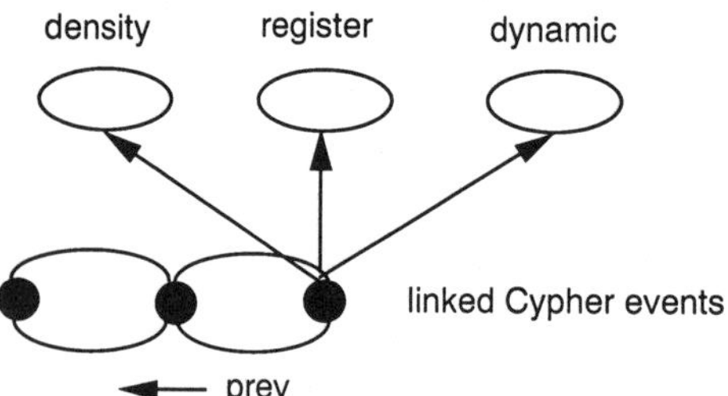

Figure 7.2

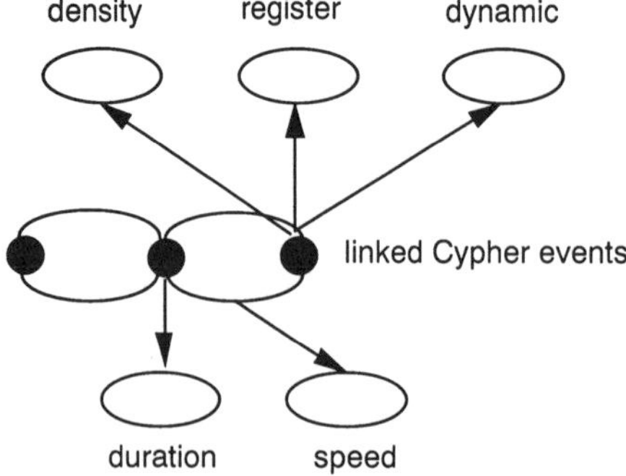

Figure 7.3

events closer to their release than to their attack. It can happen, however, that a new event will arrive before the previous one has been released. Each event is assigned a provisional duration at attack time. In the situation just mentioned, the provisional duration will be the one analyzed for the last complete event; even though this duration may correspond to an event played some significant amount of time previously, it will still have more resonance with the current context than would some arbitrary constant.

Chord Agency

The next step in the classification of an input event is the local harmonic analysis. Although the sequence of level-1 listening is presented here as a serial process, note that all of the analyses described so far could be done by the same collection of agents working in parallel. As shown in figure 7.4, the chord agency accesses the new Cypher event directly to find the values of the pitch information associated with it. At the same time, the other featural agents report their classifications of the event to the chord agent, guiding the evaluation of the raw pitch data. The chord agency uses a connectionist network to find a plausible root for the incoming pitches. The network is assisted by the feature agents, whose reports will change the weights associated with certain pitches according to their classifications. As an example, recall that pitches with a low register classification will tend to receive more weight than pitches higher in the range.

The formation of an agency incorporating a specialized, connectionist network, informed by the reports of other agents, gives the first real ordering to the processing of the level-1 listener. The low-level, perceptual feature agents (register, density, etc.) must complete their work before they can accurately inform the chord agency of their classifications. In a parallel implementation, then, a two-stage process would result: first, the feature agents arrive at their classifications in parallel; then, the chord agency accesses those classifications and the raw note data to find the dominant pitch of a local harmonic area.

Local Memories

The agency responsible for detecting beat periodicities shows an organization strongly paralleling that of the chord agency. Once again, a connectionist core is informed by featural agents, such that certain

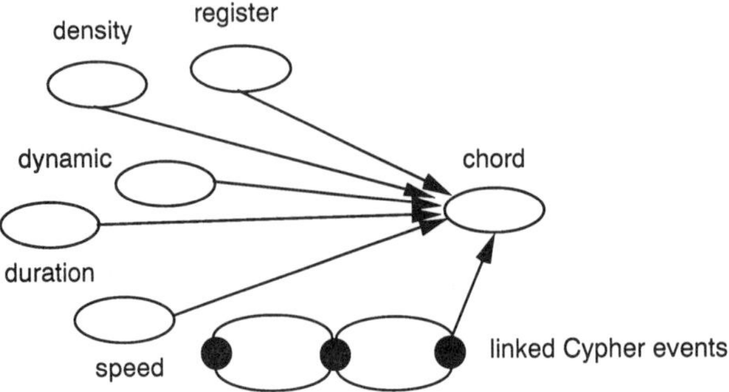

Figure 7.4

weights will be altered according to the classifications reported. Both the beat agency and the chord agency maintain separate, private memories, which record the activation levels of various theories. Further, there may be several copies of the listener active at the same time, and each copy will maintain separate memories for its constituent agencies.

For every distinct stream, the beat and chord agencies communicate results with each other. In figure 7.5, we see the beat and chord agencies, each coupled with its own local memories and receiving information from the low-level feature agents. Again, this organization reinforces the pattern of two-stage processing on level 1 that we noted earlier: first the perceptual feature agents (register, density, etc.) arrive at independent classifications. Information from these features, from the raw event data, and from the other second-stage agency are processed by the chord and beat agencies after the perceptual agents have finished, making use of contexts recorded in their local memories.

Mutual Reinforcement

In figure 7.5, we see the first two-way connections, signifying communication paths where each end can be the source or destination of information traveling across the connection. Obviously such communication holds between an agency and its memory; the presence of two-way communication between agencies, such as between the chord and beat agencies, is a more problematic issue.

When two agencies are cooperating, making their calculations interdependent, a situation arises in which the ordering of execution and communication between the two sides becomes unclear. In the case of

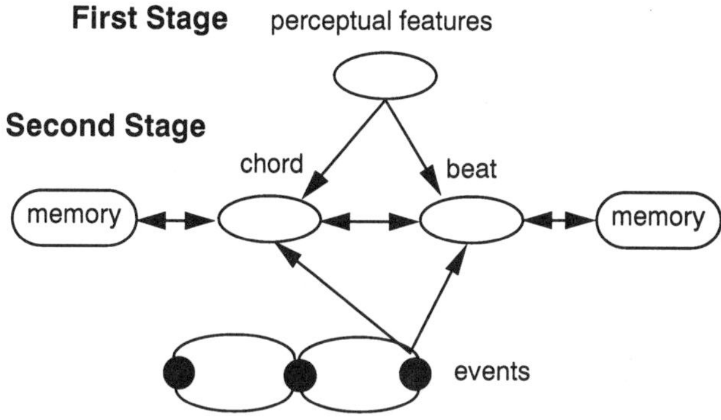

Figure 7.5

the beat and chord agencies, certain types of results arrived at by either agency can further some interpretation calculated by the other. If the beat agency reports that a new event was on the beat, the pitch information associated with that event is given more weight by the chord agency. Conversely, if the chord agency finds evidence of a new local harmonic area, that finding tends to influence the beat agency to find a beat boundary. The problem then becomes one of deciding which agency should have a stronger influence on the other or what message should be passed in which direction first.

In this case, a plausible way to arbitrate the communication between the chord and beat agencies is to use the confidence levels each of them maintains: messages with a high confidence rating are given more weight by their recipient than low-rated messages. Still, the question of execution order remains. Because the interagency influence is mutual, there is no clear way to decide whether partial results should be communicated from the chord agency to the beat agency first, or vice versa.

In a single processor implementation, like this one, the question must be decided: in Cypher, the beat tracker sends a message to the chord identifier first, followed by a message in the opposite direction. I regard a beat boundary as stronger evidence for the significance of the associated harmonic information than I regard the identification of a new chord as evidence for a beat boundary. Further, the beat tracker is making predictions about the arrival of the next beat. The chord agency can therefore plausibly influence the belief in the beat prediction after an initial estimate has been made. The processing chain proceeds as follows: the beat tracker uses the event and feature data to make an initial prediction, and to classify the current event as on or off the beat. Second, the chord agency decides on a classification, referencing the beat tracker's *onbeat* decision. Third, a change in chord will send a message to the beat tracker, altering the confidence in the current theory according to whether or not the chord change coincided with a beat boundary.

Attachment of Classifications

At this point, the raw Cypher events processed so far are assigned a featurespace classification, which records values for the perceptual features and local harmony. In figure 7.6, the featurespace word is shown as an added layer of information surrounding the original event. Attaching the classification to the event allows us to accomplish two objectives: (1) detailed information about the nature of the event is made available to level-2 processes, which observe the way such information changes over time, and (2) the judgment of all individual agents concerning an event can be ascertained by referencing it, to further the processing of any agency which might require the information.

Basically, there are two ways to implement the connectivity of agents into larger agencies: either the results of the agent can be broadcast through messages to all concerned agencies, or the results can be attached to the event being analyzed, where it is available to any interested party. The first method is advantageous for parallel architectures, when the results can be sent out to many processes working simultaneously; the second is more efficient for serial implementations, where the desired result can be simply read off of the event, rather than obtained through a message.

In figure 7.6, notice the addition of two agencies, one that tracks key (the phrase-level harmonic analysis) and another that looks for phrase boundaries. Again, these agencies maintain local memories, which are also kept distinct per event stream. In other words, the key agency has access to a local memory, which communicates with no other process. Further, there are separate local memories for the key agent associated with all active event streams. In Cypher, then, there will be two local memories for the key agency, because there are two active listeners: one corresponding to the stream of events coming from the outside world, and another associated with the event stream produced by the composition section. The key agency is involved in a mutual commu-

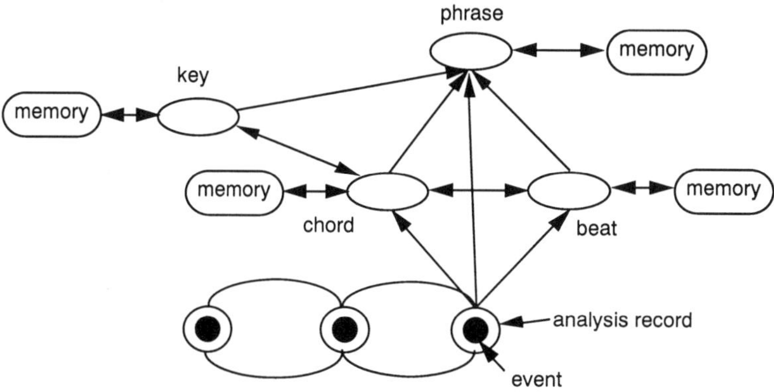

Figure 7.6

nication link with the chord agency; the phrase finder communicates with chord, key, and beat, as well as referencing the featurespace classification for the current event—thereby effectively communicating with the feature classification agents as well.

The information attached to Cypher events is one of the fundamental representations of music used by the program. Representational and processing choices make some conceptions of music easily expressed, whereas others can be approached only with difficulty. The featurespace representation, which plays such a fundamental role here, tends to treat parameters of the sound-pressure waves carrying musical percepts as central. Register, loudness, and density are all primary components of the representation.

Level 2

The listener on level 2 characterizes the way lower-level classifications change over time. The analysis record attached to each Cypher event is used to make this calculation, and the results are added to it as well. In figure 7.7, notice that the regularity detection agent has been added to the picture of the listener.

The regularity agent refers to the featurespace word, the difference between the current featurespace and the previous one, the running statistics of classification change during the current phrase, and the chord, key, and phrase agencies. A detailed description of how this analysis works can be found in chapter 5: the point to be noticed here is the connectivity and quasi-hierarchical arrangement of the various

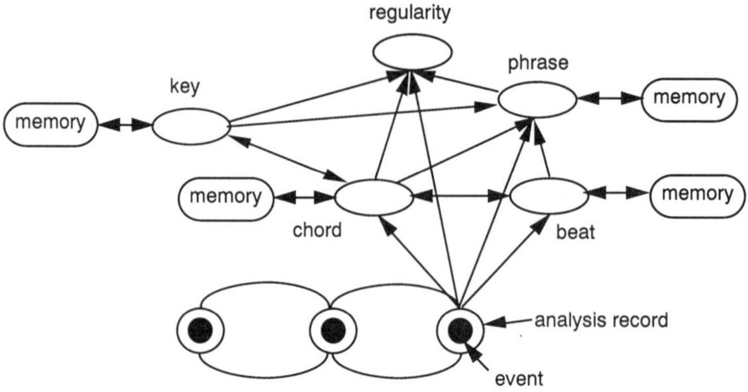

Figure 7.7

processes involved in a listener. The important characteristics of this architecture are preservation of the progressive perspective—that is, continual access to information associated with events proximate in time; maintenance of local memories on a per-stream basis for each agency; mutual reinforcement of cooperating agencies; and the attachment of analytic results to the events classified, where they can be read by other interested processes.

The illustration in figure 7.7 provides a reasonable picture of the architecture of Cypher's listener. However, it is at a significant level of abstraction. As we have built up this picture, lower-level details (such as the feature agents) have been boiled down to the analysis record attached to the original events. With the understanding that the figure is a useful reduction of the entire collection of calculations carried out, we see the real outline of the type of organization I referred to earlier as a "layered network." Recall the claim that the listener embodied a hierarchical analysis of an event stream but that the hierarchy was treelike in only a very restricted sense. Here we see the structure behind the claim: the organization can be considered hierarchical in the sense that the regularity description subsumes individual events in a characterization of a group of events. At the same time, the progressive and communication links between events and the processes analyzing them render the architecture as a whole more like a network of interconnected agents. And this is only half of the story. Next we will look at composition networks and will finally sketch the structure encompassing both competences.

7.2 Composition and Communication

In chapter 6, we examined the building blocks of compositional networks as they are constructed in Cypher. In this section, we will consider in more depth the nature of the networks linking these blocks together. Recall that there are three strategies available for generating music from the composition section: playing sequences, generating new material, or transforming received material. In contrast to the parallelism of the listener, compositional agencies built from these elements tend to link many processes together in chains, with the music that is generated being passed along from one link in the chain to the next.

Serial Processing

The way several transformations of some material are invoked is the most obvious manifestation of the chainlike behavior of many Cypher composition networks. When several transformations are due to be applied to a block of events, they are executed in series, with the output of one transformation passed along to the input of the next (figure 7.8).

It is remarkable that the processing networks on the composition side are organized so differently from those of the listening side. Both competencies use many small agents to build up more complex behaviors, but on the listening side these can operate largely in parallel, whereas on the composition side they function largely in series. A reliance on the idea of transformations engenders such a structure. Applying a set of transformations to some base material in parallel is, first of all, not possible on the current hardware platform, and, second, would produce highly variable results from event to event. We have already seen that the order of transformations can make a big difference in the eventual result; transformations all operating on the same material in parallel would have no fixed order, and the sounding result at the output would show wide deviations for even identical input material.

Figure 7.8

With the model of composition implemented in Cypher, there really is no way around a significant amount of serial processing; however, the real interest of the composition section lies in the way decisions are made to apply some transformations and not others, and in the way some material is chosen as the basis for transformation. The way these decisions are expressed, evaluated, and altered is where the parallelism of the architecture as a whole again comes into play. In the next section, I will explore the question of how the operation of one or more listeners is coordinated with that of the composer.

Execution Conditions

A Cypher listener performs several levels of analysis and maintains a record of the classifications calculated for many different musical features and their behavior over time. The record containing this information is sent on to a process that organizes the invocation of composition methods, making the output of all listener components available for compositional decisions. According to the response connections established between incoming listener messages and composition methods, anywhere from zero to a dozen or more methods will be called in series, in the order of their priority.

In figure 7.9, we see on the left a stylized version of the listener representation built up in the previous sections. At the bottom of the listener we see incoming events, with their attached analysis records. The *connections manager* box is receiving the analysis record for the current event. According to the connections maintained there, certain transformations will be called up and ordered by priority. These are

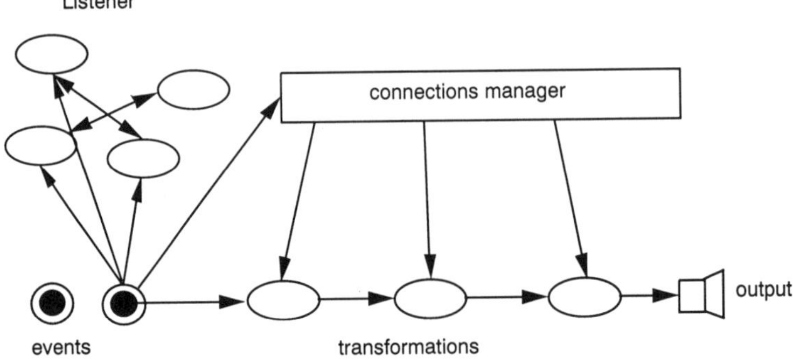

Figure 7.9

then applied to the same input event classified by the analysis record, and the result of all transformations is sent on to the output. In this example, the seed material for transformations is the input itself; another function called by the connections manager might decide to choose other material as a base, in response to some listener message.

The connections between listener messages and composition methods are established as logical expressions on the features and regularities reported by the listener. Consider the following example: High OR Loud → Trill. Here, the *triller* transformation is queued up to be applied to some seed material, if the analysis record associated with the current event shows the event to be either high or loud. The job of the connections manager, then, is to parse and evaluate the logical expressions on the left-hand side of such a connection and prepare for execution the appropriate composition methods found on the right-hand side.

The connections as represented on the graphic interface allow only inclusive OR as a logical operator. Attaching two features to some method means that when one or the other feature is found, the method will be readied for execution. Any number of features can be tied to responses in this way; however, they are all related to each other by this OR relation. The interface is not, however, the only way to specify connections. The scripts of response connections executed during score orientation allow the connections manager to be programmed using a slightly wider range of logical operators. Through the script mechanism, inclusive OR and NOT operators are available for connecting any feature or regularity report to a method. For each feature, the connection manager searches two lists: if the feature is asserted in the analysis record for the event under consideration, all methods in the OR list will be queued for execution. If the feature is negated in the analysis record, all methods in the NOT list are readied.

The full range of logical expressions should be supported by the connections manager. The path to completing it is clear; what we need is a fully developed parser, a compact representation of the notated expressions, and extensions to the connection manager that, for each incoming event, would evaluate the appropriate parts of the analysis record to see if any active expressions are satisfied. Further, full nesting of expressions should be handled by the same mechanism, so that compound statements such as (Soft OR High) AND NOT Fast could be specified as well.

Aesthetic Productions

Another component in the collection of processes establishing interaction between listening and composing has been added to figure 7.10. The listener/connections manager interaction described in the previous section is shown at the left of the figure. Now, we see two more stages added between the transformations applied by the connections manager, and the output of data to the synthesizers: first, a second copy of the listener analyzes the output emanating from the collection of methods called up by the connections manager. This second copy of the listener is labeled "critic" in the figure. Actually, the second listener is only half of the critic. The other half is made up of the rules shown in the box marked "productions." The critic includes a number of production rules, which examine the output of the composition section, and apply further modifications to it when conditions specified in the productions are satisfied.

There are two major differences between the operation of the connections manager and the critic's productions. First, the compositional methods invoked by the connections manager in response to listener messages are specified by the user, either in a script of connections, which is stepped through by the score-orientation mechanism, or by using the graphic interface, which allows the user to draw connections between messages and methods on the screen. The critic, in contrast, maintains a number of rules associating responses with listener messages under certain conditions. These connections, then, are applied automatically according to the musical context. Often, the interface will be used to try out several analysis/response combinations, the

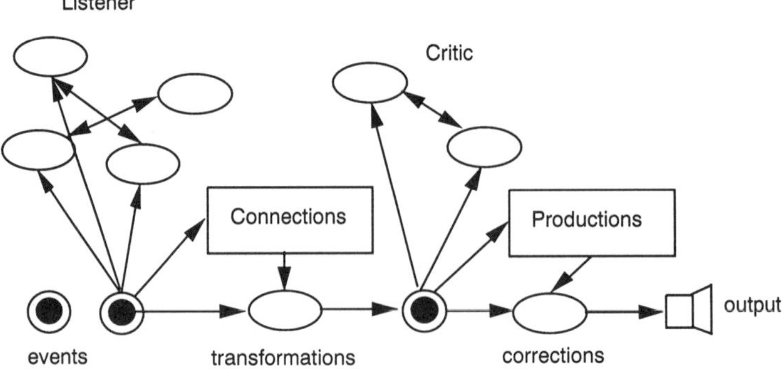

Figure 7.10

most useful of which is saved to the productions for automatic application in performance.

The second difference is that the critic's connection rules can use the full range of logical expressions on listener messages. Whereas the logical operators available to the connection manager are currently limited to inclusive OR and NOT, in the critic any arbitrary expression can be written as the conditional part of a production rule. A set of classification-reading routines can get the analysis results from the information attached to any event. Using these routines, conditional statements such as

```
if ((LoudVal(featurespace)>0) && (RegVal(featurespace)<3))
```

can be written to any level of complexity, taking advantage of the normal C language evaluation mechanisms. The example expression means that the action associated with this condition should be executed if the output of the composition section is louder than the quietest possible value and not in the highest register. Accordingly, critic production rules can be sensitive to more complicated conditions and combinations of input features than can the connections manager links.

7.3 Production Systems

Rule-based, or production, systems rely on a collection of rules with the form if <condition> then <action>. The two halves of production rules are also commonly referred to as the antecedent and consequent parts. In choosing an action to perform, a representation of the current situation will be examined to see if features mentioned in the condition part of the rule are in the state required. If so, the action part of the rule fires and makes some change to the state.

A musical application of this approach is Stephan Schwanauer's *Music Understanding System Evolver* (Schwanauer 1988). MUSE uses a generate-and-test method to perform tasks such as supplying a soprano voice to an unfigured bass. "Generate and test" means that the system first proposes (generates) a partial solution to the problem, such as positing the next note in a nascent soprano line. Production rules then test the proposal and accept or reject it according to the knowledge represented, which has to do with traditional music-theoretic concepts such as voice leading. When a generated step is found defective, another is proposed and evaluated. Sometimes problems are severe enough that several previous steps must be undone, until the system returns to a point where generation can again be continued successfully. These additional generations are known as *backtracking*, which is a common strategy in production systems for working out of failure.

Production systems lead into one of the main subtopics of artificial intelligence: planning. If a robot needs to achieve some goal, it must devise a plan to accomplish it. Production systems are basically a means of satisfying constraints; there are many others. Planning has often been approached from such a standpoint; one of the earliest efforts, hubristically called the *General Problem Solver* (GPS), employed a method henceforward termed *means-ends analysis* to choose a plan of action and execute it (Winston 1984, 146–157). In this scheme, the robot compares the current state of the world with a goal state, and then applies operations in an effort to reduce the difference between the two. In effect, GPS is employing a depth-first search of the state space; when the goal state is found (if it can be found), the search ends. GPS is recursive, in that it applies itself to subproblems as it works through the search. Further, some versions of the technique allow it to defer solving subproblems until an overall solution path has been found—a rudimentary kind of planning.

We can see here an affinity with production systems; a state is examined, and under certain conditions, actions are called up to modify the state. Planning in this sense has been explored in music expert systems, such as Schwanauer's or Kemal Ebcioglu's chorale harmonizer. A GPS-like engine has received little attention in interactive systems, though it might well be a fruitful strategy. One hurdle is that these mechanisms in their classic formulations are assumed to be working outside of real time; backtracking works well when there are no time constraints on producing an action. Production-style strategies can function in real time if one is reasonably confident that correct operations will be chosen at each juncture—in other words, if backtracking is kept to a minimum. The other solution would be to buffer the results of a calculation until all possible backtracking has completed. Although it is interactive, such a solution would not have the immediacy of many systems now in use.

The Max patch of figure 7.11 is a production system reduced almost to the point of caricature. There are two number boxes in the middle of the patch; when the left one is moved, it is compared with the value of the number box to the right. Whenever the left value passes below

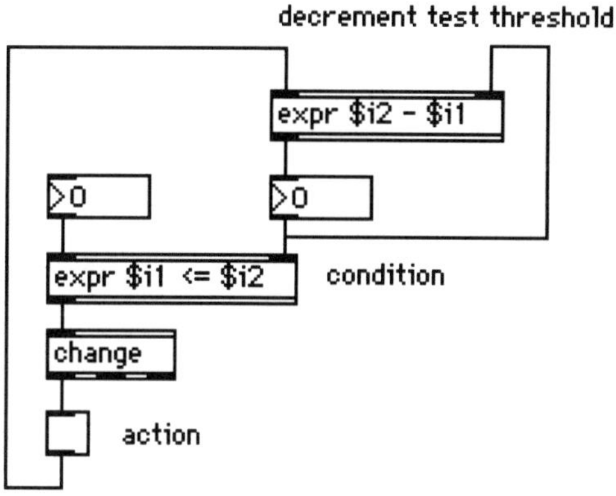

Figure 7.11

the value of the box on the right, the right box's value is decremented by one. Some of the fundamentals of production systems can be seen from this: the state of the system is held in the two number boxes. A test is made on this state, with the *expr* object marked "condition" and the *change* object beneath it. When the left box passes below the right one in value, the condition is true, and a change is made to the state of the system: the threshold value stored in the right box is lowered.

The above patch is caricatural because it has no provision for dealing with error, through backtracking, for example. Further, the maintenance and manipulation of state is an area in which graphic languages built for the control of data flow, such as Max, are less adept than other systems designed for that purpose, such as PROSPECTOR (Duda, Gaschnig, and Hart 1979) or Dendral (Buchanan and Feigenbaum 1978). For that reason, the programs we will now review have been implemented in either specialized production system environments or text-based development languages such as Lisp.

Peter Beyls

Peter Beyls's program *Oscar* is an interactive music system composed of three parts: a pattern-directed inference system, a planner, and an executer. The inference system is a collection of production rules, where the antecedent parts of the rules are patterns stored in the working memory of the program, against which input from the outside world is matched. When a match is found for any production rule, the consequent part of the rule is executed. The program has available a number of methods of response, most of which generate MIDI data and concern such musical issues as melodic contour or variation of incoming material (Beyls 1988).

Beyls has organized the memory of the system into long-term and short-term components. The long-term memory saves melodic intervals. The short-term memory is split into two halves, one maintaining salient events from the input stream and the other recording the recent behavior of Oscar itself. Because the program separates its own behavior from the nature of incoming material, Oscar is able to make comparative judgments about its place in the context. Further, the melodic patterns saved in the long-term memory are sometimes used in conjunction with more recent contours for melodic interpolations. Patterns lying between the two stored melodies are produced to create variations related to but showing novel deviations from already heard material.

Oscar develops opinions about the world in a musical sense, concerning both its own activity and the behavior of stimuli arriving from the outside world. On one axis, the program changes between states of boredom or interest. Interest is excited by unexpected events, while boredom is induced by repetition or the lack of any stimulus at all. On another axis, Oscar is able to adjust its sensitivity to stimuli, producing a fit between the kinds of information being received, and the responses those stimuli evoke. The adjustment of stimulation thresholds implements a process of focus on the strength of musical input, where strength is measured in terms of the stimuli Oscar expects and the ways they deviate from patterns stored in memory.

The planning component maintains a goal state and a list of steps to be taken in achieving it. Each successive step accomplishes a subgoal on the way to the overall desired state. In this respect, the planning part of Oscar uses means-ends analysis. In Oscar this general mechanism is extended to allow interrupts from the perceptual part of the program: if new information arrives that causes a goal to be superseded, the current path may be abandoned for a new line of subgoal processing.

Interactive Production Systems

Rule-based systems have found some use in interactive systems: a notable example is the *Interactor* program designed by Morton Subotnick and Mark Coniglio. In Interactor, scenes are constructed that consist of a set of production rules. The conditions of each rule are matched against the state of MIDI input and the program's internal state: the first rule whose condition matches is executed. One possible action for a rule is to jump to another scene, activating a new set of conditions and actions. The similarity to production systems is limited to the form and processing of the rules; there is no generate-and-test cycle, nor any backtracking.

The ideas of Interactor are evident in such Subotnick works as *A Desert Flowers*, written for chamber orchestra and computer. In performance, the conductor leads the ensemble with a MIDI baton, which is tracked by the computer. The software is able to detect changes in direction, and the velocity with which the conductor moves the baton (Dreier 1991). Further, information from a MIDI piano provides cross-referential confirmation of the ensemble's place in the score. These cues are used to advance the computer processing, through the system of scene changes previously described. Among the manipulations the computer then performs are timbral transformations, spatialization, and harmonic mutation from one synthesized chord to another.

In this limited sense of productions, Cypher can be regarded as another example. The messages from the listener to the player are sent as a function of features found in the environment; certain player processes are invoked when messages corresponding to particular feature configurations are sent. This again is a form of production rule: the <if> part is made up of listener states, and <then> corresponds to the player processes called by the listener. Generate-and-test or backtracking mechanisms are again absent. Cypher is in one respect even further removed from the realm of production systems than Interactor: in the consequent part of a Cypher production, the player processes invoked have no effect on the state examined by the <if> condition. The only exception to this observation arises when the program is running introspectively: then the compositional operations produce events that are fed back into the listener, effecting changes in the state. Two sets of productions are maintained in Cypher. The first set is manipulable directly by the user, either through the interface or through a score-orientation script. The second set makes up the program's internal critic, which reviews output about to be played and alters it according to the production rules representing its aesthetic preferences.

7.4 Knowledge Representation

An important subfield of artificial intelligence known as *knowledge representation* is concerned with methods and structures for capturing and manipulating knowledge. Again, several techniques derived from knowledge representation have been applied to musical problems and have already affected, or seem likely to affect, the evolution of interactive performance as well.

Object-Based Representations

Object orientation is usually recommended as a programming discipline: objects can inherit functionality from one another and can communicate by passing messages that invoke methods local to the receiving object. Max is an object-oriented programming language. Objects are built into larger groups by describing relationships between them. As part of the Kyma system for programming computer music compositions, Carla Scaletti and Kurt Hebel propose an object-based representation for digital audio signals, where a signal is taken to be a sound ranging in complexity from a single sonic event to entire compositions. Sound objects have a duration and a method for computing their next sample. Atomic sound objects compute the following sample directly; compound objects derive a sample from the results of all their constituent atomic objects.

The use of variables within a sound object definition produces *lifted sound objects*. Lifted objects represent a higher level of abstraction than completely instantiated ones (hence they are "lifted" relative to specific objects). By substituting values for the variables of lifted objects, specific objects can be instantiated. Lifted objects therefore represent classes of sound objects, and instances of that class can be produced by substituting values for variables.

Stephen Travis Pope's *Musical Object Development Environment* (MODE), is a large collection of object-oriented software components for composition, performance, and sound processing (Pope 1991a). Like Kyma, MODE uses objectlike structuring for sound and compositional representations. The system combines real-time sampled sound, software synthesis, and interactive performance capabilities on UNIX workstations running Smalltalk-80. Pope has developed MODE as an examplar of a class of interactive systems he calls the *Interim DynaPiano* (IDP), which feature large memories, real-time sampled sound and MIDI drivers, C-based music and DSP software libraries, and interactive graphical software development environments running under a multitasking operating system (UNIX) on a commercial engineering workstation. Kyma also falls into the IDP systems class.

MODE objects can behave differently according to context; for example, the behavior can depend on what the object represents, or on how its value is stored. Sounds are described with such classes as pitch, loudness, and duration. These magnitude models are then represented in several ways, for use in various contexts: Pitch can be accessed as a MIDI key number, a floating point frequency, a note name string, or a harmonic series ratio. Time is represented with relative durations, and as is the case with the other magnitudes, it may be expressed in a variety of ways: "Duration objects can have simple numerical or symbolic values, . . . or they can be conditions (e.g., the duration until some event *x* occurs), Boolean expressions of other durations, or arbitrary blocks of Smalltalk-80 code" (Pope 1991a, 75–76). This flexibility extends to virtually all of the objects MODE includes and allows events, for example, to have as properties envelope functions, digital signal-processing scripts, compositional algorithms, or any other complex behavior that may be appropriate to the kind of musical structure being modeled. MODE and Kyma offer the power and clarity of object-oriented programming environments in the context of interactive performance, giving the system designer (composer) enormous latitude over the behavior and relations of defined musical entities. The reader is referred to Pope 1991b for further information.

Frames

The artificial intelligence community, and several music applications as well, has a long tradition of investigation into the concept of a *frame* (Minsky 1986). A frame is a collection of related information, representing typical features of some situation, that will be used to direct processing whenever a variant of that situation is encountered. A frame consists of a number of *terminals* (or *slots*), which correspond to features usually found in the frame's reference situation. For example, a frame for a chair might have terminals representing legs, a seat, a back, etc. "Much of the phenomenological power of the theory hinges on the inclusion of expectations and other kinds of presumptions. *A frame's terminals are normally already filled with 'default' assignments.* Thus a frame may contain a great many details whose supposition is not specifically warranted by the situation" (Minsky 1985, 246–247).

This observation sparked a great deal of interest in the development of languages such as KRL (Bobrow and Winograd 1977), which facilitate the expression of related information in a frame notation. It is in fact this style of grouping information together, and relating different frames through *frame arrays* (Minsky 1986), or other chunking schemes, that has endured. Patrick Hayes, for example, questions whether the frame proposal ever described a representation scheme: "A more serious suggestion is that the *real* force of the frames idea was not at the representational level at all, but rather at the implementation level: a suggestion about how to organize large memories. Looked at in this light, we could sum up 'frames' as the suggestion that we should *store* assertions in nameable 'bundles' which can be retrieved via some kind of indexing mechanism on their names" (Hayes 1981, 457).

A distinct but related proposal is the *semantic net*, which links concepts through relations of inheritance and specialization. The KL-ONE language (Brachman and Schmolze 1985) was developed to describe semantic nets, and extended by Antonio Camurri and his colleagues for musical purposes in the HARP system (Camurri et al. 1991). An important extension was to include temporal primitives, which allow objects in the system to be situated, and related to one another, in time. For example, music objects in HARP have *begin* and *end* terminals, which can be used to define temporal relations between them.

A basic relation in semantic nets is the IS-A link, which defines some concept as an example of one or several others. For instance, in the HARP knowledge base, a canon at the unison IS-A canon. That is, *canon-at-unison* is understood as a specialization of the more general concept *canon*. *Canon-at-unison* will inherit the terminals of the *canon* concept, with some additional ones describing its specialized function. Another relation associates a terminal with some concept. In the semantic net describing Corrado Canepa's composition *Anceps Imago*, the concept *three-part-concerto* IS-A *compound-music-action*. At the same time, the concepts *1st-part* and *2nd-part* fill terminals of *three-part-concerto*, indicating two of the sections of the piece.

Scripts

The passage of time is a critical concept to be included in any computational model of musical activity. We need to be able to manipulate operations on many temporal levels and to indicate their starting time, duration, rate of speed, etc. A *script* is a representation that defines an ordering for events. A restaurant script, for example, describes the typical situation of entering the restaurant, examining the menu, ordering, eating, paying, and leaving (Schank and Abelson 1977).

For a moment let us consider the generation of a musical phrase, with the realization that similar questions will arise on other temporal levels, such as groups or parts of phrases. If we can specify the kind of motion traversed by the phrase in terms of its harmonic, textural, and rhythmic functions, we can be directed to operations appropriate to it. A cadential phrase could include a pointer to a time map that might shape the rhythmic events to effect a slight ritardando leading to the cadential point. Again we will want to have representations of typical situations, as in the preceding example.

We can combine the idea of a script with that of the frame in a representation known as a *trans-frame*. A trans-frame is a frame including certain kinds of terminals: actor, origin, trajectory, destination, and vehicle are examples. Some questions a trans-frame will be used to address are, "Where does the action start? Where does it end? What instrument is used? What is its purpose or goal? What are its effects? What difference will it make?" (Minsky 1986, 219). Trans-frames represent some kind of transfer or transformation. They would be useful for interactive systems on higher levels of both listening and composing tasks, and for the same reasons: to the extent that a musical discourse shows a goal-oriented behavior, or makes recognizable variants of some preexisting material, such behavior could be represented, at least in part, by a trans-frame representation.

7.5 Neural Networks

The term "neural network" refers to a class of computer programs that learn to associate output states with input vectors, through a network of interconnected processing units whose patterns of connectivity are modified by a learning rule. Other terms describing the same basic idea are "connectionism," or "parallel distributed processing (PDP)" (Rumelhart and McClelland 1986). A neural network is made up of layers of units, or nodes, of which there are at least two: input and output units. Some networks include another layer between these, of so-called "hidden" units. Input units are set to values corresponding to some features of the situation being modeled. Output units reflect the result of the network computation. Hidden units form a layer between the input and output nodes and are not seen by anything outside the system.

Within the system, units have associated with them a level of activation. Activation is propagated between connected units, and an activation rule indicates how the levels of activation arriving from all inputs to a unit are to be combined with the unit's own level to arrive at a new activation state. Depending on the nature of the problem, different numbers of input, hidden, and output units are used. Further, a connectivity pattern will be specified among all units in the system, designating which units will propagate activation to which others.

The simplified network shown in figure 7.12 has three input units, two hidden units, and one output unit. Again, the topology of any working network is determined by the nature of the situation being modeled and the facility with which the network is able to capture the necessary relations. Our example network is fully connected: between successive layers, each lower unit is connected to all the units in the layer above it.

The network in figure 7.12 can be trained to generate values at the output node corresponding to certain sets of three values at the input. The training process involves defining a set of examples showing "correct" associations between input vectors and output values. These examples are presented to the network, where all of the weights on the connections between units are initially random. A learning rule then adjusts the weights on unit connections according to the contribution of each unit to a correct, or incorrect, result. For instance, in the learning regime known as back propagation, the input vector of a training set is presented to the net. According to the activation rule, activation percolates up through the hidden units to the output node. Then, the output value achieved is compared with the desired training value. The difference between the two is used to modify the connection weights in a traversal back down the net. Repeating this process yields a set of connection weights that, if successful, ensures that the network will associate the output values from the training set with the input vectors.

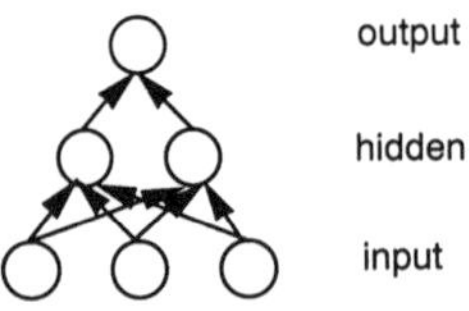

Figure 7.12

An extensive literature on training and using neural networks covers these issues in much greater depth; the reader is referred to Todd and Loy 1991 and Rumelhart and McClelland 1986. What is important to notice here is that neural nets are able to perform tasks such as associative learning, or the discovery of regularity, without rule sets. Everything the system "knows" is captured by the connection weights between processing units. Artificial intelligence has repeatedly run up against the brittleness of rule sets, which are explicitly formulated plans of action that break down when confronted with contexts outside their area of specialized expertise. For some purposes, particularly perceptionlike tasks such as pattern completion, neural networks are able to function well in a variety of contexts, without the rule orientation that can lead to a limiting specialization.

Neural networks have found their way into several music programs, including interactive ones. Michael Lee, Adrian Freed, and David Wessel report on a new Max object developed at the Center for New Music and Audio Technologies, called MAXNet, that performs neural net computations. The net has successfully been trained to recognize gestures from MIDI keyboards, guitar controllers, the Boie radio drum, and the Buchla Lightning controller (Lee, Freed, and Wessel 1991). In the following sections we will look at the application of neural networks to several musical problem areas, particularly as they relate to outstanding problems in interactive music systems.

Modeling Tonal Expectancies

Several researchers have used neural networks to model human perception of tonal relationships. The neural networks at the center of Cypher's chord and key recognition agencies were derived from work reported in Scarborough, Miller, and Jones 1989. Another major contribution can be found in an article titled "Modeling the Perception of Tonal Structure with Neural Nets," by Jamshed Bharucha and Peter Todd (1989). In it they discuss the cognitive issue of acquiring tonal competence—how untrained listeners are able to learn expectations about tonal harmonic relationships in normal Western music. Several perceptual experiments have shown that listeners without musical training are able to recognize departures from normal tonal patterns, identify distance relationships between chords, and decide whether chords are tuned or mistuned. Since this competence did not come from formal musical training, it must have been acquired passively through exposure to numerous examples of the style.

Bharucha and Todd discuss two kinds of expectancy: *schematic* and *veridical*. Veridical expectancies are learned for specific pieces of music. Schematic expectancies are culturally based, arising from the knowledge of typical sequences built from exposure to a number of veridical experiences. Bharucha and Todd were able to train neural networks to exhibit both schematic and veridical expectancies. They take this as evidence for a theory of harmony learning that should supersede rule-based models, because the neural net version acquires expectations through passive learning, rather than by accumulating a collection of ad hoc rules.

The first network they describe maps from some musical scale presented at the input units to the same scale at the output. Once trained, the net can fill in missing tones in the scale when presented with a subset or variation of the scale at the input. Further, such self-organizing networks can learn hierarchical harmonic relationships, such as those arising among tones, chords, and keys. A net called MUSACT, developed by Bharucha, showed emergent recognition of the importance of the circle of fifths in distance relationships between chords in a key (Bharucha 1987).

Bharucha and Todd then trained a sequential network to develop expectancies concerning chord progressions. The network was made sequential as follows: each input node had a self-recurrent connection, with an identical constant weight of between 0.0 and 1.0. The self-recurrent connection fed the activation of each input node back to itself on successive input steps, thereby providing the input layer with a decaying memory of the preceding context. The input nodes corresponded to the six most common major and minor chords of a key. For each successive chord in a sequence, the input node for that chord was activated, and all nodes received their own previous activation level from the previous step, modified by the decay weight on their self-recurrent links.

After training on a number of typical Western harmonic chord progressions, the network developed a schematic expectancy for the probability of some chords following certain others. In other words, for each input chord, the activation of output nodes matched a probability distribution showing the likelihood of the six chord types as a successor. The tonic chord was likely to be followed by the subdominant or dominant, for instance, while the dominant itself aroused a probability distribution strongly favoring the tonic. Whereas the sequential network did not learn veridical expectancies for specific progressions in the training set, it did develop a schematic expectancy for the most probable transitions in Western chord sequences.

The network was then extended to include "additional context" units in the input layer. These context units were clamped to some values uniquely identifying particular chord progressions. With the addition of this information, essentially the name of the sequence being learned, the expanded network could learn veridical expectancies: it predicted successive chords in particular examples. Once a number of examples had been learned, two new sequences were presented to the net: one followed normal harmonic transitions, and the other did not. The net learned the typical sequence much more rapidly than the other, demonstrating the schematic expectancies acquired by the net in the process of learning specific examples.

The work reported by Bharucha and Todd shows that neural networks that learn regularities in harmonic behavior can be developed through exposure to examples in a style. Particularly, networks trained to recognize specific sequences learn normative harmonic behavior as an emergent property. The techniques of neural network design and training tend to be well suited to tasks concerned with recognition, pattern completion, and expectation: Bharucha and Todd have shown that tonal expectancy is one such area in computer-based music perception.

Connectionism and Algorithmic Composition

In work closely related to that reported in the previous section, Peter Todd (1989) developed some sequential net designs for experiments in algorithmic composition. Again, this work was not developed for interactive systems, but could certainly be adapted for such use. Todd notes, "In contrast to the slow learning these networks often exhibit, their performance once trained is practically instantaneous" (Todd 1989, 38). He describes his method thus:

> Our new approach to algorithmic composition is first to create a network that can learn certain aspects of musical structure, second to give the network a selection of musical examples from which to learn those structural aspects, and third to let the network use what it has learned to construct new pieces of music. We can satisfy the first step by designing a network that can exactly reproduce a given set of musical examples, because being able to reproduce the examples requires that the network has learned a great deal about their structure. (Todd 1989, 27–28)

The network Todd used to learn melodic sequences shows some features in common with the tonal expectancy nets reviewed in the previous section. Again *plan units* (called in the other work "additional context" units) are clamped to a unique identifying value for each individual sequence being learned. These plan units allow the net to learn specific progressions, rather than only generalizing from all of the training examples presented. Context is preserved in two ways: First, each input unit feeds back to itself, modified by a decay, so that more recent inputs are represented more strongly than more distant ones. Second, the output units are fed back to the input, eliciting the production of the next pitch in the sequence. During training, the *target* values are fed back to the context units, rather than the outputs. Once the targets are learned, attaching the outputs instead is equivalent, since now the targets and the outputs will be the same. Training proceeds much more quickly, however, if incorrect outputs are not maintained in the context units during each trial (Todd 1989, 37).

Input and output units represent absolute pitches, rather than some more key-independent quantity such as intervals. This is because when the network makes an error in the intervallic representation, the rest of the sequence is suddenly thrown into another key, producing a quite jarring effect. When each unit corresponds instead to one pitch, errors are kept local to one wrong note, rather than affecting the remainder of the example. Duration is represented as well: the output of the network is assumed to be quantized to some minimum time slice. Then, pitches that sound for more than one slice are presented in succession, for the full duration of the note.

Once the network has been trained, it can be made to produce new melodies simply by altering the plan units. We have seen that the plan units identify particular melodies, such that when the plan units have the same values they did during training, the network will reproduce the same sequence of notes. If a network has been trained to produce a single melody, new ones can be made by setting the plan units to some value other than the one used during training. Peter Todd shows examples from this method and another approach in which the network learns several sequences, after which the plan units are varied to produce interpolations between two known melodies.

In my view the fallacy in Todd's compositional model is the belief that "being able to reproduce the examples requires that the network has learned a great deal about their structure" (Todd 1989, 28). This is rougly equivalent to maintaining that a neural network capable of reproducing the letter sequence of a sentence has learned a great deal about what the sentence says. In fact, the net knows virtually nothing about the structure of the passages it has learned, and the shallowness of its understanding is quite clear from the variations produced. Meter, in particular, is ignored by the network; the simple 2/4 meter of the training melodies is routinely changed into essentially random combinations of eighth- and quarter-note durations. Harmonic considerations do not fare much better. Interpolations between two sequences, for example, consist of the beginning of one sequence and the close of the other, with some quasi-random selection of pitches from both in the middle. Peter Todd is correct in noting that the interpolated melodies produce unpredictable combinations of the originals; however, they also bear little relation to traditional variations.

Connectionism and Music Cognition

In his essay "Understanding Music Cognition: A Connectionist View," Christoph Lischka (1991) directly discusses the application of artificial intelligence techniques to modeling music cognition. He is, as a point of departure, skeptical about the theoretical power of music cognition: "Both concepts, music as well as cognition, involve such complexities that it seems hopeless to clarify their mutual interaction" (Lischka 1990, 417). However, positing the view that the very idea of music cognition is culturally conditioned and therefore problematic, Lischka sets out to explore the possibilities for modeling musical thought through artificial intelligence, and, in particular, he examines how some of the underlying assumptions of AI limit the sphere of cognition that can be so treated.

As a case study, Lischka considers the harmonization of Bach chorales. He distinguishes three design paradigms from the AI tradition that might be applied: (1) decomposition of chorale harmonization into subtasks, which are individually solved and put back together for an overall solution; (2) case-based reasoning, in which situations are matched against known cases and the known cases are modified to suit the new problem; and (3) constraint satisfaction, where harmonization is modeled as a network of interacting constraints. Reviewing implementations built using some techniques from all three design paradigms, for instance those of Ebcioglu 1988 and Lischka and Güsgen 1988, Lischka reports, "Our implementation exhibits interesting behavior; the proposed harmonizations, for instance, are (in a sense) correct. But they are not exciting. What is lacking, for instance, is some kind of global coherency. Also, the examples are not very specific to J. S. Bach's practice" (Lischka 1990, 427). He concludes that the difficulty lies in capturing the cognitive processes actually used by expert harmonizers: the techniques reported in knowledge acquisition interviews seem closest to case-based reasoning, but the perceptionlike nature of the thought processes involved makes it extremely difficult to elicit a chain of inference, particularly in the terms required by a symbolic, information-processing model.

Neural net models can skirt the knowledge acquisition problem by providing a system itself able to learn the necessary relations between input and output. Particularly for perceptionlike tasks, neural nets can be trained to recognize contexts and complete patterns—areas where elicitation of rules from knowledge acquisition is notoriously difficult. Rather than accept the relative advance of connectionist models for some kinds of information-processing tasks, Lischka goes on to question information processing itself as a paradigm for cognition. In arguments reminiscent of Winograd and Flores 1986, he notes problems with the information-processing paradigm's reliance on representations, on inference as a general approach to problem solving, and on the idea that behavior can be decomposed into constituent parts approached individually and recomposed into an overall solution. He concludes,

> If we are interested in building truly cognitive systems there is strong evidence to pursue a general paradigm shift. The usual consequence drawn from the previously mentioned insights is to yield to resignation concerning the possibility of AI. The argument runs more or less as follows: Because cognition seems to be inevitably bound to biological organisms, there will be no way to construct artificial systems that exhibit comparable functionality. On the contrary, we think that there exists a much weaker conclusion: Because cognition is probably bound to biological organisms, the only possible way to build artificial cognitive systems is to ground them on artificial organisms. (Lischka 1991, 436)

The research program Lischka proposes to reach a new paradigm involves implementing Piagetian schemata in artificial organisms, where complex behavior will emerge from the interaction of many small, simple elements. Because these interactions are nonlinear in organic systems, precise analysis is impractical. Rather, simulation on massively parallel machines with cellular automata or neural networks would provide a path to implementation. Lischka suggests simulation of the rise of auditory imagery in Piagetian terms, where sensorimotor schemata are interiorized in the development of an inner voice, as a research objective. Such an agenda is certainly not idle speculation; Gary Drescher reports on recent work implementing a Piagetian schema system in a computer program inhabiting a microworld, "The mechanism learns from its experiences by processes of empirical learning and concept invention, and uses what it learns to plan actions, often for the sake of explicit goals" (Drescher 1991, 1). The learning processes embedded in the program develop concepts increasingly independent of immediate perception, recapitulating some of the classic stages in Piagetian development.

Christoph Lischka's provocative essay suggests a direction for AI-based interactive systems that would take the performer paradigm to a new level of independence. We know that many of the techniques he advocates (cellular automata, neural nets, etc.) can, once trained, function in real time. Finding ways to allow such systems to learn their own interactions with the musical world would produce programs that could not only be thought of as separate personalities but that would have ways of interacting with their environment that are unpredictable by their maker; they would truly decide on the basis of their own, nonsymbolic mode of perception, what to make of a musical context.

7.6 Pattern Processing

Pattern processing encompasses two goals: (1) learning to recognize important sequential structures from repeated exposure to musical examples, and (2) matching new input against these learned structures. I will refer to processing directed toward the first goal as *pattern induction*; processing directed toward the second will be called *pattern matching*. In pattern induction, we want to find sequences—strings of numbers representing such things as harmonic progressions, rhythmic patterns, or melodic fragments—that gain significance either through repeated use, or because of their relation to other known structures. Pattern matching, in contrast, is an algorithm for comparing new input to the known sequences found from pattern induction and signaling new instances of the stored strings.

The two kinds of processing have different effects. A successful application of pattern induction will yield a new pattern, to be added to a database, which is retained in the program's long-term memory

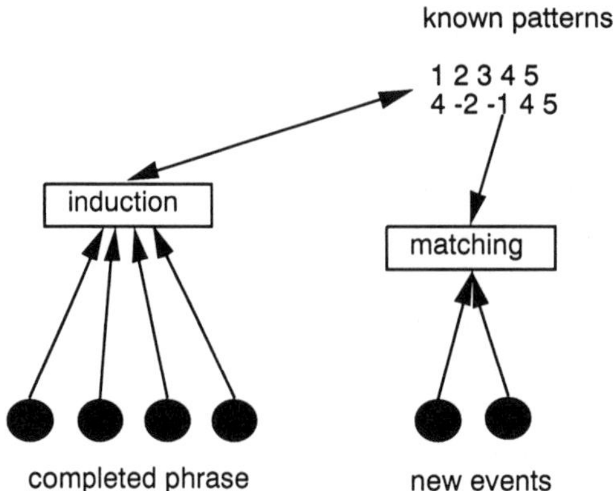

Figure 7.13

from execution to execution. The pattern-matching process can send out several different messages, depending on its progress through a match. For example, the matcher will emit one message at the completion of a successful match, identifying which pattern was found; another kind of message will signal an ongoing match, when the beginning of some pattern has been seen. In figure 7.13, we see the information from a completed phrase being taken up into the induction process, which compares the phrase with known strings and new strings recently heard by the program, to see if the phrase should be added to the database. Pattern matching compares incoming events with the known strings, to see if there is a match.

Precedents of this kind of pattern processing are found in several sources, musical as well as nonmusical. Pattern recognition, a field that would seem to bear a strong resemblance to pattern induction, is in fact quite distinct; pattern recognition's most common area of inquiry is computer vision, and it encompasses several techniques developed for finding objects in a raw image. The patterns dealt with here differ in two important respects from vision problems: first, the patterns we seek to find are played out over time, and second, our patterns gain significance through repetition and their resemblance to known structures, rather than through the intrinsic qualities of any individual instance. Similarly, strict matching of precisely defined patterns is only a beginning for the processing needed to deal with musical sequences. Deviations from an exact repetition of stored patterns can arise from many causes, and a musical pattern matcher needs to be able to accommodate them: examples could include transposition, change in ordering, omissions, and variations.

Cope

In our parlance, pattern induction is the assertion that certain sequences of numbers have been repeated to such a degree that they should become marked as significant and remembered for later use. David Cope's *Experiments in Music Intelligence* (EMI) are an example of pattern induction in this sense: large samples of music from particular composers are analyzed by the program to extract patterns, or "signatures," that exceed frequency thresholds maintained by the software. "This article assumes that 1) pattern matching is a powerful technique to use in attempting to discover some of the reasons why composer's styles sound as they do; 2) patterns judged as alike which occur in different works of a composer are valuable and constitute what the author will call signatures; 3) re-using such signatures in music composed following standard chord protocols and voice leading can lead to replications in the style of the composer" (Cope 1990, 288).

In Cope's view, culling patterns from large collections of data representing several examples of a particular composer's work captures significant features of that composer's style. Demonstrations of the learned styles are built by pressing signatures into a prepared substrate of tonal material. For example, an EMI composition in the style of Mozart begins with a template of textbook sonata-allegro form and adds signature patterns such as motives and cadences to provide the proper Mozartian stylistic traits.

What I call induction Cope refers to as matching: the heart of his system is a group of routines that exhaustively search number sequences to find repeated series. The number sequences that are processed represent chains of intervals. The first step in the induction process reduces strings of pitches to strings of the intervals separating those pitches. In this way the same material beginning on different scale degrees will have an identical, intervallic representation. Cope's algorithm then performs an exhaustive search of melodic sequences to find those considered identical, within certain tolerances.

One tolerance he uses is a *range tolerance*, which will allow intervals falling within the specified range to match. During the search part of the algorithm, each successive interval in the two strings being matched is compared. Identical intervals will, obviously, be considered a match; intervals whose absolute difference does not exceed the range tolerance will match as well. For example, setting the range tolerance to 1 will produce matches between major and minor mode versions of a melody, because the scale degrees of the major and minor modes usually differ by no more than one half step.

Another tolerance, or "tuner," as Cope calls them, is the *error tolerance*, which is the maximum number of times interval matches can fall outside the bounds of the range tolerance without aborting the match as a whole. If the error tolerance is nonzero, patterns with some small number of significant deviations in intervallic structure will still be recorded as patterns. This tuner allows variants of some sequence to be recognized as similar, where the variations go beyond the simple major/minor discrepancies handled by the range tolerance.

David Cope's EMI experiments are interesting because they implement a proven method for finding significant sequences, where significance is regarded as a function of frequent repetition—in other words, an algorithm for pattern induction. This evaluation is somewhat different from Cope's own; he considers the program to be finding fundamental elements of a composer's style. That claim I find overblown: style is a combination of processes operating on many levels of harmonic, rhythmic, and formal structure. Cope's signatures correspond, in my view, to an inventory of a composer's clichés rather than to the essence of her style.

Simon and Sumner

In their 1968 article "Pattern in Music" Herbert Simon and Richard Sumner outline a method of describing alphabets and their manipulation that represents significant features of temporal sequences. Moreover, Simon and Sumner consider patterns to be among the fundamental structures of music cognition and in particular to be a strong determinant of the expectations and goal-directed motion that are a basic part of the experience of Western music. "We are led by these studies to conclude that pattern-seeking is a common activity of people faced with temporal sequences, and that the vocabulary, or stock of basic concepts they have available for describing patterns is parsimonious, involving only a few elementary notions together with rules for combining them, and also is relatively independent of the specific stimulus material" (Simon and Sumner 1968, 222).

Simon and Sumner's agenda assumes that patterns are the primary building blocks of music—if an exacting notation of patterns and transformations could be developed, entire pieces of music could be described and generated from their basic pattern structure. Though I regard pattern processing as one perspective on musical experience, which only gains coherence in conjunction with other modes, I am nonetheless struck by the terms they employ to describe patterns and their function in music:

> Patterns involve *periodicity*—repetition (in a generalized sense) at intervals that occur periodically (in a generalized sense). Patterns make use of *alphabets*—sets of symbols ordered in a definite sequence. Patterns can be *compound*—made up of subpatterns which can themselves be represented as arrangements of symbols. Patterns generally possess *phrase structure*, which may be explicitly indicated by various forms of punctuation. Patterns, as we have already seen, may be *multidimensional*. Repetition in pattern generally involves *variation*. (Simon and Sumner 1968, 228)

Their treatment of patterns comprises two stages of processing, which bear some resemblance to my own: the first is called *pattern induction*, finding structure in a sequence of elements (I have adopted their terminology for an analogous operation). The second process is termed *sequence extrapolation*, the generation of an extension to some pattern according to the structure found through pattern induction.

"The pattern inductor may be thought of as a 'listener,' since it accepts the music (or the score) as input, and detects the melodic, harmonic, and rhythmic relations implicit in it" (Simon and Sumner 1968, 244). The work reported in this article is an intriguing approach to pattern processing, which relates the cognitive machinery of music perception to such tasks as letter sequence completion. I think, however, that the "magic bullet" status Simon and Sumner accord to pattern processing is too optimistic: the predictive power they describe accounts for only a part of the full experience of music. Their technique, in particular, does not learn or retain any sequences, regardless of their importance or frequency in the examples it has seen. Moreover, it is not clear how their rules should be applied in real time; the rules for finding phrase boundaries, for example, require much more backtracking than is possible for a system trying to find boundaries as they occur.

CompAss

The CompAss project developed at the Institut für Informatik in Stuttgart is a system for editing musical compositions on the phrase level (Mahling 1991). Built on top of Smalltalk-80, CompAss includes two groups of editors: the first group is used to modify time-independent relationships between musical objects, and the second group defines a composition's form. The time-independent editors are coordinated in a PhraseStructureEditor window, allowing different views on musical objects. The output of some chain of operations can be seen, for example, in common music notation, or a MIDI event list. A PhraseArrangementEditor window manages the second group of editors, laying out in time the phrases defined with the first group.

Musical objects are organized into a hierarchical knowledge base, in which concepts are related to one another through taxonomy networks and *PlayContexts*. A *PlayContext* provides all the information necessary to perform a composition from the computer system, including MIDI-level details such as synthesizers and program changes. The processing layer provided by a *PlayContext* reinterprets MIDI information coming from the rest of the system according to the nature of the device to which it is routed. For example, Note On messages routed to synthesizers will have the customary effect. The same messages routed to a drum machine will select different drum sounds by the pitch number. Note On messages routed to a MIDI mixer will select channel numbers through the pitch field and fader settings with the velocity value.

The analytical function of CompAss is meant to abstract essential characteristics of musical phrases from several examples. The abstracted patterns are found by a procedure called *constant matching*. In constant matching, two phrases are compared with each other. Any elements that differ between the two phrases are replaced with variables. This procedure can be continued with any number of example phrases: the pattern abstracted is guaranteed to match all examples from the training set. CompAss uses patterns found in this way as part of the compositional process. Arbitrary new phrases can be matched against the stored patterns; if similar phrase patterns are found, aspects of the stored abstraction can be used to guide further elaboration of the new phrase. Constant matching is complemented by a set of incremental abstraction editors, which allow a user to pull salient relations out of a single phrase interactively. The abstractions supported by CompAss are directed toward representing such processes as voice leading: relationships among tones in a phrase can be abstracted as intervallic networks, as groups of scale degree members, or in terms of duration ratios.

Though CompAss is not a real-time interactive system, the motivations behind it lead us to consider it here. The constant matching algorithm, coupled with user-directed pattern abstraction editors, provides mechanisms for the system to learn phrase types and for a musician to improve on those representations. As it stands, new phrases can be matched against the stored patterns in a session of computer-assisted composition. One can easily imagine CompAss-style patterns incorporated in a real-time pattern matcher, where associated rule sets determine how the system will react to matches between the known patterns and incoming or machine-generated phrases.

7.7 Induction and Matching

Pattern induction is a form of unsupervised learning; the goal is to identify patterns in a musical sequence that have been repeated to such a degree that they should be remembered as significant and used in constructing responses. The learning is unsupervised because it occurs in the course of performance—another approach would be to teach the system the patterns required to function in some context. This would bias the computer performer towards sequences known in advance, however, and would limit its capacity to pick up on and use regularities introduced in the course of an improvisation. For this reason, induction explores the more difficult, unsupervised situation. Patterns can be induced from any number sequence; such sequences could be interpreted as representing melodies, rhythmic patterns, harmonic progressions, etc. In Cypher, patterns are induced and matched for melodies and harmonic progressions. A similar procedure has been implemented as part of the McGill University TMax project.

Basic Algorithm

In their article "Real-Time Computer Accompaniment of Keyboard Performances," Joshua Bloch and Roger Dannenberg describe techniques for matching monophonic and polyphonic performances against stored scores representing the expected performance. The patterns Cypher currently considers are strings of numbers, which may be interpreted in various ways: as chord progressions, for example, or progressions of rhythmic durations. The patterns considered in Bloch and Dannenberg 1985 are the Note On messages arriving from the performance of some musical score. Therefore, Cypher's problem corresponds to their monophonic matching case: the program does not try to coordinate the reports of multiple listeners or consider simultaneous harmonic or rhythmic streams, and so it is able to avoid the polyphonic matching problem they describe later.

Briefly, the Bloch and Dannenberg algorithm computes a matrix relating score events (the stored representation) to performance events (the notes coming from the live player). Each time a new performance event arrives, the next column of the matrix is computed: finding the maximum rating of possible score to performance correlations will point to the most likely position in the score of the current performance. This approach maps well to the pattern matching task: we want to match incoming information against stored strings to see if any known pattern is being followed. The known pattern, then, corresponds to the score in the Bloch and Dannenberg application, and new input corresponds to their performance. There are, however, significant differences as well. First of all, pattern processing requires matching against many different patterns simultaneously. Second, there is no a priori way to know when a pattern may begin; new input must be continually matched against the head of many patterns to find incipient pattern instances.

Pattern induction is basically a matter of pattern matching, but with different kinds of data preparation and different interpretation of the results. Following this idea, the pattern-matching algorithm of Bloch and Dannenberg was made neutral enough to accommodate the demands of both induction and straight matching. There are two main advantages to this strategy: One is that a single matcher can be maintained, with the differences in processing required for induction and matching reflected in the way the process is called and the way its return value is used. Second, this pattern-matching algorithm is much more efficient than the exhaustive search employed by Cope. Cope's intention was certainly not to develop a real-time pattern matcher; further, his exhaustive methods will turn up patterns not found by the algorithm described here. The point of pattern processing in Cypher, however, is to coordinate the induction and matching of patterns with other kinds of analysis in real time. Therefore, the constrained method developed by Bloch and Dannenberg is more appropriate to both the induction and matching problems.

The induction process is called twice, once for each type of data that can spawn a pattern, at every phrase boundary. Phrase boundaries are demarcated in the manner explained in chapter 5; once a boundary has been found, the harmonic progression and melodic intervals for the most recently completed phrase are sent to the induction process to be matched against progressions and melodies from earlier phrases. The TMax environment developed at McGill University employs a similar task division: as MIDI data arrives, it is first sent to a process called the segmenter, which uses several heuristics to identify possible phrase boundaries. When such a boundary has been located, a *k mismatch* pattern-matching algorithm is trained on the events of the phrase. When a pattern is successfully matched against the stored collection of known patterns, the matcher reports back to the main process the location of the found pattern in the phrase. Otherwise, the new material is saved as a pattern in the collection (Pennycook and Lea 1991).

As noted above, the Bloch and Dannenberg algorithm maintains a matrix of score-to-performance matches. The basis of their technique is described thus:

> An integer matrix is computed where each row corresponds to an event in the score and each column corresponds to an event in the performance. A new column is computed for each performed event. The integer computed for row *r* and column *c* answers the following question: If we were currently at the rth score event and the cth performance event, what would be the highest rating of any association up to the current time? The answer to this question can be computed from the answers for the previous column (the previous performance event) and from the previous row of the current column. The maximum rating up to score event *r*, performance event *c* will be at least as great as the one up to $r - 1, c$ because considering one more score event cannot reduce the number of possible matches. Similarly, the maximum rating up to r, c will be at least as great as the one up to $r, c - 1$, where one less performance event is considered. Furthermore, if score event *r* matches performance event *c*, then the rating will be exactly one greater than the one up to $r - 1, c - 1$. (Bloch and Dannenberg 1985, 281)

Because the only information needed to compute the next column of the matrix is the previous column, the storage required for each pattern is simply twice the largest pattern size. Further, the computation can be centered around the highest rating achieved so far, limiting the necessary processing to a constant as well. These characteristics of the algorithm make it eminently suitable for our real-time requirements.

The Cypher routine StringMatcher(s, start, newelement)—where *s* is a pointer to a string, *start* is the position in the matrix of the highest match, and *newelement* is the next element to be processed—is an implementation of the algorithm described by Bloch and Dannenberg. To induce harmonic progressions or melodic intervals, the matcher is handed two patterns: one from the current phrase, and one from the previous phrase. The larger pattern plays the role of the performance, in the Bloch and Dannenberg sense, and the smaller pattern is used as a score. In other words, the larger pattern is matched against the smaller one. Each element from the larger pattern is successively sent to the matcher, always to be matched against the smaller pattern. After all elements from the larger pattern have been processed, the highest rating achieved in the smaller pattern's matrix is the last element in the smaller pattern's array that was actually found. If this rating is larger than 4, that is, if at least 4 elements from the smaller pattern were also found in the larger one, the induction is successful, and an attempt is made to add a new entry to the list of known patterns. Now the newly induced pattern must be compared to those already known; accordingly, it is matched against all patterns already in memory. If the rating after matching the new pattern against a known pattern is 4 or more, the patterns are considered to be the same. In that case, the known pattern's strength is incremented, and the process ends. If the new pattern does not match any known pattern, it is added to the list to be saved in the program's long-term memory.

Representations

The Cypher analysis record for every event in a listening stream includes a representation of the event's harmonic function relative to the active key. As each successive event is read from the stream and added to the phrase, the root of the local harmonic area and the current key are obtained from their respective agencies. With these two pieces of information, a simple calculation provides the function. Both chords and keys are stored as an integer between 0 and 23. Major and minor modes of the same root are stored adjacently; chord and key number zero are both c major. Therefore, for both chord and key, C major is 0, C minor is 1, C# major is 2, C# minor 3, and so on. With this system, we can use the following define statement to calculate chord function within the key:

```
#define Function(key, chord) (((chord+24) – (key – (key%2)))%24)
```

The effect of the defined Function statement is to move the position of 0 across the collection of chord theories. If both key and chord are already 0, for example, the position of 0 in the chord theories will remain on C major and will indicate that chord as the tonic of the key. If the key is 4 (D major) and the chord 8 (E major), Function will return a value 4, indicating a major chord based on the scale degree a major second above the tonic. If the key is minor, however, Function subtracts the value of the major key on the same root; this keeps minor functions on odd values and major functions represented as even values, which is the convention for all harmonic reports in the program. Relating local harmonies to the key effectively removes key from consideration in storing and matching harmonic progressions. A functional progression of tonic to dominant to tonic will look identical, in this representation, regardless of the key in which it was originally presented. Chord progressions are sent through the induction process at each phrase boundary. When a phrase boundary is found, Cypher makes a list of the chord functions by reading from the beginning of the just completed phrase to the end, appending to the list function values for every event along the way. If a function for some event is found to be identical to the one before, it is discarded.

The other current source of sequences is melodic activity. Melodies are strings of single-note events; the phrase boundary demarcation is used again to identify melodic groups to be submitted to the pattern inducer. Preprocessing of melodic information into a pattern requires two steps: First, we are currently considering only monophonic melodies, so as the preprocessor steps through the events in a phrase, events with a vertical density greater than 1 are discarded. Second, as in the case of harmonic progressions, it is desirable to give the pattern some degree of independence from the specific context in which it is embedded. In the case of melodies, this is done by casting specific pitch sequences into sequences of intervals. Each new pitch appended to the melody list is compared with the previous one: the difference between the two note values is the value added to the list. So a rise of a major third from C3 to E3 (MIDI notes 60 to 64) is represented as +4, an ascending major third. Descending intervals will produce negative intervals. Intervallic representation allows melodic contours beginning on different scale degrees or in different registers to be successfully matched. Note that this representation means that there will be one fewer interval generated than the total number of events in the phrase.

As patterns are induced, they are added to a list of known patterns. Two lists are maintained: one for melodic patterns, and the other for harmonic progressions. Every time Cypher ceases operation, it writes out a file storing a record of the patterns it knows. This file represents the long-term memory of the program. Then whenever Cypher starts up again, it loads in the patterns from long-term memory and activates them for matching. In this way, the program incrementally learns and uses patterns found in the music played to it.

Each known pattern has an associated strength: the strength is an indication of the frequency with which the pattern has been encountered in recent invocations of the program. Whenever the inducer notices a pattern, it attempts to add the pattern to the known list. Before such an addition will succeed, the pattern is matched against those already on the list. If the pattern is similar to one already known, that is, if it matches most of the known pattern, the new copy will not be appended. In that case, however, the strength of the already stored pattern will be increased. Pattern strengths are used for two purposes: First, strong patterns will be used more often by the composition section as seed material. Second, pattern strength decays slightly with every program execution. If a pattern is not seen again through a sufficient number of executions, it will be deleted from the list. In other words, if a pattern is learned but then not seen again for a long time, it will be forgotten—dropped from the long-term memory file.

Evaluation

The pattern induction process just described works, after a fashion: it has successfully found chord progressions and simple melodies from listening to music. These successes, however, are limited to what I would call "toy" examples. Induced chord progressions, for instance, are found by repeating the progression literally several times in succession until the program notices it. Similarly for melodies, simple sets of intervals not more than eight notes long can be found by pattern induction if they are repeatedly played to the machine.

Much more desirable, of course, would be pattern induction that could function in the real world. Finding chord progressions and melodic patterns from improvisation or performance of compositions not geared to the algorithm is where this work is intended to lead. The reasons such "real-world" functionality remains elusive, in fact, have much less to do with finding an efficient matching algorithm than they do with good preparation of data to present the matcher as input. There are at least three major problems here: (1) building patterns on the right level, (2) successfully grouping information into patterns, and (3) storing good candidates for repeated matching attempts.

Different pattern types will present meaningful sequences of data on different levels. Melodic information, for example, will most often be found on level 1, in the succession of events; however, some evaluation of the data should be done before building a candidate pattern, to remove ornaments, for example. A "real-world" pattern inducer should be able to find melodies repeated with some ornamentation. Having a speed feature classification at the grace-note level would be a first approximation: events with the highest speed rating could be discarded when building melodic patterns for induction. Harmonic progressions, however, are most likely not found on the event level. Rather than trying to match chord sequences presented in a phrase, the progression preparation should try to identify an important, or dominant, chord or two within each phrase. Sequences of important chords could then be built into patterns and presented as candidates for induction.

The second problem, finding good groups, is related to the workings of the phrase boundary agency. As it is now, induction takes place at the end of each phrase, comparing the just completed phrase with the one before it. This works reasonably well, as long as the phrase boundary finder is reliably finding boundaries in the same place when presented with similar music. Particularly before the phrase threshold has stabilized, this is not always the case. Perfectly plausible patterns, then, may not be found, because a spurious phrase boundary would interrupt the construction of exactly the pattern we might wish to notice.

The third problem involves the question of how to identify sequences that are worth saving for future matching attempts. In "real-world" music, interesting patterns will rarely be literally repeated end to end. Normally, some melody, for example, will appear and reappear, but with each occurrence separated from the others in time. In a pattern inducer looking for matches between adjacent phrases, such sequences will not be found. What we need is some way to select melodic or harmonic strings that are interesting in their own right, so they will be kept around and matched against future sequences even when an immediate match is not found. This is the main lesson to be learned from the induction process reported here: repetition alone is an insufficient heuristic for finding good sequences. Using only repetition means that all sequences will have to be stored and tried out for induction, in an exhaustive search that could quickly drop out of real time. Melodies and harmonies must also be recognized as interesting because of some intrinsic qualities and tested repeatedly for matches against subsequent material.

Matching

The pattern-matching algorithm described in the beginning of section 7.7, in connection with the induction process, is the same one used for the related problem of matching induced patterns against incoming data. StringMatcher(), the routine responsible for matching patterns and returning a rating of the highest matched element between them, is the same one used here. In this section, I will review the differences in the way data is prepared, and results interpreted to handle the matching problem.

Because of the properties of StringMatcher(), every incoming event can be tested against the known patterns: there is no need to wait for a phrase boundary to find groups, as in the case of pattern induction. When the rating of a known pattern becomes nonzero, after exposure to incoming events, some part of it has been matched. Therefore, the general strategy is this: When a new event arrives, it is matched melodically and harmonically against known patterns. If more than half of a known pattern is found, a message is sent to the composition section along with the remainder of the pattern. If all of a pattern is recognized, another message is sent to the player, the rating matrix is reset to zero, and the process begins again.

Though the matrix-rating algorithm of Bloch and Dannenberg has proved to be a useful starting point, significant adaptations have been made to it for Cypher's pattern-matching tasks. The algorithm has been changed, because our demands are significantly different. For example, in the score-following case, an assumption is made that the performance will not go backward. That is, once the matcher is relatively sure of having matched some part of a score, it will try to continue on from that point. In matching melodic patterns, however, we can never be sure when a pattern might start, and we have less reason to believe that matching any part of it means we will not see that part again before the rest of the pattern. Therefore, the ratings of the original algorithm have to be modified if a partial match has not been continued for some time.

One of the efficiencies of the Bloch and Dannenberg algorithm is that a window can be centered on the highest-rated event found with the matrix and continued from there. The same convenience is adopted here as is evidenced by the *start* argument to the StringMatcher() routine. The deviations from the Bloch and Dannenberg version come when no new match is found. In that case, one is subtracted from the rating of all of the elements in the matrix. Our window begins at the point of the latest match, represented by the *start* argument; however, it continues from there to the end of the pattern. Therefore, when we subtract one from all ratings on an unsuccessful match, we effectively start looking from one element further back in the target sequence with the next match. If the next element is found on a subsequent attempt, nothing is lost—because we continue to search to the end, it will match in the same place as if no decay of the ratings had taken place. If the next element is not found for several events, however, the decay in ratings means that the matcher will again be searching from the beginning of the pattern. In other words, if the continuation of some pattern is not detected, the decay in element ratings will gradually return the matcher to the start condition, where it is again looking for the head of the sequence.

We have seen that the matcher returns a rating representing the number of matches of the new pattern against a known one. Because of the way this matcher uses the rating matrix, the first location in the matrix of the maximum rating reached by the match equals the position of the last matched element in the known pattern. With this information, the composition section can schedule the rest of the pattern for performance or for further elaboration from a compositional network. The routine FinishMelody(String *s) is called when the rating and number of matches returned for some pattern is greater than half its length. FinishMelody() will then examine the *maxrating* array to find the last matched element. The rest of the elements after that last match will be scheduled to play on successive beats after the invocation of FinishMelody(). This is a crude but effective way to test the matcher: a frame representation storing the number of beats associated with each remaining element of the pattern would preserve the rhythmic integrity of remembered material. Still, playing out the remainder on the beat is already much preferable to playing it back at an unchanging speed whenever the beginning is found.

8 Outlook

In this book, we have examined the underpinnings of interactive music systems both in terms of their technical implementation and the musical possibilities they advance. The specific realizations reviewed here are unquestionably quite diverse; still, a number of recurring trends emerge. To many interactive systems, the transfer of some degree of musical intelligence to the machine is central. In fact, virtually all computer programs dealing with musical issues could benefit greatly from such a transfer; however, the degree to which musicianship can be functionally captured by a computer program is still an open question.

Researchers in several fields, including music theory, cognitive science, and artificial intelligence, are each considering this question from their own perspective. Composers and performers working with computers onstage are another source of the development of machine musicianship. Some kinds of music are effectively made this way; in fact, much of the music made with computers today could not be produced in any other way. The development and interpenetration of these differing movements as they transfer musical sensibility to a computer will continue to show the ways in which human music cognition can be so modeled and what parts of musical skill will continue to defy any computable formulation. The search will continue under many of the rubrics we have already seen; as with any vital undertaking, it will also branch into new paths that are unsuspected now or whose outlines are just coming into view. The remarks in this chapter will identify some of those paths and provide a motivation for undertaking the effort at all.

8.1 Cooperative Interaction

An important goal for interactive systems is to devise artificial musicians able not only to respond to human players but to cooperate with them. The programs we have reviewed here demonstrate a style of interaction we can refer to as *call and response*: the human user initiates some action, and the computer system responds. To arrive at a more sophisticated interaction, or *cooperation*, the system must be able to understand the directions and goals of a human counterpart sufficiently to predict where those directions will lead and must know enough about composition to be able to reinforce the goals at the same moment as they are achieved in the human performance. Programs are now forced to rely on call and response because they are unable to predict what a performer will do next. The only exceptions to this observation are score followers, an example of limited cooperative music systems: their derivation of tempo is in fact a prediction of the future spacing of events in a human performance based on an analysis of the immediate past.

Although endowing a computer with the clairvoyance to know what a human will do next seems a formidable undertaking, many kinds of music are highly predictable. If they were not, even humans would not be able to play together. The example of rhythm is a clear one: music to which one's foot can be tapped is displaying a predictable rhythm —otherwise, you would not know when to put your foot down. For a cooperative system to be equally prescient, it must pick up on regularities, or near regularities, in the onset times of external events. Once it has detected such a regularity, it can assert a continuation of it and begin scheduling events to coincide with the found pulse. The beat-tracking schemes we examined in chapter 5 do just this.

For example, the algorithm proposed in Dannenberg and Mont-Reynaud 1987 does not rely on a stored representation of the music to be followed and could form a component of a generally cooperative system. Mont-Reynaud's tracker is sensitive to "healthy" notes, that is, notes exceeding a minimum time threshold and not significantly shorter than the preceding note. To build a predictor, the program then tries to notice arithmetic regularities in the offset times of three successive healthy notes. If roughly equal offset times are found, they are brought into a typical eighth-note range and taken to be the current beat. George Lewis has a technique for beat following that depends on the detection of a "subtempo," some short duration that, when added to itself some integer number of times, will account for most of the actual durations being heard. In other words, the Lewis algorithm is additive, looking to find large durations from combinations of short ones, rather than looking for a tempo of longer values and subdividing it to account for the quick notes.

Extrapolating from the beat detection case, we can see that what we need to predict the future of a musical performance is the construction of high-level recognizers: processes watching the results of event-to-event analyses and searching for regularities and directions. Once we have a pattern, predicting the future reverts to the score-following case: not in the strict sense of matching tempi but in the general sense of comparing incoming material with what we believe to be an ongoing pattern and notifying response processes about the goodness of fit. If our follower is matching well, the responders can schedule output events to coincide with events in the remainder of the stored pattern. The work on pattern induction and recognition, and the use of scripts and frames reported in chapter 7 form fragments of the mechanism needed to accomplish such behavior.

Once such prototype induction/matching mechanisms are formed, we will learn whether correlations of patterns found by beat tracking, chord finding, and key recognition might allow the cooperative performance of some musical styles. If a listener has informed a generation section that "we are following a harmonic pattern (I-IV-I-V-I), in which the chords change every four beats. The current chord is tonic in the key of C, and the next chord change will occur two beats from now," the generator could schedule events consonant with the upcoming chord to be played in relation to the found beat pattern.

Recognition of directed musical motion can take place in two ways, performed independently or in combination: either direction can be detected in the event-to-event behavior of the input, or the input can be recognized as following a stored template of typical musical patterns. The first kind of recognition is the one addressed by the work of Simon and Sumner 1968: they assume certain fundamental alphabets, such as scales, and a small number of way of organizing the elements of those alphabets. Building on these assumptions, they write processes to find patterns arising from manipulating the alphabets with the given operations. Once such a pattern has been found, they can extrapolate (predict) the extension of the sequence by continuing to apply the discovered operations on the underlying alphabet.

The second kind of direction detection would be an extension of the pattern induction/matching mechanism. The same script representations carrying information about typical harmonic and rhythmic behavior could be fitted with additional slots describing motions of intensification and relaxation along some dimension. Again, it remains to be seen whether scripts with sufficient subtlety and variability to be musically useful can be devised.

8.2 Parallel Implementations

Current generations of high-end computers are based on some degree of parallelism, where several processors are used simultaneously to attack engineering and scientific problems. The interactive music systems discussed in this book are usually implemented on personal computers, for reasons of access, transportability, and cost. As parallel hardware implementations begin to move down into the personal computing class, interactive systems will start to take advantage of the higher power offered by collections of CPUs. With the power of parallel processors, however, comes the problem of programming them effectively, to make use of the opportunities for simultaneous execution of several processes. The software architecture of interactive systems, in other words, then needs to be split into two or more subtasks, which can be treated in parallel.

T-MAX

One of the first efforts in this area is the T-MAX project, developed by Bruce Pennycook and his colleagues at McGill University. T-MAX stands for Transputer Max and is a software environment based on Max, running on a Macintosh computer platform extended with three transputers (25 MHz. floating point devices) and a Digidesign Sound Accelerator card. In a related development, a team from the Durham Music Technology center has developed a parallel architecture for real-time synthesis and signal processing, also built around Inmos Transputers (Bailey et al. 1990).

A primary task of the T-MAX project is to implement an Automatic Improviser, an interactive system capable of tonal jazz improvisation. On a parallel hardware platform, one of the first decisions is how to divide the task across the available processors. For the Automatic Improviser, three partitions were devised—listening, pattern matching, and playing. The partitions were spread across the processor resources as follows: (1) the Macintosh host handles MIDI transfers and system IO, (2) one T805 transputer directs communication between the transputers and the Macintosh, (3) one T805 performs real-time analysis (listening), and (4) one T805 handles pattern matching and performance algorithms.

The devotion of one transputer to directing communication traffic to and from the Macintosh host allows transparent access to the processing power of the other T805s from within the T-MAX environment. When a T-MAX object is loaded in Max, T-MAX loads the executable code onto the appropriate transputer, and sets up a communications channel between the affected transputer and the Max window. In this way, a user can generate as many instances of a T-MAX object as are needed, with the system taking care of all of the details of allocating processor resources, and passing messages across the machine boundary.

The listening part of the Automatic Improviser project is an adaptation and extension of Cypher. Incoming MIDI data is packaged into events and sent to the T-MAX listener object. This object was originally developed from the C code of Cypher's listener, then elaborated by the T-MAX developers. The T-MAX listener performs the two-level analysis described in chapter 5, the results of which become available from two outlets on the object, one outlet for each level of analysis. Separate objects called *extractors* then accept the analyses coming from the listener object and pull out the classifications for each separate feature, or regularity report. These classifications, available at the outlets of the extractors, can then be further processed in any way by the full Max environment.

The patch shown in figure 8.1 is one of the first implementations of this idea, showing an early test of the listener in a Max environment. Here, the *listener* object is a straight import of the Cypher listener. Pitch and velocity information from *notein* is sent to the inlets, and the level-1 and level-2 listener classifications come from the two outlets. The companion objects *fextract* (for feature extract) and *rextract* (for regularity extract) then make the various classifications available for other processing. In figure 8.1 a collection of dials and buttons show the classifications emanating from the two extractions.

8.3 Signal Processing

To this point we have considered signal processing as an emanation from some black box generically called a synthesizer, or sampler. The

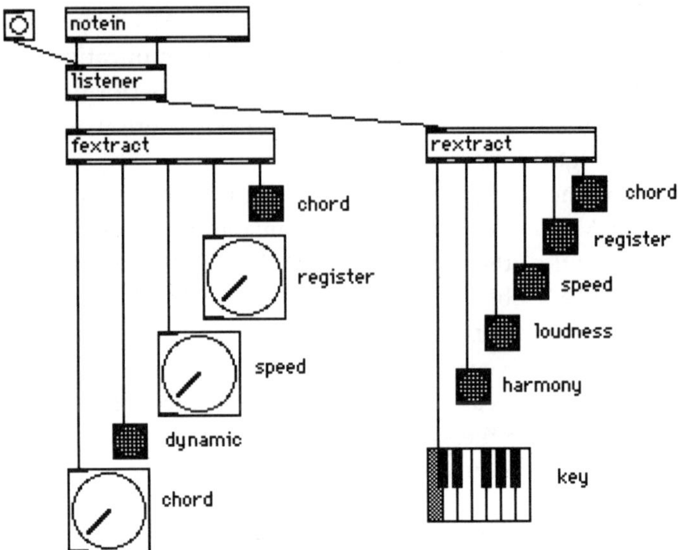

Figure 8.1

use of commercially available synthesis devices tends to encourage standardized approaches to signal processing, typified in the worst case by the exclusive use of factory presets. In fact, the ubiquitous insinuation of a small subset of synthesis techniques into the sonic arsenal, or even the repeated use of exactly the same sounds, is a recent development in the history of real-time or interactive systems. Earlier examples tended to be built around high-speed signal processing devices, among which the 4X machine, developed at IRCAM by Giuseppe di Giugno and his team, is the most prominent example (Favreau et al. 1986).

Now, after a period of relative domination by commercially supported synthesis techniques, signal processing is again being opened to more widespread experimentation by the appearance of such devices as the Digidesign Sound Accelerator (Lowe and Currie 1989), the NeXT machine's digital signal processing (DSP) capabilities (Jaffe and Boynton 1989), and the M.I.T. Media Laboratory's Real-Time Acoustic Processing (RTAP) board (Boynton and Cumming 1988). All of these devices are built around high-speed DSP chips, such as the Motorola 56001, which is at the heart of the aforementioned hardware packages. As the design and manufacture of digital signal processors pass to large chip makers, these devices will become cheaper, more powerful, and more widespread, and the processors, as well as the synthesis techniques, will become standard.

The example of the 4X machine is instructive, as it relates to the kinds of interaction widespread DSP capabilities will make possible. The main differences between the 4X and the current generation of DSP devices are that the 4X was much more powerful but the new chips have been well integrated with personal computer platforms such as Apple's Macintosh family or the NeXT machine. The 4X was most often used as a high-powered synthesis engine, or real-time sound processor. But what made the 4X clearly superior to a rack full of specialized boxes was not its suitability to any particular synthesis technique, but that it was programmable and could implement whatever mix of functionalities was necessary in the way that was most appropriate to the piece at hand (Baisnee et al. 1986).

On the control level, the addition of signal-processing capabilities leaves the composer's task largely unchanged—organizing the processing and arrangement of sound through the course of the composition or improvisation. It is at the level of the input and output to the control algorithms that the choices will be multiplied. On input, DSP capabilities allow access to aspects of instrumental sound not well represented by MIDI, most notably continually varying timbral information. On output, the composer can use flexible combinations of processing algorithms and an expanded range of real-time sound transformation techniques. Although using DSP devices is more demanding than selecting presets or even using a sound librarian, the sound world expressed and understood by interactive systems is already being enriched through the incorporation of real-time digital signal processing.

The Hierarchical Music Specification Language (HMSL), developed at Mills College, is a Forth-based, object-oriented programming language that supports the development of interactive music compositions. Recently HMSL has been extended to include digital signal processing objects, which are realized on several Motorola 56000-based architectures. The language itself makes few assumptions about the nature of the devices that will be used to realize any particular piece: "HMSL compositions have used electric motors, graphics devices, solenoids, text files, and MIDI synthesizers, as output devices" (Burk 1991, 15). To use the DSP capabilities, a composer concatenates various sound units, such as oscillators, filters, reverb units, envelopes, and the like. These units are realized with small code resources installed on a resident 56000 processor.

Max and DSP

IRCAM has again set a standard for the incorporation of digital signal processing in interactive systems, with the recent IRCAM Signal Processing Workstation. One of the most novel aspects of the ISPW is that it is built around a high-powered but general-purpose processor (the Intel i860), rather than a device designed particularly for signal processing (such as the Motorola 56000 series). Indeed, as processor speed generally increases, the need for specially designed devices will generally diminish. And in any case, the market for fast processors is so much larger than the one for signal processing devices that development efforts in the first realm will tend to overwhelm those in the second sooner rather than later.

The Max patch in figure 8.2, provided by Cort Lippe, shows a simple example combining control and audio level objects in a single patch. The *notein* and *stripnote* objects are familiar by now; a transition from control to audio level information is effected with the *mtof* object, which converts MIDI note numbers into a frequency value, to control an audio oscillator. Every Max object whose name ends with the "~" character, is operating in the audio realm. Therefore, in the audio portion of the patch in figure 8.2, a simple oscillator is multiplied with the output of a simple line segment generator to control the amplitude. The result is sent to both channels of a stereo digital-to-analog converter, which can be enabled and disabled with start and stop messages, shown connected to the left inlet.

The composer Todd Winkler has explored the use of Max for processing live acoustic sources, through the use of commercial digital signal processing devices, such as the Yamaha SPX-1000 or DMP-11 mixer. Many of the same effects realizable with the ISPW can be achieved in this way, though the configuration again must confront a machine boundary between the computer and the DSP device and a concomitant reliance on MIDI. In Winkler's work, a Max patch sends continuous controller data to affect parameters of signal-processing algorithms programmed in the commercial devices and modifying the sound of an acoustic instrumental performance.

For example, a module called "Capture Gesture" uses EXPLODE to record the dynamics and rhythm of a 6-second violin phrase. Using velocity as break points, the MAX "line" object creates a function that is sent as continuous controller data to change reverberation time. By lengthening the overall time

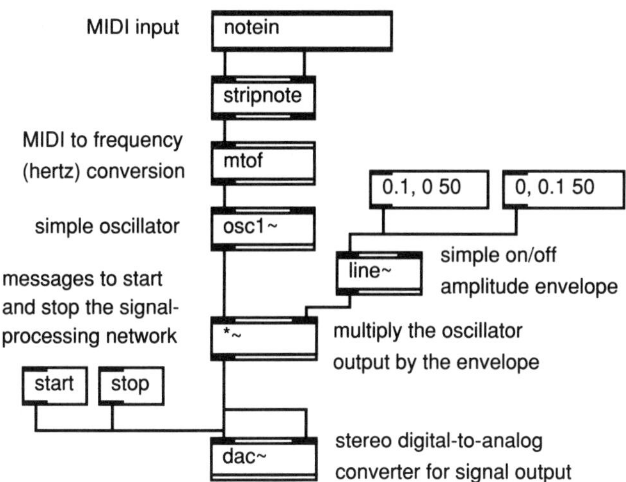

Figure 8.2

of the function, the apparent size of the hall changes continuously over the next two minutes of the piece, with the same proportions as the original phrase, thus enabling the performer to "phrase" the apparent size of the hall. (Winkler 1991, 547)

8.4 Conclusion

Trouble would begin, however, if mechanical music were to flood the world to the detriment of live music, just as manufactured products have done to the detriment of handicraft. I conclude my essay with this supplication: May God protect our offspring from this plague!
—Bela Bartok, "Mechanical Music"

Bartok's (1976) supplication concerns primarily the introduction of recording technology, though he does cite the example of one determined composer who attempted a kind of synthesis by etching his own grooves into the vinyl of a phonograph record. With the application of ever more powerful technologies to the production of music, the ways music is composed, performed, and experienced have changed radically. The fears about the future of music, particularly music performance, have grown as well. In an article in the *New York Times* of May 13, 1990, titled "The Midi Menace: Machine Perfection is Far From Perfect," Jon Pareles (1990) notes with distress the burgeoning use of sequenced MIDI material as a substitute for human players in the performance of pop music. He writes, "If I wanted flawlessness, I'd stay home with the album. The spontaneity, uncertainty and ensemble coordination that automation eliminates are exactly what I go to concerts to see; the risk brings the suspense, and the sense of triumph, to live pop."

Similarly, I have often heard professional musicians complain that soon all the performance work will go to machines. At first, I took such complaints as evidence of a lack of familiarity with the field: it seemed to me there is little danger of machines taking over the concert stage as long as they remain such remarkably poor musicians. And yet, as Pareles notes, machines are assuming an ever-increasing role in the performance of music. Because of the nature of the machine's participation, such occasions come to resemble less a live performance than the public audition of a tape recording.

As this book has demonstrated, however, interactive systems are not concerned with replacing human players but with enriching the performance situations in which humans work. The goal of incorporating humanlike music intelligence grows out of the desire to fashion computer performers able to play music with humans, not for them. A program able to understand and play along with other musicians ranging from the awkward neophyte to the most accomplished professional should encourage more people to play music, not discourage those who already do.

It is in this respect that interactive music programs can change the way we think about machines and how we use them. We do not currently expect a machine to understand enough about what we are trying to do to be able to help us achieve it. Many problems must be solved to make a music machine able to show such sensitivity. But the means, the technical and intellectual foundations, and the people needed to address these problems are already engaged. Now we must concentrate on improving the musicianship of our emerging partners.

In developing my own computer musician, I attempt to make human participation a vital and natural element of the performance situation —not because I am concerned about putting performers out of work but rather because I believe that if the numbers of humans actively, physically making music declines, the climate for music making and the quality of music will deteriorate. Pareles concludes, "Perhaps the best we can hope for is that someone will come up with a way to program in some rough edges, too." I hope we can do better than that: develop computer musicians that do not just play back music *for* people, but become increasingly adept at making new and engaging music *with* people, at all levels of technical proficiency.

References

Ames, C. 1989. "The Markov Process as a Compositional Model: A Survey and Tutorial" *Leonardo* 22(2): 175–187.

Bailey, N.; Purvis, A.; Bowler, I.; and Manning, P. 1990. "An Highly Parallel Architecture for Real-Time Music Synthesis and Digital Signal Processing Applications." In *Proceedings*, ed. S. Arnold and G. Hair. Glasgow: ICMC Glasgow.

Baisnee, P. F.; Barriere, J. B.; Koechlin, O.; and Rowe, R. 1986. "Real-Time Interaction between Musicians and Computer: Live Performance Utilisations of the 4X Musical Workstation." In *Proceedings of the 1986 International Computer Music Conference, The Hague*, ed. P. Berg. Berkeley: Computer Music Association.

Barlow, C. 1987. "Two Essays on Theory." *Computer Music Journal* 11(1):44–60.

Barlow, C. 1990. "AUTOBUSK: An Algorithmic Real-Time Pitch & Rhythm Improvisation Programme." In *Proceedings*, ed. S. Arnold and G. Hair. Glasgow: ICMC Glasgow.

Bartok, B. 1976. "Mechanical Music." In *Bela Bartok Essays*, selected and edited by Benjamin Suchoff. London: Faber & Faber.

Berry, W. 1976. *Structural Functions in Music*. New York: Dover Publications, Inc.

Beyls, P. 1988. "Introducing OSCAR." In *Proceedings of the 14th International Computer Music Conference, Cologne*, ed. C. Lischka and J. Fritsch. Cologne: Feedback Studio.

Bharucha, J. J. 1987. "MUSACT: A Connectionist Model of Musical Harmony." In *Proceedings of the Ninth Annual Meeting of the Cognitive Science Society*. Hillsdale, N.J.: Erlbaum Press.

Bharucha, J. J., and Todd, P. M. 1989. "Modeling the Perception of Tonal Structure with Neural Nets." *Computer Music Journal* 13(4):44–53.

Bloch, J. J., and Dannenberg, R. B. 1985. "Real-Time Computer Accompaniment of Keyboard Performances." In *Proceedings of the International Computer*

Music Conference, 1985, ed. B. Truax. San Francisco, Calif.: Computer Music Association.

Bobrow, D. G., and Winograd, T. 1977. "An Overview of KRL, A Knowledge Representation Language." *Cognitive Science* 1(1):3–46.

Boynton, L. 1987. "Scheduling as Applied to Musical Processing." Cambridge, Mass. MIT Media Laboratory report.

Boynton, L., and Cumming, D. 1988. "A Real-Time Acoustic Processing Card for the Mac II." In *Proceedings of the 14th International Computer Music Conference, Cologne*, ed. C. Lischka and J. Fritsch. Cologne: Feedback Studio.

Brachman, R. J., and Schmolze, J. G. 1985. "An Overview of the KL-ONE Knowledge Representation System." *Cognitive Science* 9:171–216.

Buchanan, B., and Feigenbaum, E. 1978. "Dendral and Meta-Dendral: Their Applications Dimension." *Artificial Intelligence* 11(1,2):5–24.

Burk, P. 1991. "The Integration of Real-Time Synthesis into HMSL, the Hierarchical Music Specification Language." In *Proceedings*, ed. B. Alphonce and B. Pennycook. Montreal: ICMC-1991 Faculty of Music, McGill University.

Camurri, A.; Canepa, C.; Frixione, M.; Innocenti, C.; Massucco, C.; and Zaccaria, R. 1991. "A High-Level System for Music Composition." In *Proceedings*, ed. B. Alphonce and B. Pennycook. Montreal: ICMC-1991 Faculty of Music, McGill University.

Chadabe, J. 1989. "Interactive Composing: An Overview." In *The Music Machine*, ed. C. Roads. Cambridge, Mass.: The MIT Press.

Chafe, C.; Mont-Reynaud, B.; and Rush, L. 1982. "Toward an Intelligent Editor of Digital Audio: Recognition of Musical Constructs." *Computer Music Journal* 6(1). Reprinted in *The Music Machine*, ed. Curtis Roads. Cambridge, Mass.: The MIT Press, 1989.

Chung, J. 1989. "An Agency for the Perception of Musical Beats, or, If I Only Had a Foot . . . " Cambridge, Mass. MIT Media Laboratory report.

Clarke, E. F. 1987. "Categorical Rhythm Perception: An Ecological Perspective." In *Action and Perception in Rhythm and Music*, ed. A. Gabrielsson. Stockholm: Royal Swedish Academy of Music.

Clarke, E. F. 1988. "Generative Principles in Music Performance." In *Generative Processes in Music: The Psychology of Performance, Improvisation, and Composition*, ed. J. A. Sloboda. Oxford: Clarendon Press.

Clifton, T. 1975. "Some Comparisons between Intuitive and Scientific Descriptions of Music." *Journal of Music Theory* 66–110.

Cook, N. 1987. *A Guide to Musical Analysis*. New York: George Braziller.

Cooper, G., and Meyer, L. B. 1960. *The Rhythmic Structure of Music*. Chicago: University of Chicago Press.

Cope, D. 1990. "Pattern Matching as an Engine for the Computer Simulation of Musical Style." In *Proceedings*, ed. S. Arnold and G. Hair. Glasgow: ICMC Glasgow.

Dannenberg, R. B. 1989. "Real-Time Scheduling and Computer Accompaniment." In *Current Directions in Computer Music Research*, ed. M. V. Mathews and J. R. Pierce. Cambridge, Mass.: The MIT Press.

Dannenberg, R. B. 1991. "Software Support for Interactive Multimedia Performance." In *Proceedings of The Arts and Technology III*. New London: Connecticut College.

Dannenberg, R. B., and Mont-Reynaud, B. 1987. "Following an Improvisation in Real Time." In *Proceedings of the 1987 International Computer Music Conference*, compiled by J. Beauchamp. San Francisco, Calif.: Computer Music Association.

Dannenberg, R. B.; Sanchez, M.; Joseph, A.; Saul, R.; Joseph, R.; and Capell, P. 1990. "An Expert System for Teaching Piano to Novices." In *Proceedings*, ed. S. Arnold and G. Hair. Glasgow: ICMC Glasgow.

Demers, L. P. 1991. "A Performance Instrument for Lighting." In *Proceedings*, ed. B. Alphonce and B. Pennycook. Montreal: ICMC-1991 Faculty of Music, McGill University.

Desain, P., and Honing, H. 1991. "Tempo Curves Considered Harmful." In "Music and Time," ed. J. D. Kramer. *Contemporary Music Review*. London: Harwood Press.

Dobrian, C., and Zicarelli, D. 1990. *MAX Development Package Manual*. Menlo Park: Opcode Systems Inc.

Dreier, R. 1991. "Notes on the Program." *Stagebill*. Program to October 13 performance of the American Composers Orchestra. New York: B&B Enterprises Inc.

Drescher, G. L. 1991. *Made-Up Minds: A Constructivist Approach to Artificial Intelligence*. Cambridge, Mass.: The MIT Press.

Dreyfus, H. L. 1979. *What Computers Can't Do: The Limits of Artificial Intelligence*. Rev. ed. New York: Harper Colophon Books.

Duda, R.; Gaschnig, J.; and Hart, P. 1979. "Model Design in the Prospector Consultant System for Mineral Exploration." In *Expert Systems in the Microelectronic Age*, ed. D. Michie. Edinburgh: Edinburgh University Press.

Ebcioglu, K. 1988. "An Expert System for Harmonizing Four-Part Chorales." *Computer Music Journal* 12(3):43–51.

Favreau, E.; Fingerhut, M.; Koechlin, O.; Potacsek, P.; Puckette, M.; and Rowe, R. 1986. "Software Developments for the 4X Real-Time System." In *Proceedings of the 1986 International Computer Music Conference, The Hague*, ed. P. Berg. Berkeley: Computer Music Association.

Glinsky, A. 1992. "The Theremin and the Emergence of Electronic Music." Ph.D. dissertation, New York University.

Hamlin, P., with Roads, C. 1985. "Interview with Herbert Brün" In *Composers and the Computer*, ed. C. Roads. Los Altos, Calif.: William Kaufmann, Inc.

Handel, S. 1989. *Listening: An Introduction to the Perception of Auditory Events.* Cambridge, Mass.: The MIT Press.

Hayes, P. 1981. "The Logic of Frames." In *Readings In Artificial Intelligence*, ed. B. L. Webber and N. J. Nilsson. Los Altos, Calif: Morgan Kaufmann Publishers, Inc.

Jaffe, D. 1985. "Ensemble Timing in Computer Music." *Computer Music Journal* 9(4):38–48.

Jaffe, D., and Boynton, L. 1989. "An Overview of the Sound and Music Kits for the NeXT Computer." *Computer Music Journal* 13(2):48–55.

Jaffe, D., and Schloss, A. 1991. "Wildlife." Manuscript.

Koenig, G. M. 1971. *Summary Observations on Compositional Theory.* Utrecht: Institute of Sonology.

Kramer, J. D. 1988. *The Time of Music: New Meanings, New Temporalities, New Listening Strategies.* New York: Schirmer Books.

Krefeld, V. 1990. "The Hand in The Web: An Interview with Michel Waisvisz" *Computer Music Journal* 14(2):28–33.

Krumhansl, C. L. 1990. "Melodic structure: Theoretical and perceptual aspects." Paper presented at the International Wenner-Gren Symposium: Music, Language, Speech, and Brain. Stockholm, Sweden.

Lee, M.; Freed, A.; and Wessel, D. 1991. "Real-Time Neural Network Processing of Gestural and Acoustic Signals." In *Proceedings*, ed. B. Alphonce and B. Pennycook. Montreal: ICMC-1991 Faculty of Music, McGill University.

Lenat, D. B., and Guha, R. V. 1990. *Building Large Knowledge-Based Systems: Representation and Inference in the Cyc Project.* Reading, Mass.: Addison-Wesley Pub. Co.

Lerdahl, F. 1988. "Cognitive constraints on compositional systems." In *Generative Processes in Music: The Psychology of Performance, Improvisation, and Composition*, ed. J. Sloboda. Oxford: Clarendon Press.

Lerdahl, F., and Jackendoff, R. 1983. *A Generative Theory of Tonal Music* Cambridge, Mass.: The MIT Press.

Lewis, G. 1989. Lecture at the MIT Media Laboratory, Cambridge, Mass.

Lindemann, E.; Dechelle, F.; Smith, B.; and Starkier, M. 1991. "The Architecture of the IRCAM Musical Workstation." *Computer Music Journal* 15(3):41–49.

Lippe, C. 1991. "Using MAX on the IRCAM Musical Workstation: A Musical Study." Manuscript.

Lischka, C. 1991. "Understanding Music Cognition: A Connectionist View." In *Representations of Musical Signals*, ed. G. De Poli, A. Piccialli, and C. Roads. Cambridge, Mass.: The MIT Press.

Lischka, C., and Güsgen, H. W. 1986. "Mvs l c—A Constraint-Based Approach to Musical Knowledge Representation." In *Proceedings of the 1986 International Computer Music Conference, The Hague*, ed. P. Berg. Berkeley: Computer Music Association.

Longuet-Higgins, H. C., and Lee, C. S. 1984. "The Rhythmic Interpretation of Monophonic Music." *Music Perception* 1(4): 424–441. Reprinted in *Mental Processes: Studies in Cognitive Science*, ed. H. C. Longuet-Higgins. Cambridge, Mass.: The MIT Press.

Lowe, B., and Currie, R. 1989. "Digidesign's Sound Accelerator: Lessons Lived and Learned." *Computer Music Journal* 13(1):36–46.

Loy, G. 1985. "Musicians Make a Standard: The MIDI Phenomenon" *Computer Music Journal* 9(4). Reprinted in *The Music Machine*, ed. Curtis Roads. Cambridge, Mass.: The MIT Press, 1989.

Loy, G. 1989. "Composing with Computers—a Survey of Some Compositional Formalisms and Music Programming Languages." In *Current Directions in Computer Music Research*, ed. M. V. Mathews and J. R. Pierce. Cambridge, Mass.: The MIT Press.

McAdams, S. 1987. "Music: A Science of the Mind?" In *Music and Psychology: A Mutual Regard*, ed. S. McAdams. *Contemporary Music Review* 2(1):1–62. London : Harwood Academic Publishers.

Machover, T., and Chung, J. 1989. "Hyperinstruments: Musically Intelligent and Interactive Performance and Creativity Systems." In *Proceedings: 1989 International Computer Music Conference*, ed. T. Wells and D. Butler. San Francisco: Computer Music Association.

Machover, T.; Chung, J.; Hong, A.; and Gershenfeld, N. 1991. "Hyperinstruments: Musically Intelligent/Interactive Performance and Creativity Systems." Yearly Report to the Yamaha Corporation. Cambridge, Mass. The MIT Media Laboratory.

Mahling, A. 1991. "How to Feed Musical Gestures into Compositions." In *Proceedings*, ed. B. Alphonce and B. Pennycook. Montreal: ICMC-1991 Faculty of Music, McGill University.

Mathews, M. V. 1989. "The Radio Drum as a Synthesizer Controller." In *Proceedings: 1989 International Computer Music Conference*, ed. T. Wells and D. Butler. San Francisco: Computer Music Association.

Meyer, L. B. 1956. *Emotion and Meaning in Music*. Chicago: University of Chicago Press.

Minsky, M. 1985. "A Framework for Representing Knowledge." In *Readings in Knowledge Representation*, ed. R. J. Brachman and H. J. Levesque. Los Altos, Calif.: Morgan Kaufmann Publishers, Inc.

Minsky, M. 1986. *The Society of Mind*. New York: Simon and Schuster.

Minsky, M. 1989. "Music, Mind, and Meaning." In *The Music Machine*, ed. Curtis Roads. Cambridge, Mass.: The MIT Press.

Moore, F. R. 1988. "The Dysfunctions of MIDI." *Computer Music Journal* 12(1):19–28.

Moore, F. R. 1990. *Elements of Computer Music*. Englewood Cliffs, N.J.: Prentice Hall.

Narmour, E. 1977. *Beyond Schenkerism: The Need for Alternatives in Music Analysis*. Chicago: University of Chicago Press.

Narmour, E. 1984. "Some Major Theoretical Problems Concerning the Concept of Hierarchy in the Analysis of Tonal Music." *Music Perception* 1(2):129–199.

Narmour, E. 1990. *The Analysis and Cognition of Basic Melodic Structures: The Implication–Realization Model*. Chicago: University of Chicago Press.

Oppenheim, D. V. 1991. "SHADOW: An Object-Oriented Performance System for the DMIX Environment." In *Proceedings*, ed. B. Alphonce and B. Pennycook. Montreal: ICMC-1991 Faculty of Music, McGill University.

Palmer, C. 1988. "Timing in Skilled Music Performance." Ph.D. dissertation, Cornell University.

Palmer, C., and Krumhansl, C. L. 1987. "Independent Temporal and Pitch Structures in Determination of Musical Phrases." *Journal of Experimental Psychology: Human Perception & Performance* 13:116–126.

Pareles, J. 1990. "The Midi Menace: Machine Perfection is Far From Perfect." *New York Times*. May 13.

Pennycook, B. 1991. "Machine Songs II: The PRAESCIO Series—Composition-Driven Interactive Software." *Computer Music Journal* 15(3):16–26.

Pennycook, B. 1992. "Tracker: A Real Time Music Listener." Montreal: McGill University. Manuscript.

Pennycook, B., and Lea, C. 1991. "T–MAX: A Parallel Processing Development System for MAX." In *Proceedings*, ed. B. Alphonce and B. Pennycook. Montreal: ICMC–1991 Faculty of Music, McGill University.

Pope, S. T. 1991a. "The *Interim DynaPiano*: An Integrated Computer Tool and Instrument for Composers." In *Proceedings IX Colloquium on Musical Informatics Genova*, ed. A. Camurri and C. Canepa. Genova: Associazione di Informatica Musicale Italiana.

Pope, S. T., ed. 1991b. *The Well-Tempered Object: Musical Applications of Object-Oriented Software Technology*. Cambridge, Mass.: The MIT Press.

Posner, M. I., ed. *Foundations of Cognitive Science*. Cambridge, Mass.: The MIT Press.

Pressing, J. 1988. "Nonlinear Maps as Generators of Musical Design." *Computer Music Journal* 12(2):35–47.

Pressing, J. 1991. "Quaternmusic: A Quaternion-Based Nonlinear Map Music Generator." Manuscript.

Puckette, M. 1990. "Amplifying Musical Nuance." Paris: IRCAM document.

Puckette, M. 1991. "Combining Event and Signal Processing in the MAX Graphical Programming Environment." *Computer Music Journal* 15(3):68–77.

Reese, G. 1959. *Music in the Renaissance*. New York: W. W. Norton & Company Inc.

Rich, R. 1991. "Buchla Lightning MIDI Controller." *Electronic Musician* 7(10):102–108.

Risset, J. C. 1990. "From Piano to Computer to Piano." In *Proceedings*, ed. S. Arnold and G. Hair. Glasgow: ICMC Glasgow.

Ritter, D. 1991. "A Method for Sound-Image Correspondence." Manuscript.

Roads, C. 1985. "Improvisation with George Lewis." In *Composers and the Computer*, ed. C. Roads. Los Altos, Calif: William Kaufmann, Inc.

Rosenthal, D. 1989. "A Model of the Process of Listening to Simple Rhythms." *Music Perception* 6(3):315–328.

Rumelhart, D. E.; McClelland, J. L.; and the PDP Research Group. 1986. *Parallel Distributed Processing: Explorations in the Microstucture of Cognition*. Cambridge: The MIT Press.

Scarborough, D.; Miller, B.; and Jones, J. 1989. "Connectionist Models for Tonal Analysis." *Computer Music Journal* 13(3):49–55.

Schank, R. C., and Abelson, R. P. 1977. *Scripts, Plans, Goals, and Understanding*. Hillsdale, N.J.: Erlbaum.

Scheidt, D. 1991. "Action/Reaction." Notes to compact disc IMED-9105-CD Montreal: empreintes DIGITALes.

Schenker, H. 1933. *Five Graphic Music Analyses*. Reprint, with an introduction by F. Salzer. New York: Dover Publications Inc., 1969.

Schenker, H. 1979. *Free Composition*. Translated and edited by E. Oster. New York: Longman.

Schwanauer, S. 1988. "Learning Machines & Tonal Composition." In *Proceedings of the First Workshop on Artificial Intelligence and Music*. Minneapolis/St. Paul, Minn.: AAAI-88.

Serafine, M. L. 1988. *Music as Cognition: The Development of Thought in Sound*. New York: Columbia University Press.

Simon, H. A., and Sumner, R. K. 1968. "Pattern in Music." In *Formal Representation of Human Judgement*, ed. B. Kleinmuntz. New York: John Wiley & Sons., Inc.

Sloboda, J. 1985. *The Musical Mind: The Cognitive Psychology of Music* Oxford: Clarendon Press.

Teitelbaum, R. 1984. "The Digital Piano and the Patch Control Language System." In *Proceedings of the International Computer Music Conference, 1984*, ed. W. Buxton. San Francisco, Calif.: Computer Music Assoc.

Teitelbaum, R. 1991. "Improvisation, Computers, and the Unconscious." Manuscript.

Todd, P. M. 1989. "A Connectionist Approach to Algorithmic Composition" *Computer Music Journal* 13(4):27–43.

Todd, P. M., and Loy, D. G., eds. 1991. *Music and Connectionism*. Cambridge, Mass.: The MIT Press.

Vercoe, B. 1984. "The Synthetic Performer in the Context of Live Performance." In *Proceedings of the International Computer Music Conference, 1984*, ed. W. Buxton. San Francisco, Calif.: Computer Music Assoc.

Vercoe, B. 1990. "A Realtime Auditory Model of Rhythm Perception and Cognition." In *Proceedings*. Cambridge: International Conference on Music and the Cognitive Sciences.

Wessel, D. 1991. "Improvisation with Highly Interactive Real-Time Performance Systems." In *Proceedings*, ed. B. Alphonce and B. Pennycook. Montreal: ICMC–1991 Faculty of Music, McGill University.

Winkler, T. 1991. "Interactive Signal Processing for Acoustic Instruments." In *Proceedings*, ed. B. Alphonce and B. Pennycook. Montreal: ICMC-1991 Faculty of Music, McGill University.

Winograd, T., and Flores, F. 1986. *Understanding Computers and Cognition: A New Foundation for Design*. Reading, Mass.: Addison-Wesley Publishing Company.

Winsor, Phil. 1991. "PAT-PROC: An Interactive, Pattern-Process, Algorithmic Composition Program." In *Proceedings*, ed. B. Alphonce and B. Pennycook. Montreal: ICMC-1991 Faculty of Music, McGill University.

Winston, P. 1984. *Artificial Intelligence*. 2nd ed. Reading, Mass.: Addison-Wesley Publishing Company.

Wyatt, D. 1991. *Opcode MIDI System (OMS)*. Menlo Park: Opcode Systems, Inc.

Yadegari, S. D. 1991. "Using Self-Similarity for Sound/Music Synthesis." In *Proceedings*, ed. B. Alphonce and B. Pennycook. Montreal: ICMC–1991 Faculty of Music, McGill University.

Zicarelli, D. 1987. "M and Jam Factory." *Computer Music Journal* 11(4):13–29.

Index